PITKIN COUNTY
library
inspire growth

 1

D0349969

120 North Mi.

812.54 H232   28.00
Hampton, Wilbor.
on route

WITHDRAWN

*f*P

HORTON FOOTE

America's Storyteller

Wilborn Hampton

FREE PRESS

New York   London   Toronto   Sydney

Free Press
A Division of Simon & Schuster, Inc.
1230 Avenue of the Americas
New York, NY 10020

Copyright © 2009 by Wilborn Hampton

All rights reserved, including the right to reproduce this book or portions thereof
in any form whatsoever. For information address Free Press Subsidiary Rights Department,
1230 Avenue of the Americas, New York, NY 10020

First Free Press hardcover edition September 2009

FREE PRESS and colophon are trademarks of Simon & Schuster, Inc.

For information about special discounts for bulk purchases,
please contact Simon & Schuster Special Sales at 1-866-506-1949
or business@simonandschuster.com.

The Simon & Schuster Speakers Bureau can bring authors to your live event.
For more information or to book an event contact the Simon & Schuster Speakers Bureau
at 1-866-248-3049 or visit our website at www.simonspeakers.com.

Manufactured in the United States of America

1   3   5   7   9   10   8   6   4   2

Library of Congress Cataloging-in-Publication Data

Hampton, Wilborn.
Horton Foote : America's storyteller / Wilborn Hampton.
p. cm.
1. Foote, Horton. 2. Dramatists, American—20th century—Biography. 3. Screenwriters—
United States—Biography. 4. Texas—Intellectual life—20th century. 5. Wharton (Tex.)—
Biography. I. Title.
PS3511.O344Z63 2009
812'.54—dc22
[B]   2009007387

ISBN 978-1-4165-6640-3
ISBN 978-1-4165-6691-5 (ebook)

Grateful acknowledgment to Barbara Hallie Foote and the Estate of Horton Foote
for permission to quote from his works and to reproduce selected photographs

For

LuAnn

The leading lady of my life

Contents

HORTON FOOTE

CHAPTER 1

Wharton: Front Porches
and Kitchen Tables

THE TOWN of Wharton, Texas, lies forty-five miles inland from the Gulf of Mexico on an alluvial plain formed by the Colorado River and a smaller waterway called Caney Creek because of the giant switch cane that once grew along its banks. It resides on part of two leagues of land ceded by the Mexican government in 1824 to William Kincheloe, one of the original three hundred settlers who came to Texas from Louisiana with Stephen F. Austin.

The town was officially put on the geographic map in 1838, when the fledgling Republic of Texas added it to a mail route and named the community for two brothers, John and William Wharton, who fought in the Texas war of independence from Mexico. It first appeared on the literary map a hundred years later in a one-act play called *Wharton Dance*, written by an aspiring young actor named Horton Foote, a native son.

Over the course of the ensuing seventy years, Wharton became the setting, under a variety of names, for a canon of work that includes more than sixty plays, films, and television dramas and that defined twentieth-century America. The man responsible for turning it into a metaphoric Hometown, U.S.A., was the firstborn child of the fourth generation of extended families on both sides of an unlikely union.

The forebears on his father's side had a lofty local pedigree. A decade after Kincheloe received his land grant from Mexico, Albert Clinton Horton arrived on the Texas Gulf Coast from Alabama

1

with his wife, Eliza. Within a year he organized a group of volunteers who fought for Texas's independence and, after it was won, served in the first Republic of Texas Congress. After that war, Horton bought some land near the Kincheloe plantations and built a two-story house on it that he called Sycamore Grove.

Albert Clinton Horton remained active in politics, and when Texas was admitted to the Union in 1845, he was elected lieutenant governor of the new state. He even served as acting governor for a year, from 1846 to 1847, while the governor, J. Pinckney Henderson, fought in the Mexican War. For the rest of his life and after, he was known among friends and relations as Governor Horton.

The governor and his wife had six children, but only two—a daughter named Patience Louisiana Texas and a son named Robert John—survived a yellow fever outbreak in the 1850s. In his will, Governor Horton left Sycamore Grove and half of his 170 slaves to his daughter and her husband. He left his son, who was unmarried and away fighting with the Confederate army at the time, the other half of his slaves.

Patience herself died shortly afterward, and she left all her property, including the plantation house, to her daughter. When Robert returned from the Civil War, he found that his young niece had inherited Sycamore Grove. Since the eighty-five slaves he inherited had all been freed, he was left with nothing. Robert Horton married the year after the war ended, and he and his wife had six children—one son and five daughters, the eldest of whom was named Corrella.

In 1889, Corrella Horton married a young lawyer named Albert Harrison Foote. Foote's father had been a cotton dealer in Galveston, but the business, like so many in the South, went bankrupt after the Civil War, and when his father died, Foote moved with his mother and five brothers and sisters to Wharton. He and Corrella eventually had two children—a son they named Albert Horton, after Corrella's grandfather, and a daughter, Lily Dale.

The marriage, however, was not a happy one. Foote, a lawyer who loved books and read Greek and Latin, had a hard time supporting not only his new family but also his mother and siblings, and he began to drink heavily. Corrella divorced Albert Harrison Foote and moved to Houston, taking her daughter with her. She left her son, Albert Horton, to live with her parents.

From the start, young Albert was something of an outsider at Sycamore Grove, a daily, living reminder of his profligate father. He was embraced by his four aunts—his mother's younger sisters, all of whom still lived at home—but his grandparents treated him almost as an orphan. Soon after his mother left town, Albert's lawyer father died, penniless, and was buried in an unmarked grave (his only legacy was a collection of books that went to the local saloon keeper to satisfy his bar bill). Young Albert's mother married Pete Cleveland, a man she met in Houston.

If Albert was hoping his mother would send for him after her remarriage, he was to be disappointed. Although Cleveland accepted Lily Dale as part of the family, even doted on her, he refused to acknowledge Albert.

When he was twelve years old, Albert Horton Foote ended his formal education in the sixth grade, moved out of his grandparents' house, and went to live with an uncle on a farm outside Wharton. The farm had a country store that catered mostly to black sharecroppers, and the boy was often left in charge of it while his uncle caroused in town. Young Albert eventually left his uncle and ended up living most of his adolescence with a black family who farmed some land nearby. He would later say that it was the happiest time of his childhood.

Although Albert maintained close familial ties with his four aunts into adulthood, he remained estranged from his mother. Corrella Cleveland refused to challenge her new husband on the issue of her son. Once, when Albert attended a six-week business course in Houston, his stepfather refused to let him stay in the house; Albert had to sneak over to visit his mother when Cleveland was away at work.

Unlike on the father's side, the family of Horton Foote's mother were relative newcomers to Wharton. Tom Brooks was born in East Columbia, Texas, in 1865, the year the Civil War ended. He was one of ten children born to John and Harriet Brooks, only five of whom survived infancy. Tom was the brightest, and he won a scholarship to Texas A&M College. After his graduation in 1886, rather than return home, he took a job as a clerk in his uncle's grocery store in Wharton, a fast-growing community about thirty miles northwest of his hometown that had just been added to the New York, Texas and Mexican Railway line.

Brooks was an industrious young man and within a year he had bought his uncle's store outright. Abolition had greatly changed the economy of the South, and the old plantations that had been its backbone were being abandoned or foreclosed. Brooks used the profits from the grocery store to buy up several of these plantations and divided them into smaller farms, reselling some of them and managing others on a sharecropping arrangement. Soon, he was the leading landowner in Wharton.

Brooks opened an office in the town and hired a young woman named Daisy Speed—who had been born on a plantation in Brooks's home county—as his secretary. She was the first woman ever employed in such a position in Wharton. Within a year, Tom and Daisy were married.

Over the half century since it was settled, the original Kincheloe plantation had been divided and subdivided, sold off parcel by parcel, and in 1896 Tom Brooks bought fifteen acres of what remained of it and moved his wife into a six-room house that was standing on it. Tom and Daisy Brooks had eight children, six of whom survived infancy—three daughters and three sons. The eldest girl was named Harriet Gautier but was always called Hallie.

For reasons that were never clearly expressed, Tom Brooks was opposed to any of his daughters marrying. Perhaps it had something to do with his disappointment at his sons, all three of whom spent most of their adult lives running up saloon bills and gambling debts that the family had to pay off. If pressed on the matter, he would simply say he could provide for his daughters, so why did they need husbands? To support his argument, he would point to all the disastrous marriages around town, ignoring the fact that his own was an extremely happy one.

4

Tom Brooks had intervened once before to break up a romance his daughter Hallie had pursued with a young man he deemed unacceptable. But he had not objected when young Albert Foote first began to call at his house, possibly because he thought Foote was too old to have any romantic interest in his daughters.

After returning to Wharton from the business course in Houston, Albert had taken a job as a clerk in town and had ambitions about having his own store. He eventually opened a cleaning and pressing shop, from which he would also take measurements for mail-order tailored suits. He also began to acquire a reputation as something of a wild young man, a chip off his father's block, a bit too fond of drink and cards and not always scrupulous in his choice of friends.

Foote had seen Hallie Brooks around town from the time she was a girl in high school, and as she grew older his interest became more amorously inclined. In the spring of 1914, Albert and Hallie started to go out together, to the picture show, as movies were called, and to dances and parties. He began to spend more time at the Brooks house.

Wharton was a small town, and the Brooks family was by now one of its pillars. Every time Albert and Hallie were seen together in each other's company, especially at dances, which were supposedly forbidden to Hallie, a churchgoing Methodist, it was duly reported back to Tom and Daisy Brooks. When it became apparent that Hallie and Albert Foote were becoming serious about each other, Brooks forbade Foote to come to his house. Hallie pleaded with her father not to stand in their way, but Tom Brooks was resolute. He said young Foote was a ne'er-do-well who would bring only heartache to any woman unlucky enough to become his wife.

Myriad are the paths of love, however, and as lovers inevitably do, Albert and Hallie found other ways to meet. With a little help from friends, they would often find themselves at the same social gathering or just happen to go to see the same movie at the same time. They began to talk of marriage. They soon realized, however, that if they went forward with their plans, they would have to do it secretly and elope.

When the wedding day finally arrived, it was carried out with all the secrecy and precision of a military operation. Although Wharton was growing—its population had nearly tripled in a decade—it was still a small town in which everyone knew everybody else, and gossip raced around the main square faster than one of the new automobiles that were fast replacing horse and buggies.

Albert and Hallie told only their closest friends about their marriage plans, fearing that if word got out ahead of time, Hallie's parents would find a way to stop it. Albert got a friend to go to the jewelry store to buy the wedding rings. He even went to a neighboring town to get the marriage license, knowing that if he applied for one at the Wharton courthouse, one of Mr. Brooks's many friends there would report it to Hallie's father.

Hallie sneaked her wedding dress over to a friend's house the day before the planned ceremony. On the actual day, she left her house early in the morning, telling her mother she was going to spend the day with her friend. Thus she was able to dress for her wedding without arousing her parents' suspicion.

Although an actual church wedding was out of the question, both Albert and Hallie wanted to be married by a minister. The pastor at the Methodist church the Brooks family had attended all of Hallie's life refused to conduct the ceremony. Finally, they asked the town's Baptist preacher if he would marry them, and he agreed to perform the service on the condition that Hallie tell her parents what she was doing beforehand.

The wedding was scheduled for five o'clock in the afternoon in the front parlor of the home of Allie and Archie Elmore, two of their friends. Ten minutes before that time, as the minister insisted, Hallie picked up the phone and dialed her home number. She thought it would be easier to tell her mother rather than her father.

The phone rang and rang, but no one answered. Her mother was clearly not at home. So Hallie had to call her father at his office. He pleaded with her over the phone not to go through with the marriage, saying she would regret it the rest of her life. She did not heed his advice, however, and with only their friends as witnesses, Albert Foote and Hallie Brooks were married on St. Valentine's Day 1915.

For the first month of their marriage, the newlyweds lived in a spare bedroom at the Elmores' house, then rented a single room of their own in a rooming house and took their meals at a boarding-house across the street.

Hallie's parents refused to speak to her for nearly a year after she defied them by marrying Albert Foote. Once, when Hallie was walking on the sidewalk in town, she saw her mother approaching from a distance. Her mother turned on her heel and walked back in the direction from which she had come.

The estrangement ended as abruptly as it began. In the summer after her marriage, Hallie became pregnant. As was then common, pregnant women rarely went out in public. After Hallie began to show she was with child, she mainly stayed indoors at the rooming house where she and Albert lived. As a result, she was close to term before Tom and Daisy Brooks learned their daughter was expecting. One day while a friend was visiting, the landlady of the rooming house knocked on her door and told Hallie she had a telephone call. As she went downstairs, the landlady whispered, "I think it's your mother."

Hallie's heart was pounding and she tried to mask the nervousness she was feeling as she picked up the receiver: "Hello."

"Hallie, this is your mother," the voice on the other end of the line said.

At first, Hallie couldn't think of anything to say in return and she felt like she was going to start crying, so she swallowed and replied, "Hello, Mama, how are you?"

"I'm fine, thank you. I thought I would come over and see you this afternoon if you're going to be at home."

"Yes, ma'am. I'll be here."

Daisy Brooks arrived about three in the afternoon and went straight to Hallie's room. She strode in and began talking to her daughter as though they had seen each other the day before and hadn't finished the conversation. No apologies were asked or given, and the subject of the rift between them was not mentioned, then or ever.

The reconciliation was completed the following day. Hallie's father showed up at the rooming house. As soon as he saw his daughter, he started telling her about his plans to build a house on a lot adjacent to his own, so that she and her husband would have a place to take the baby. Albert agreed to his father-in-law's plan, provided the house be kept in his wife's name.

On March 14, 1916, Hallie delivered a baby boy in the single room she and her husband had rented and lived in since shortly after their elopement. The child was named after his father: Albert Horton Foote Jr.

The following year, the Footes and their son moved into a six-room house built by Hallie's father on three-quarters of an acre of land, with the backyard adjoining that of the Brookses. They lived in that house their entire lives, and although he left it at the age of sixteen to pursue his dream of being an actor, it is the house Horton Foote regarded as home for the next ninety years.

The house was built high off the ground, like that of the Brookses, to protect it from the frequent flooding of Caney Creek, which ran nearby. It was said that when Caney Creek flooded, the town's main square turned to mud so thick that it took a team of four mules just to pull a wagon across it. In the summer, Caney Creek usually ran dry, leaving its banks covered with dead fish, and spawning outbreaks of malaria, typhoid, and yellow fever. In the 1920s, Wharton's two main doctors prevailed on the town's leaders to drain Caney Creek in an effort to prevent the perennial outbreak of disease, and the crawl spaces underneath the two houses were covered over.

The house also had a wide front porch that ran nearly halfway around it. The front porch, or gallery as it was sometimes called, was a central part of American society in the early twentieth century and beyond. Almost without exception, front porches were furnished with a swing, a rocking chair, a love seat, and an array of other chairs and stools. It was where families gathered after the evening meal to discuss the day's affairs and tell stories. Even after the radio made its way into most American homes, the front porch remained a family room. It was only in the second half of the century, when televisions became pervasive, that families moved indoors permanently. The den replaced the front porch, and Americans became content to let TV take over the storytelling.

The front-porch ritual was very much a fixture at the Foote

household during Horton's childhood. It would begin each night with Foote's mother asking his father about the day's business. The elder Foote had sold his cleaning business and opened a clothing store on the main square. After an accounting of the day's sales and the visitors who came into the store, the talk would turn to town gossip. Once that was exhausted, the evening was spent recalling old tales, usually prefaced with a rhetorical question, such as "Whatever happened to . . . [so and so]," or "Do you remember the time . . . ?" Foote's father, who had been a traveling salesman during the time he courted Foote's mother, would sometimes recount stories from the places he had visited, beginning each with the phrase "When I was on the road . . ."

Unlike most boys his age, who preferred to run outside and play after supper, young Foote relished listening to the stories, even when they were told over and over. Albert and Hallie later had two more sons, but Foote was never particularly close to his brothers growing up. For one thing, there was a difference of several years in their ages. Tom Brooks, the middle son, was born in 1921, when Foote was five and already in the first grade. The third son, John Speed, was born two years later. But it was not only the age differences, and the natural resentment of an eldest son toward siblings who steal the attention of his parents and relatives; the two younger Foote boys simply did not share their elder brother's fascination with old family tales. While they were off playing baseball or hide-and-seek with other kids, their brother stayed at home or visited his grandmother or aunts, or the black families who lived on his grandmother's property and worked for her, prompting them to repeat yarns he had heard many times but that changed slightly with each retelling. And even in Wharton, Texas, there was a wealth of stories.

The town was expanding. The arrival of a second railroad around the turn of the twentieth century had brought another population boom. Wharton, a hamlet of only a couple hundred people at the time Foote's grandparents married, had a population of over three thousand by the time Foote started school. And like the Naked City with its eight million inhabitants, every one of Wharton's three thousand had a story to tell.

Many of the stories involved his own family. The Foote and Brooks family trees had more branches than the giant pecans that grew everywhere in Wharton. There was a plethora of aunts and uncles, great-aunts and great-uncles, and cousins by the dozens. Even for a family member, it was hard to keep them all straight. To an outsider, it was like reading a nineteenth-century Russian novel in which all the characters have three given names, in addition to one or more nicknames.

There were, for example, his mother's three brothers. They were Thomas Henry Brooks, John Speed Brooks, and William Smith Brooks. The eldest was known in the family as Brother, or Uncle Brother, or sometimes as Harry. The second one was known by his middle name, Speed, and the youngest was usually called Billy, although he had other nicknames as well. His grandmother, who was born Mary Phelps Speed, was called Daisy all her life by friends and relations, and dubbed Baboo by Foote when he was a child. On his father's side, Foote had two aunts and two uncles in addition to four great-aunts—sisters of the paternal grandmother he saw only infrequently in childhood, usually when he would visit her in Houston for two weeks in the summer. The eldest of these women was named Louisiana Texas Patience Horton, but always known as Loula, and she was one of young Foote's favorites.

It was Loula who had the most stories, and many of them involved his three maternal uncles, whose misguided lives brought their mother and their sisters much heartache. It is not unusual for a respected family to have at least one black sheep in it. But for a family as highly regarded as the Brookses to have all three male offspring turn out to be profligate was a subject of more than idle gossip.

The Brooks boys, as they were collectively known around town, each began drinking as adolescents, and they were never far from trouble. The drinking led to gambling and the gambling to debts that their father had to pay off. There was a scandal over a girl one got pregnant; there were fights and arrests. Speed was once involved in a drunken brawl in a neighboring town in which a man was killed; there was a trial, but both Speed and the man who struck the fatal blow were freed. Each was found a variety of jobs or set up in a business in the hopes the responsibility would instill some discipline in their lives, but it never did.

Family tragedy struck when Foote was only nine years old. Tom Brooks, Foote's grandfather, collapsed and died one March afternoon on a street in Wharton. For the nine-year-old boy, the biggest loss at the time was the sense of security he had always felt being the number one grandson of the town's leading and wealthiest citizen. If his grandfather had lavished attention on him, his now widowed grandmother took him under her wing almost as though he were her own.

The boy began to spend nearly as much time at his grandmother's house as his own. Possibly because her own sons had turned out the way they had, his grandmother began to place all of her hopes on young Horton. She would have catered to his every whim if Foote's father had not insisted against it. Instead, she rewarded him with capital of a different kind—more of the stories that he would later turn into plays and movies.

There were other stories to tell as well. The Ku Klux Klan was still active in Wharton in the 1920s, as it was throughout the South, and one incident involved a local man who was rumored to be living with a black woman. He was pulled from his horse one afternoon in the middle of town, carried off in a car, then returned a couple of hours later, naked, shaved bald, and covered with tar and feathers. Another involved the lynching of a black man, a trustee from a prison farm who had been working in a neighbor's yard the same day a white woman was raped and murdered. There was a cousin, Mabel Horton, a celebrated beauty whose husband shot and killed himself on their honeymoon. Whether it was an accident or suicide was a source of family speculation for years to come. Then there was an aunt who was engaged to be married but called it off practically at the church door when she learned on her wedding day that her fiancé had "outside children," meaning he had fathered children with a black woman. Another aunt had wanted to marry her first cousin but was forbidden, and the cousin used to walk by her house every evening just so he could see her sitting on the front porch and wave to her.

There was the story about the president of a local bank and his son-in-law, who were discovered to have been helping themselves to their customers' savings. There was the married neighbor who had been keeping a woman in the next town, and the wife of another local man who ran away with a traveling salesman. There was another cousin whose husband killed his father-in-law, and yet another who walked out into a lake in Florida, even though he couldn't swim, and drowned. There was Archie Elmore, in whose home his parents had been married, who put a gun to his head one day and blew his brains out. There was one of young Foote's classmates whose father ran off with another woman, leaving the boy's mother destitute. There was the neighbor who would get drunk and walk into town and climb the pecan trees in the courthouse square. And there was the mysterious story of Miss Minnie Mae, the prettiest girl in the county, who once went to all the dances and was the belle of all the balls, but married a handsome layabout who never worked a day in his life. She ended up a recluse, refusing to answer the door, and was often seen walking up and down in her garden at night talking to herself.

The stories went on and on, and when the stories on his own front porch ran out, he would race across his backyard to his grandmother's house, or across the street to his aunt's, to hear more. If his own relations were too busy, Foote would visit the two homes that his grandparents had built for their black retainers, where he would often hear the same stories, but from the servants' point of view rather than the masters'.

At the time, the population of Wharton was about evenly divided between white and black families, and although racial segregation was still the rule in public places and in schools and churches, and the black and white neighborhoods were in separate parts of town, young Horton was welcomed into the black homes as though he were one of the family. This was partly due to the regard the black townsfolk had for his father.

Having been partly raised by a black family during his teen years, Foote's father had a strong empathy with the plight of black people in the South, most of whom worked as sharecroppers on small farms or at the cotton gin or as domestic help. The local black population shopped for their clothes almost exclusively at Foote's haberdashery, and on Saturdays they would wait in line outside the store for the elder Foote to wait on them personally. There once was a small scandal in town when Foote senior refused to stop assisting a black customer when a white woman came in and demanded to be served immediately. The woman stalked out and tried to organize a boycott of the store, but it had no effect.

During his childhood, Foote visited the houses of black families and played with their children almost as much as with those of white neighbors. Many of the black people he knew only by their first names, but one with whom he felt great kinship was Stant Powell. Stant had worked for Foote's father when Foote senior ran the cleaning business with the sideline in mail-order suits. When Foote was a baby, Stant would carry him around on his shoulders. Stant always called young Foote "Little Horton" and his father "Big Horton." Little Horton and Stant had a special bond.

One of Foote's early lessons in the realities of racial relations in the South came when he was sixteen. Foote had spent the summer in Dallas with his aunt and grandmother, and when he returned to Wharton and saw Stant on the street, the now aging black man addressed him as "Mister." Young Horton said nothing, but felt a sadness at the change and asked his father about it. "That's because you are both in the South," his father replied. "And that's the way things are done in the South."

It was in the kitchens and yards of black families that he heard tales of the supernatural that were rife in the black community. A major source for these stories was Walter, who worked for Foote's grandmother as yardman and chauffeur, both in horse-and-buggy days and after the arrival of automobiles. Walter claimed to have the gift of second sight, which allowed him to see spirits that no one else could see. Walter, who had been sent overseas in a Negro regiment in World War I, loved to recount how he had seen mermaids during his ocean voyage to Europe. Another story Walter was fond of telling was how he had once been driving the Brooks family in a buggy when the horse suddenly shied, reared, and refused to go forward. No one could figure out what was wrong except Walter, who saw there was a fiery chariot standing in the middle of the road and the horse wouldn't go around it.

From the black servants of the town's white families Foote often heard the unvarnished versions of the local scandals. He heard, for example, how the wife and daughter of a prominent businessman refused to talk to him or even eat meals with him because he was discovered to be keeping a mistress. The maid had to take a tray of food to him in his room and carry notes to and from his family. If he walked into a room, the other family members would walk out. Or, how another lady called her children into the dining room, sat them down in the presence of their father (and the maid), and proceeded to tell them in detail what he had been up to with a woman he was keeping in Houston.

Another source of stories for young Foote was Outlar's Drugstore. If the front porch was the family room of small-town America, the drugstore was its forum. Everybody stopped in the drugstore at some point during the day. It was the place where one could pick up a soda pop and all the latest news bulletins about anything that happened in the town. The drugstore was such a predominant social institution that Foote set his first full-length play in one much like Outlar's.

Through what Faulkner once called the "means of childhood's simple inevitable listening," Foote stored away all of the stories that would one day make their way into his plays. That the veneer of genteel Southern society covered a tawdry reality steeped in alcoholism, gambling, and sex is not surprising. That Foote's plays could have occurred in any town in the country only serves to make them universally relevant. What sets his stories apart are not the details themselves, but the compassion for human frailty and the struggle for dignity in the face of adversity and failure that runs through them.

It is probably only natural that a young man so enamored of stories should find an affinity for the theater and the movies. Discovering that connection, however, was not easy in a small town like Wharton. While there was a cinema in Wharton and young Foote saw many motion pictures, his only exposure to live theater was a traveling troupe called the Dude Arthur Comedians that came to town every summer for a week of performances staged in a tent. His only childhood acting experience came in the third grade, when his teacher enlisted his class to perform scenes from *A Midsummer Night's Dream* for a charity social she was organizing. Young Foote was cast as Puck, and the scenes were presented one night in the backyard of his teacher's home. Eighty years later he would say it was one of the happiest memories of his childhood.

When he was twelve years old, Foote told his parents that he wanted to be an actor when he grew up. If his parents did not immediately try to dissuade him from such a notion, it was probably because they thought it was a childhood fantasy he would soon outgrow. In an effort to provide his stagestruck son with a taste of reality, Foote's father put him to work in his store as a clerk on Saturdays and after school.

His father never employed a full-time clerk in his haberdashery, and the only time he might have needed one was on Saturdays. There were days during the week when Foote would not sell a single item all day long, although people might drop by to pass the time of day. As with most farming communities, the opening of any conversation usually had to do with the weather and how cotton was faring, since the entire economy relied on the success of the year's crop. On Saturdays, when nearly everyone in town did their shopping, Foote often kept his store open until ten or eleven o'clock at night, especially during the cotton season, which ran from July until late October. Dozens of customers would crowd into the store, visiting and chatting with other customers while waiting their turn to buy shirts, socks, hats, ties, or maybe to be measured for a mail-order suit.

Horton senior's decision to bring his son into his store as a clerk, however, failed to dissuade Foote from his theatrical pursuits. Two events in the town helped keep young Foote's aspirations alive: the first was the formation of a theater company in Wharton, and young Foote saw every play it mounted; the second was the arrival of Eppie Murphree, who was hired to teach speech classes at Wharton High School.

Ms. Murphree had traveled, loved the theater, and had seen numerous productions in big cities. In addition to teaching speech, she began to direct plays at school. Foote confided in her about his desire to become an actor, and she encouraged him by casting him in all the school plays during his sophomore, junior, and senior years.

It was also about this time that Foote began going steady with a girl in his class, Martha Jay Winn. Apart from going to the movies, the main entertainment for young people in Wharton, as in many small towns, were dances, and if a young man didn't know how to dance, he was pretty much regarded as a social outcast. Although his mother's family had long been pillars of the local Methodist church, which condemned dancing as sinful, Foote had by the time he was thirteen learned the waltz, the fox-trot, and a scandalous new dance known simply as "belly rubbing."

Since the Footes did not own a car, Horton and Martha Jay had to double-date when they went out on the weekends. There was a dance every Friday night at the Norton Opera House, a large, barnlike structure originally built for touring Chautauqua shows, the summer programs of concerts and lectures, named for the New York lakeside town where they were first organized. At one end of the hall was a stage where an orchestra, usually a six- or seven-piece band from a neighboring town, played. Occasionally, a black orchestra from Houston would appear, but usually it was a white group. Admission was normally twenty-five cents, though it could go up to as much as a half-dollar if there was a larger band.

The dances were not just for high school students. Young couples, married or single, attended the weekly dances. There was a lot of traffic in and out of the dance hall, and invariably someone had some bootleg liquor in a car in the parking lot. Sometimes there were arguments or fights outside, but chaperones, usually mothers of the school-age crowd, were on hand to make sure nothing untoward occurred inside the dance hall.

Foote himself was abstemious with regard to drinking—his uncles had set a vivid example of the pitfalls of liquor—and he would spend his time dancing to the hits of the day, such as "Stardust," "Dream a

Little Dream of Me," "I'll Get By," and everybody's favorite swing number, "Tiger Rag."

Since Foote had started public school when he was five and the high school ran only through the eleventh grade, he graduated when he was sixteen. For most of his senior year, he had rebuffed his parents when they spoke of him going to college, insisting that he only wanted to be an actor and that the only place for an actor was New York City.

While not rejecting him outright, his father kept referring to his plans to be an actor as a "notion" and insisted that New York City was no place for a sixteen-year-old boy to be on his own. Another consideration was money. It was 1932, and the Depression was by now being felt in every town in America; Wharton and Foote's haberdashery were no exceptions. The economy of Wharton, like much of the agrarian South, was based on cotton. If cotton was not selling, it meant that fewer shirts were being made. If fewer shirts were being made, fewer shirts were being bought. It was an unending cycle that affected farmers, manufacturers, retailers, and everyone in between. While Foote senior was managing to keep food on his family's table, he did not have money to send his son off to New York to study acting.

Finally, a compromise was reached. Foote agreed to wait one year after his graduation to be sure that was what he wanted to do with his life. If he still wanted to pursue acting, his father would pay for him to study for two years, but not in New York City. Miss Murphree had some brochures from other acting schools around the country, and after looking them over, Foote's father told him he could attend the Pasadena Playhouse in California, mainly because Foote had a great-aunt who lived in Los Angeles. In the interim, his father said, he could spend the off year with another aunt, Laura, who lived in Dallas, and take acting lessons there.

When his grandmother heard of the plan, she devised one of her own to help him and, possibly, to straighten out her own youngest son, Billy, in the process. Mrs. Brooks announced she had decided to spend a year in Dallas herself. She would take Billy with her and he could go to night school and study to become a lawyer while young Horton studied acting.

The August after his graduation, Foote, his grandmother, and his uncle Billy all went to Dallas and settled into a house his grandmother had rented in the Oak Cliff section of the city. She even found him a drama academy called the Woodward School. Under the agreement his grandmother had reached with his father, Horton could stay at the house she had rented, but he would have to find a job to pay his tuition to the acting school. Within his first week in Dallas, he got a job as an usher at the Majestic movie theater on Elm Street. It paid three dollars a week, which just barely covered school fees and his pocket expenses. It also allowed him to see free movies. Every day he would take a streetcar to his job, and twice a week he went to his classes at the Woodward School.

As it turned out, Miss Woodward gave little in the way of acting instruction. The school was more an elocution class than anything else, but there was to be a recital in the spring in which her students would perform scenes they had worked on during the term. She assigned Foote a part in a two-character Chekhov play called *Swan Song*, in which he, at the age of sixteen, was to play a washed-up, alcoholic actor in his sixties who, one night after a performance, recalls his glory days by reciting speeches from *King Lear, Hamlet,* and *Othello*.

When spring rolled around, Foote's mother came up from Wharton to see him in the recital. It was the first time she had spent a night away from her husband since they had married, and she planned to stay several days. The evening went well, and they all celebrated at a dinner out that evening. But the next day, Foote's mother received a phone call from his father saying that Foote's brother Tom had fallen out of a tree and broken his collarbone. Foote's mother took the bus back to Wharton the following morning, her break from domestic life cut short.

If anything, the Woodward School only made Foote more determined than ever to take proper acting lessons at a proper acting school, and with his parents' blessing he enrolled in the Pasadena Playhouse for the fall. To pay for his tuition, Foote's father sold a small house he had bought years earlier and had been renting to bring in extra money.

As Foote recounted in *Farewell*, a memoir of his childhood, his father called him out on the front porch on the night before he was to leave and gave him a new billfold with some money for his trip inside it.

"Be careful with that wallet, son," his father admonished him. "There are pickpockets on those buses, and—"

"Daddy, I'm going to be careful. Don't worry."

"I'm not worrying," his father said. "I have every confidence in you. I'm very proud of you, son. I know you'll do just fine."

There was a brief silence, then his father continued.

"You'll get to see mountains. Do you realize that? I envy you. I've never seen a mountain in my life. I guess now I never will. I'm glad you're going, son. Sometimes I wish your mother and I could get up and go and live some other place."

The following morning, Foote and his mother were driven to Houston by his uncle Billy to catch the bus to Dallas, where he was to spend one night with his aunt Laura before catching another bus the next day to Los Angeles.

Although he would return for one more summer, Foote knew he was leaving home for good. But rather than escaping his family, Foote ended up carrying them all with him, and it was they who became his collective muse.

CHAPTER 2

Pasadena:
The Actor Prepares

THE PASADENA PLAYHOUSE was founded in 1917 when a man named Gilmor Brown took over an old burlesque house and began putting on plays there. Although he had little talent as an actor or a director, he had a great passion for the theater, and he staged new and interesting plays that found an audience in Pasadena. By 1925, Brown's success prompted the town to raise funds to build a new theater for his enterprise, which was originally called the Pasadena Community Playhouse. Brown soon added a second stage, a small theater-in-the-round called the Play Box, and established a school that offered classes in acting and other theater arts.

By the time the seventeen-year-old Horton Foote arrived in the fall of 1933, it was a well-known academy that attracted aspiring actors from across the country. The school had a two-year curriculum and charged a fee of five hundred dollars for the first year and two hundred fifty dollars for the second, a lot of money during the Depression. The fee included a room at a boardinghouse near the school, but any other expenses were out of the students' pockets.

One of the reasons Foote's father agreed to his studying in Pasadena was that he had a great-aunt, his maternal grandmother's sister, who lived in Los Angeles. Foote had been told that this aunt, Mag, and her husband, Walt, would meet him when he arrived in Los Angeles, and he would spend the weekend with them before reporting to the school the following Monday.

He arrived at the Greyhound bus terminal in the middle of Los

Angeles after dark on a Saturday evening. Aunt Mag and Uncle Walt were indeed waiting for him. His aunt asked if he was hungry. He said he was, and they drove to a cafeteria for a meal. After dinner, his aunt and uncle suggested they drive around the city, and Foote readily agreed, eager to see his new hometown. After a brief time, however, Aunt Mag told Walt it was late, and they should drive to Pasadena so Horton could find a room at the YMCA. Foote was surprised. He started to remind her that he was supposed to stay at their apartment until Monday, but he was too polite, so he said nothing.

When they parted at the YMCA in Pasadena, Foote's aunt told him that they wanted him to come spend Thanksgiving with them. Foote thanked them, but was still puzzled over why they did not take him home with them as planned. He was also starting to worry about how long his money would last. The room at the Y was an expense he had not counted on. It was a small room but clean, and by this time Foote was so tired, he lay down on the bed and went to sleep with his clothes on.

The next day, Foote spent twenty-five cents on a breakfast of bacon and eggs and coffee at a drugstore, then asked directions to the Playhouse. He walked there, but it was locked up like a jail. He sat outside for a while, thinking someone might come out, but no one did. He walked along an empty Colorado Boulevard, the main street in Pasadena.

At one intersection, he heard church bells ringing and thought that his mother was likely sitting down to play the organ at the Methodist church in Wharton. For some reason, he thought of Miss Barclay, the woman who played the organ at the church until she committed suicide by hanging herself in her bedroom. He then remembered that California time was two hours behind Texas time, and that church services in Wharton were over, and his family was probably sitting down to Sunday dinner of fried chicken, mashed potatoes, biscuits, and gravy. The thought made him hungry again, but he knew he couldn't spend the money on another meal so soon.

An incident on the bus trip had made him acutely mindful of his finances. A woman who sat next to him had told him how she and her husband had lost their house, their car, and all their savings in the Depression. She asked him why he was going to California, and when Foote told her he was going to study acting at a drama school, she wanted to know how much it cost. When he told her, she exclaimed, "My God, that's a fortune. Seven hundred and fifty dollars is a fortune to me." And she proceeded to tell just about everyone else on the bus that he was going to California to study to be an actor and that it cost seven hundred and fifty dollars.

By late afternoon, he was tired of walking and was getting hungry again. He saw a cafeteria, but he didn't know how much the dishes cost, so he decided not to risk it. He found a diner that had the price of items they offered on signs behind the counter, and he got a hamburger for ten cents. After eating, he returned to his room at the YMCA. He lay down on his bed for a nap and when he awoke it was after nine o'clock at night. He thought again of his parents and realized they would be asleep by now.

To pass the time as much as anything else, he began writing a letter to his parents, telling them how much he loved Pasadena and how beautiful it was with its huge palm trees and flowering bougainvillea, although at that moment he was beginning to wonder why he had ever thought of becoming an actor in the first place: how he'd really like to be home at that very moment, sleeping in his own bed. He had only half finished the letter when sleepiness again overtook him and he lay down. The next thing he knew it was Monday morning, and the world looked a little brighter.

He paid his bill at the YMCA and walked with his one suitcase to the same diner for breakfast, then to the Pasadena Playhouse. When he got there it was still padlocked. It was only seven thirty in the morning, and the school didn't open until nine. There was one other person in front of the theater, clearly another student who had arrived early. Foote introduced himself.

The other student was named John Forsht, and he had just arrived that morning on a bus from Pennsylvania. He was three years older than Foote and had attended college for two years at Bucknell. Forsht asked Foote if he had eaten breakfast. When Foote said he had, Forsht told him he hadn't eaten in two days because his wal-

PITKIN COUNTY LIBRARY
120 NORTH MILL STREET
ASPEN, COLORADO 81611

let had been stolen when he changed buses in Denver, and he didn't have a cent. Foote loaned Forsht a quarter so he could eat breakfast.

The class was comprised of twelve girls and seven boys, all but one of whom were about Foote's age or a little older. One of the girls was very loud and kept telling anyone in earshot she was Jody Schwartzberg from Fort Worth, Texas. The students were introduced to one of their teachers, Miss Eugenia Ong, and given the addresses for their rooming houses. They were told classes would begin the following morning.

The house to which Foote was assigned was a two-story yellow frame structure only a block from the school. The landlady said another student at the school, Charles Robinson, would be staying there, but he wouldn't arrive until the next day. There were two other boarders, both older men. Foote's room was on the second floor, furnished with a bed, a table, a straight-backed chair, and one armchair.

Classes took place five days a week, from nine to five, with an hour off for lunch. There were courses in speech, theater history, scene design, makeup, and fencing, a common instruction for actors at that time, more to teach graceful movement than to prepare for swashbuckling roles. Two hours each day were spent in rehearsals. The three directors employed by the main theater took turns directing the students in different plays. Each student was assigned to a play they would present at the end of term.

For the next few weeks, Foote got to know the other class members. One to whom he paid considerable attention was named Charlotte Sturges. She was willowy and attractive in an ethereal sort of way and reminded him of Katharine Hepburn. Charlotte's great passion in life was modern dance, and she was devoted to Mary Wigman. She had wanted to go to Germany to study with the great dancer, but her parents insisted she go to the Pasadena Playhouse instead. Foote had known little of dance besides the fox-trot and belly rub when he started going out with Charlotte, but he soon learned a great deal, and modern dance would play an important part in his life within a few years.

The first play to which Foote was assigned was a Roman comedy

PITKIN COUNTY LIBRARY
120 NORTH MILL STREET
ASPEN, COLORADO 81611

to be directed by Tom Brown Henry. Henry was a harsh taskmaster who believed the best way to get a credible performance out of an actor was to scare him or her into it. On the first day of rehearsals, as Foote recalled in *Beginnings*, his memoir of his early years trying to become an actor, Henry addressed the cast:

> You are here to learn, I believe. You won't learn by my flattering you, but by my telling you what you have to do to survive in this lousy business. Now Gilmor Brown will be along one day and give you inspirational talks about how the theater is a temple and you must dedicate yourself unselfishly to it, and that's what he has done and that's worked for him, but I tell you you'll get kicked out of the temple if you don't know how to walk across the stage without looking like an automaton and talking so low you can't be heard.

Henry certainly wasted no flattery on Foote's efforts. On the second day of rehearsals, as Foote was acting in a scene, Henry stopped him after almost every line.

"Boy," he finally snapped. "Where are you from?"

"Texas, sir," Foote replied.

"Is that how they talk in Texas?"

"I guess so, sir."

"Well, I'm not from Texas and I can't understand a word you are saying."

"Is it not loud enough?" Foote asked.

"No. You're loud enough. But you'll never get anywhere with that accent."

After his speech class the following day, Foote was asked by Miss Ong to stay behind after the others had left. She told him he should have some private tutoring to overcome his drawl of a Texas accent and recommended her own speech teacher, Blanche Townsend.

In all of his budgeting and planning for his studies in Pasadena, the prospect of additional lessons had not entered into the calculations. But he figured if he went without lunch, he would be able to afford two lessons a week from Miss Townsend.

The extra speech lessons began at eight o'clock, an hour before classes started at the Playhouse. The first lessons concentrated on breathing exercises. Then Miss Townsend had him read Hamlet's speech to the players. Foote began: "Speak the speech, I pray you, as I pronounced it to you, trippingly on the tongue . . ." She interrupted him.

They concentrated on the phrase "trippingly on the tongue" for half an hour. Miss Townsend made him say it over and over and over.

"Trippingly, trippingly, trippingly," she would say.

"Trippingly, trippingly, trippingly," he would echo.

"Better. Much better," she would encourage.

Foote was not sure what all this had to do with acting, but he trusted Miss Townsend, and she was very patient with him. Also, Tom Brown Henry had stopped riding him quite so hard in rehearsals at school.

By the time Thanksgiving rolled around, Foote was looking forward to a weekend away. He called his aunt Mag early that week and she said they would be at his boardinghouse at eight o'clock on Thursday morning and all drive together to Vista, the town where Mag and Walt's grown children lived.

Foote packed a small suitcase and was waiting in the living room of his boardinghouse by seven thirty Thanksgiving morning. When eight o'clock came, he went outside to look for their car. By eight thirty, he was becoming a bit anxious. By nine, he was decidedly uneasy. His landlady asked if he was sure he had the time right. She suggested that maybe they had gotten lost trying to find the house. He doubted that was the case.

Ten o'clock came and went. At eleven, Foote tried to call them. Uncle Walt answered the phone. Foote asked if Aunt Mag was there, but Walt told him that she had gone to Vista the day before for Thanksgiving and would be gone a few days. If it occurred to Walt that she was supposed to take her grandnephew with him, he said nothing about it. Again, Foote was too polite to mention it, so he wished his uncle a happy Thanksgiving and hung up. They had simply forgotten about him.

Foote's landlady set a place for him to have Thanksgiving dinner at the boardinghouse, and he spent the rest of the weekend on his own. All the other students had departed to family and friends. He started writing a letter to his mother and father, but he didn't want to tell them what had happened with Aunt Mag and Uncle Walt, and he didn't want to lie by telling them what a wonderful Thanksgiving he had, so in the end he didn't write them at all.

Throughout the fall, in addition to classes and the plays they worked on, the students attended productions at the Playhouse's main stage and at the Play Box. Seeing these performances gave Foote as much of an education in acting as he was receiving from the teachers.

Foote took Charlotte to most of the plays at the Playhouse, although she was dismissive of all of them. For Charlotte, modern dance was the only true form of artistic expression, and the theater and acting were outdated and not worth wasting one's time on.

One night, after they had seen a production of Oscar Wilde's *Salomé* with a young actor named Lee J. Cobb in the role of Herod, their differences of opinion developed into a full-blown argument. Charlotte was particularly incensed by the actress playing the title role and her Dance of the Seven Veils.

"That vulgar display is *not* dancing," she told Foote as they left the theater.

Foote had been very taken with Cobb's portrayal of Herod and marveled that he was only twenty-five years old. Moreover, a fellow student named Joe Anthony, who was in his second year at the Playhouse, appeared in the production and Foote admired his performance as well. He wanted to talk about the play and asked Charlotte if she wanted to go for a soda.

"I'm going home," Charlotte fumed. "I hated it."

Foote offered to walk with her, but she insisted on going alone. They quarreled, then agreed to disagree, and Charlotte finally let Foote walk her home.

By dating Charlotte throughout his first year, Foote learned a great deal about modern dance. But he had to look elsewhere for any discussion about the plays and performances he saw at the school.

One of his more outspoken classmates was Jody Schwartzberg, who was as enamored of the German theater, especially Max Reinhardt, as Charlotte was of German dance and Mary Wigman. John Forsht was also devoted to German theater, as was Doc Granby, another classmate who had graduated from Princeton and had actually seen Broadway productions. In fact, Germany was pretty much at the vanguard of all artistic endeavor at the time, and many of its leading lights—actors, playwrights, directors, dancers, musicians—were beginning to emigrate to America as the Nazis brought more of German society under their repressive control.

Foote soon joined the chorus of students who extolled German theater and acting as the acme of the profession. It was, however, an American actress who made the most lasting impression on him during his two years in Pasadena. It came in the spring of Foote's first year, and it was his grandmother from Wharton who made it possible.

Early in December, Foote received a letter from his mother saying his grandmother had decided to spend some time with her two sisters in California, and, unsurprisingly, had chosen Pasadena to be her home base for the visit. Foote had since written his parents about the Thanksgiving incident with Mag and Walt. It occurred to him that his mother might write her aunt to thank her for having him for the holiday, and that would only deepen the embarrassment. His grandmother figured that Walt had gotten drunk and so angered Mag that she simply went off on her own and forgot about her grandnephew.

Foote's grandmother arrived the day before the Christmas holiday break began at the school. It was arranged that she and Mag would collect him at his boardinghouse and they would drive together to spend Christmas with their other sister, Bo, in La Jolla. Foote had not seen or heard from Mag since being stood up on Thanksgiving, and he did not know whether there would be any awkwardness. But his aunt was friendly when they met and did not mention the incident. It was as though nothing had ever happened.

Bo, Foote's other great-aunt, was a widow who lived in a house on the ocean. Her husband, Harry, had owned an insurance business that had run into financial problems, and he had hanged himself in their bedroom ten years earlier. Aunt Bo had taken over the company, turned it around, and now clearly had a lot of money.

Aunt Bo surprised Foote by announcing on the first day of their visit that since it was 1933 and Prohibition had been repealed, she would serve cocktails before dinner and wine with the meal. She also said that she smoked cigarettes. What surprised him even more was that his grandmother simply smiled and said that was fine. Foote had thought that since Baboo's own sons had such a problem with alcohol, she would have objected. His grandmother, of course, declined the cocktails and wine, and seemed pleased when Foote did as well.

After Christmas, Aunt Bo decided to join Foote's grandmother in Pasadena for a few weeks. His grandmother had rented an apartment in one of the more expensive neighborhoods in Pasadena, and she insisted that Foote move in with them. It would be a longer walk to school each day, and Foote knew there would be a problem if he left the boardinghouse before the end of the school year.

Indeed, his landlady complained to the school, saying she relied on the income from renting her rooms to acting students for her livelihood, and she expected Foote to stay there through the end of the term. But the school smoothed things over, and Foote spent the rest of the semester in the apartment his grandmother and Aunt Bo had rented.

Nearly every student in Foote's class had an idol whose artistic talents were the epitome of genius. For Charlotte, it was Mary Wigman. For Jody Schwartzberg, apart from Reinhardt's German theater, it was Eva Le Gallienne. Early in March, Jody came to school bursting with the news that Le Gallienne was going to appear in Los Angeles in three Ibsen plays and that everybody should go see her.

As Foote's birthday approached, his grandmother asked what he would like as a present. Without hesitation he said he would like to go into Los Angeles and see *Hedda Gabler* with Miss Le Gallienne. His grandmother readily agreed and bought tickets for Foote, herself, and Aunt Bo. The performance was on a Friday night, and the three of them took a train into Los Angeles proper. The evening was a revelation for Foote.

From the moment Le Gallienne entered as Hedda, Foote could not take his eyes off her. He would say years later that he could never forget how she said the word "bored," or how she insulted her husband's aunt by thinking the aunt's hat belonged to the maid, or how she burned Eilert's manuscript and then reacted to the news of his death, how she looked at Judge Brock when he threatened to blackmail her, or how she caressed her pistols.

On the way out of the theater, Aunt Bo told Foote's grandmother that there were two more performances of different plays—*A Doll's House* and *The Master Builder*—the following day. The two women decided instantly to come back and see them both, and his grandmother went to get the tickets. When she returned she was carrying a copy of Le Gallienne's book *At 33*, which had been on sale in the lobby. "Happy Birthday," she said, handing Foote the book.

"Baboo," he said. "You don't know what seeing the play has meant to me."

"I'm glad," his grandmother replied. "Very glad."

Foote, his grandmother, and his great-aunt saw *A Doll's House* at the Saturday matinee and *The Master Builder* that evening. Le Gallienne took the role of Mrs. Linde in *A Doll's House* and played Hilda in *The Master Builder.* Foote was again mesmerized, not only by Le Gallienne's performance but by Ibsen's plays. He realized for the first time how such moving drama could be made out of ordinary stories of everyday life.

The first person Foote saw at school the following Monday was Charlotte, who ran up to him, full of excitement. She was carrying a catalog she had received in the mail from Mary Wigman's school in Germany. She told him that her parents had consented for her to apply to study with Wigman in the fall if she would work to help pay the cost. Foote began to tell her about the Ibsen plays and how he had been enraptured by Le Gallienne's performances, but she interrupted him and said she had to go see if there were any part-time jobs available, since she had to start saving to go to Germany.

Next he saw Jody. He thought she, for certain, would be excited by his weekend. He showed her Le Gallienne's book and said he was so taken by her performances that he was determined to go to New York and try to work in her company.

"That will never happen," Jody sniffed, in her own pronounced Texas accent. "Not with your diction. Why, even the people who answer the phone at the Civic Repertory Theatre have perfect diction."

One night a few weeks later, Foote began to feel unwell. He spent a restless night, and the following morning had a stomachache. His grandmother and aunt fussed over him, took his temperature, and poked around his stomach where he said it hurt. He had a slight fever of 101 degrees, and his grandmother called the school to say he was ill and would not be in class that day.

Through the morning, the pain in his stomach increased, and the landlady of the apartment they were renting gave them the name of a doctor. One thought flashed through his grandmother's mind—years earlier her brother-in-law had died of a ruptured appendix, and it always haunted her that he could have been saved if he had acted in time to have it removed.

The doctor came, poked around some more, and told his grandmother and his aunt that Foote did appear to have a mild case of appendicitis, but that he did not think it was serious enough to operate. He said the pain should go away and advised Foote to stay in bed for a couple of days, but to call him if the pain increased. By Wednesday, the pain was completely gone and Foote returned to school.

Toward the end of April, Foote's grandmother received a letter that visibly disturbed her, and she announced at dinner that she would have to return to Wharton immediately. She did not tell Foote what news the letter contained, but he imagined it had something to do with some trouble one of his uncles had gotten into. Aunt Bo tried to convince her sister to stay until the end of Horton's term, but she said she had to get back to Texas at once. She paid the rent on the apartment through the end of the month and for the last few weeks of the school year he lived there alone.

On the night before the last day of classes, Foote took Charlotte to dinner. Just before leaving to return to La Jolla, his aunt Bo had given him a ten-dollar bill, and he spent a good part of it on buying Charlotte a farewell meal at an Italian restaurant. Charlotte had already lined up a job for the summer, and with the money she would earn she hoped to be in Germany by the fall studying with Mary Wigman. Foote did not know when, if ever, he would see her again. She was bubbling with excitement about her plans, but she gave him her address and each promised to write through the summer and fall.

While he was looking forward to seeing his family again, Foote was anxious about what he would find when he arrived home for the summer. His mother had written him that she and his father had moved into his grandmother's house while she was away in California. Times were getting harder, and they had decided to rent out their own house to make some extra money. Although he had treated his grandmother's house almost as an extension of his own throughout his life, it would feel strange sleeping and living there all the time.

His older cousin Nan met him at the bus station in Houston and drove him to Wharton. Nan had been another source of stories for Foote as he was growing up. She was a gossip columnist of sorts for the local Wharton newspaper, and she knew most of the town's scandals, including those she couldn't print. When she was younger she had traveled to New York and had seen plays on Broadway, which had endeared her to the stagestruck young Foote, and it was she, among all of his relatives, who had most encouraged him in his acting ambitions. On the drive from Houston to Wharton, she kept asking him about California, whether he had seen any movie stars, and whether it was as beautiful as everyone said, while Foote kept asking about his family and the situation he would find at home.

He learned that it had, indeed, been some trouble his uncles had gotten into that brought his grandmother back from California, and that she had been unwell ever since she returned. She now spent most of her days in bed. Foote asked about his father's business, and his aunt replied, "There is none." While the cotton crop had been good, there was no demand for it and it sat in warehouses, unsold. As if to emphasize the point, they drove past farm after farm where the cotton just sat in the fields unpicked.

When they arrived at his grandmother's house, he greeted his mother and asked, "Where's Baboo?" His mother told him she was in her bedroom, resting. Hearing his voice, his grandmother called out to him. When he entered the room and saw her, he could not believe it was the same woman he had stayed with until just a month earlier. She seemed to have shrunk in size, and her voice was barely an echo of its former self. It pained him to see her lying there so helpless and suddenly so old.

After visiting with her a few minutes, he went downtown to see his father at the store. There were no customers when he got there, and his father told him everything that had been happening. The crisis that brought his grandmother home from California came when two of his uncles, Billy and Speed, had gone on a bender in Houston, got into a fight, and ended up in jail. Foote's father became angry as he talked about his brothers-in-law and the effect they were having on their mother. "Their behavior is sending her nearer the grave every day."

Foote spent his first few days home looking up old high school friends and working on his speech exercises. His brother Tom began charging his friends a nickel just to hear Horton practice his diction exercises in the backyard of his grandmother's house.

Foote had been back home only a few days when he awoke one night with a severe stomach pain like the one he'd had in California. He called out to his mother. She didn't hear him, but his grandmother did, and she got out of bed and came to him. When he told his grandmother it was the same pain he had had in California, she insisted they call the Brookses' family doctor.

Soon the whole house was awake. Dr. Toxie arrived about fifteen minutes later and was told about the similar episode in California. After examining him, Dr. Toxie said it was another appendicitis attack, but that he thought it was not so severe that it required surgery. He told them to keep ice packs on his abdomen to reduce the swelling, and that the pain should subside.

For the next hour, his father chipped ice from a block, and his mother wrapped the ice in a towel and held it on his stomach. The pain, however, only increased, and at one point when Foote cried out, his grandmother called the doctor to return. This time the doctor decided to operate immediately and they took him in the doctor's car to the hospital.

The Wharton hospital had been converted from an old two-story house that Dr. Toxie had bought some years earlier. A nurse who was on night duty greeted them, and Foote heard the doctor tell her, "We're going to operate right now." He heard his grandmother tell his mother, "I can't help but think of Uncle Billy," her brother-in-law who had died of a ruptured appendix. It frightened him, and that was the last thing he remembered before he went under the anesthesia for the surgery.

When he awoke the next morning, he heard his aunt Loula and his mother talking outside his room. Loula was telling his mother, "Daisy called and said his appendix had burst and he was in the operating room, and all I could think about was Billy." Foote stayed in the hospital for ten days. His nurse turned out to be an old high school acquaintance named Ruby Davis. She told him he was lucky to be alive because his appendix had indeed ruptured and that Dr. Toxie had been so worried that he stayed in his room for the rest of the night after the operation.

For the remainder of the summer, Foote convalesced at his grandmother's house. When the time came for him to return to Pasadena, his grandmother, who seemed to revive herself just by helping to take care of him, told his father that she thought he should take the train back to California rather than the bus, and that she wanted to pay for the ticket. To Foote's surprise, his father agreed without protest.

The train was certainly a lot more comfortable than the bus and took a lot less time. His aunt Mag and uncle Walt again met him and drove him to Pasadena, but this time there was no talk of him spending Thanksgiving with them. There was also no question of him staying with them until the school opened.

During the summer, he had received communication from the

school that it had bought two houses near the Playhouse, and all students would be assigned rooms to share in one of them. Mag and Walt dropped him off at the school office, and he was given the address of the house he would be in. He would be rooming with John Forsht.

On the first day of classes, he learned that the second-year students would work on a series of plays to be performed in the Playhouse's patio theater, a third stage that was reserved for school productions. The students would act, design and build the sets, and do all the other backstage work. There would be three weeks of rehearsals for each play, which would be performed for one matinee and two evenings.

The first play was Wilde's *The Importance of Being Earnest*, and Foote was cast as Jack. John Forsht was to play Algernon and Jody Schwartzberg was assigned the role of Lady Bracknell. At the first rehearsal, their director, Janet Scott, asked the cast if they wanted to try for English accents. All eagerly said they did.

During the first reading, Miss Scott listened for a while, but when Jody began her first speech as Lady Bracknell, the director stopped her.

"Is that an English accent you're attempting?" she asked.

"Yes, ma'am," Jody replied.

"And you, Horton and John?"

They admitted it was.

"Well, let's forget the accent," Miss Scott said. "There is no time for that."

"But I want to have an English accent," Jody insisted, pouting.

"I'm sure you feel that, dear," the director said, not unkindly. "But I'm your director. Just speak naturally for me, and later, *much* later, we can try for an accent." They never attempted an English accent again.

Throughout the mid-1930s, Los Angeles experienced an influx of German actors, most of whom were fleeing the Nazi regime. One of the plays produced at the Playhouse's main stage that fall was a dramatization of Dostoyevsky's *The Brothers Karamazov*, featuring two German actors from Max Reinhardt's company. In the spring, another protégé of Reinhardt's appeared in a play about

John Brown. But she was an American, a strikingly beautiful young woman named Rosamond Pinchot. Foote was captivated by her.

Since Jody Schwartzberg was the resident expert on Reinhardt and his company, Foote asked her about Rosamond Pinchot. Jody sniffed and said she was a New York socialite from a very rich family who had been "discovered" by Reinhardt on an ocean liner between Europe and the United States. Jody thought she had no talent, but Foote said he admired her performance.

"You're just dazzled by her beauty," Jody said.

"Not just that," he said. "I find something very touching and vulnerable about her."

"Vulnerable, indeed," Jody scoffed. "That's just sheer panic, because she doesn't know what she's doing. She obviously is not much of an actress and needs a great deal of training."

Foote went to see Rosamond in the play a second time, and was as impressed as he had been the first time. Afterward, he went backstage to tell her how much he enjoyed her performance. She seemed genuinely pleased to have an admirer, and told him to wait while she changed and they could talk. They walked out together to the courtyard.

She was tall and wore her blond hair shoulder length. She was a cover-girl beauty, but very down-to-earth and friendly. They talked for nearly an hour that night, and Foote met her often during the course of the play's run. They opened up to each other, Rosamond telling him about how she was discovered by Reinhardt, but confessing that she felt insecure on the stage and thought she needed experience, which was why she was doing this play. Foote told her he wanted to go to New York and become an actor, and Rosamond encouraged him. She even suggested a Russian teacher who had been with the Moscow Art Theatre and with whom she planned to study when she returned.

When the play ended its run, Rosamond gave Foote her address and told him to write to her and look her up when he came to New York. As Foote's final year at the Playhouse drew to a close, he was in a quandary over his future. While the plays he had been in that year seemed to have been well received at the school, he did not have any confidence that he could make it as an actor in New York. He thought of all the great performances he had seen during his two years in Pasadena—from the young Lee J. Cobb to Eva Le Gallienne—and doubted he would ever be able to reach their level.

Shortly before the end of term he asked his speech teacher, Miss Townsend, if she thought he could make it as an actor in New York.

"Anything is possible, Horton," she said. "It would depend, I think, on your determination."

Foote's heart sank.

"By the way," she added, "what are you doing for the summer?"

Foote replied that he would go home to Texas, but after that he didn't know what he would do.

"I teach in the summer at Martha's Vineyard," she said. "There's a stock company there, too."

Miss Townsend explained that she directed a summer of plays at the Rice Playhouse on the Vineyard, and that the owners allowed her to bring three or four of her students to work in the theater. It paid only five dollars a week, but there was free room and board. She had already asked John Forsht, and he had accepted, and Joe Anthony, the student whom Foote had admired in the play with Lee J. Cobb, was also coming for the summer. Miss Townsend wondered if Foote would like to come as well. She told him to think about it and let her know.

"I can give you my answer now," he said. "I want to go."

Foote immediately wrote his parents about the offer, explaining he would only be able to visit them a short time. He also asked if they would be able to pay his train fare to Massachusetts. His father wrote back to say how proud he was of him and that he would pay Foote's train fare to Martha's Vineyard, but since the Depression was still going on, that would be the last time they could help him pursue his acting career.

John Forsht went home to Texas with Foote at the end of term, and they spent a week in Wharton. When they arrived on the Vineyard, they began taking classes from Miss Townsend and got to know Joe Anthony. Over the course of the summer, the three young men became close friends.

Foote and Forsht were cast together in the final play of the season, a three-hander by Paul Green called *The No 'Count Boy*, a drama about rural blacks in North Carolina. Foote played the title character in blackface, and even then wondered why Miss Townsend had chosen such a play for three white actors to perform.

Foote's familiarity with the black culture in Wharton was a big asset, however, and the play was a success, performing to sold-out audiences. By the end of the run, he and John and Joe all determined to go to New York that fall and become Broadway stars.

CHAPTER 3

Greenwich Village:
Auditions

Aт the time of Foote's arrival in New York City, Greenwich Village was the cultural center of America, a mecca of small theaters and clubs and cafés to which every aspiring writer, actor, artist, musician, and dancer became pilgrim.

When Foote left the Vineyard for New York in the fall of 1935, Foote's father sent him a check for fifty dollars and told him that would be the last he could expect. And except for gifts on the occasions of his marriage and the birth of his children, it was the last money he took from his family; though in those early years in New York, there were many nights when he went to bed hungry.

Foote, John Forsht, and Joe Anthony went in together and rented a furnished apartment on MacDougal Street, just across from the Provincetown Playhouse. It had two large rooms and one smaller one, plus a small kitchen. The furnishings were old and minimal—three beds, a sofa, and a few chairs—but the apartment was comfortable enough and the three young men thought it would only be for a short while anyway.

At the time of his arrival, Foote still had most of the fifty dollars his father had given him. John had a grand total of seven dollars he had saved from the summer and Joe had only a little more than that. They would have to get jobs quickly. Foote and John both found employment across the street, working backstage at the Provincetown Playhouse for a show called *The Provincetown Follies*, which was just going into rehearsals. It paid very little, but it was enough to keep body and soul together until they could find real acting jobs.

Once the show opened, Foote and John began the daily routine of making the rounds of Broadway production offices. Broadway was a very different beast in the 1930s and '40s. Writers, actors, singers, dancers, and just about anyone who wanted to be in the theater went from office to office looking for work. Only the top stars had personal agents who sealed deals over three-martini lunches. There were no glossy 8 × 10 photos pasted to the backs of résumés for casting agents to look at. You showed yourself and hoped you looked the part.

These agencies often consisted of only two rooms—an outer reception area and an inner office. The best agencies tried to keep abreast of every stage and film project in New York and what parts directors were looking to fill. A director or producer might send out a call that he was looking for a tall blonde or a short brunette for a role in a play or movie. If an aspiring actor walked in who looked right for a part that was open, he or she might be sent to a casting call. Other agencies might also have sent actors fitting the description, and the director would then choose one of them for the job.

Foote's days took on a certain ritual. They began with breakfast in a downtown drugstore, followed by a subway ride to Forty-second Street, then hours of visiting one office after another, along with hundreds of other actors, to ask, "Anything today?" The question almost invariably received a glance and a simple shake of the head. Foote's route usually began at Thirty-ninth Street, at the Empire Theatre building, across the street from the old Metropolitan Opera House. Several theatrical agencies had offices there, and it would take him nearly an hour to go into every one. From there, he plodded farther uptown, hitting every office on all the side streets off Broadway—Forty-fourth Street, Forty-fifth Street, Forty-sixth Street, Forty-seventh Street.

At lunchtime many actors gathered in the drugstore of the Hotel Astor. Apart from affordable sandwiches, the actors could pick up information—the short brunette might know of an agent who was looking for a tall blonde, or somebody else might know of a show that needed a rope twirler. Foote went by the Astor almost every day for lunch and then dropped in again in the afternoon for a soda, always hoping to hear any tips.

By late November, *The Provincetown Follies* had closed and Foote had been without a job for weeks. The money he had saved from working backstage was nearly gone, and he wasn't even getting a second glance at the agencies. One very cold day he was early to meet John at the Astor. He was looking forward to just being inside for a bit. Then he remembered some other offices farther uptown that he hadn't tried.

He wavered between the warmth of the drugstore and schlepping farther up Seventh Avenue. He decided to finish making the rounds. At the first two, on Fifty-fifth Street, he chatted with the receptionists, then asked, "Are you casting today?" In both offices, the young women shook their heads and replied, "Not today."

He was about to skip the last office, the Jennie Jacobs Agency, which was another two blocks north and had a reputation for never hiring off the street. But he thought, *You've come this far, you might as well go on.* When he walked into the office it was empty, and he was about to turn and leave when Henry Weiss, Miss Jacobs's assistant, came through a door. Before Foote could even ask, Weiss said, "Nothing today, son."

As Foote was about to leave, Weiss stopped and said, "Wait a minute." Weiss looked him up and down and then said, "Can you go over to the Fox Studio right now?"

Foote could and did.

The Fox Studio was in the mid-fifties near Tenth Avenue and looked more like a sweat shop in the Garment District than a movie studio. The man Foote was to contact looked him over, up and down, and walked around him for nearly five minutes, like he was about to measure him for a suit. Foote said nothing and held his breath. Then the man said, "Come with me."

The audition was for a small part in a costume film set in the fifteenth century. The man gave him a script and ten minutes to look over some lines. He then had Foote read the lines and asked him whether he would be free to shoot the scene the next day. Foote didn't need to check his calendar. "Yes, sir," he replied. The man told him to go home and he would call him that evening at seven o'clock and let him know if he had the part.

The apartment Foote shared with John and Joe did not have a telephone—they couldn't afford one. There was a pay phone on the fifth floor of the apartment building, and it was that number Foote gave out to friends and relatives or anyone to whom he might be applying for a job.

When he arrived home, John was already there and preparing their dinner. Foote left the front door to their apartment open and moved a chair over by it so he could hear the phone when it rang. When seven o'clock came and there was no call, his heart sank. It finally came ten minutes later. Foote raced up the several flights of stairs.

"Can you be at the studio at seven tomorrow morning for costume and makeup?" a voice asked.

"Yes, sir, I certainly can," Foote replied.

It was only for two or possibly three days' work, but it would pay a hundred and fifty dollars. John asked him what the name of the movie was, but Foote had forgotten to ask.

When he arrived at the studio promptly at seven the next morning, Foote was told to report to makeup. He learned that two actors who were well known on Broadway at the time—Ernest Glendinning and Paul Leyssac—were both in the film. Foote then got a crash course in one of the primary activities involved in film acting—waiting.

The director did not call for his scene until late in the afternoon, and after shooting a couple of takes, he was asked to come back the next day. When he finished at three in the afternoon the following day, he still did not know the name of the movie, and he never saw any mention of it again. He assumed it had never been released, and it was only years later he learned it was an industrial film. He never learned its name.

The money helped stave off eviction and hunger for a few weeks, but as Christmas approached, Foote had not found another job and money again was starting to run low. To add another touch to the sense of gloom, a snowstorm hit New York. Foote had never seen snow before. His father had told him stories about the one time it had snowed in Wharton, before Horton was born, but it was a new experience for Foote and he wrote his parents a long letter describing it.

Both John and Joe planned to return to their homes in Pennsylvania and Wisconsin for the holidays, and John, realizing Foote would be alone in the city, asked him to join him. John's parents had sent him some money for the trip home, and there was enough to pay for both his and Foote's bus fare.

When they arrived on Christmas Eve, they were met at the bus station by John's brother and they drove straight to his house. There was no spare room for Horton at John's parents', so it was arranged for him to stay with a family friend, a German professor who lived in the next town. John and Foote had dinner with the professor that night and John told him he would pick him up the next morning to have Christmas dinner with John's family. It snowed during the night, and when John arrived the following morning, he said that his mother had taken ill and they would not be having dinner at home. Instead, John and Foote had Christmas dinner in a restaurant on some money John's brother had given him. Afterward, Foote said he thought he would return to New York that day. John did not try to talk him out of it.

Foote arrived back in New York shortly before midnight on Christmas night and took the subway home. The next day it snowed again and a package arrived from Texas. In it were Christmas presents from his parents. There was a shirt and a pair of socks from his father's store, a fruit cake, and a box of cookies.

Both John and Joe stayed with their families through the holidays, and Foote was still alone as New Year's Eve approached. Their apartment was over a small nightclub that featured a trio—piano, drums, and sax—that played nightly from eight to midnight. It was mostly a nuisance since the trio played the same popular songs over and over.

Over the months, the boys had gotten used to the constant sound of the band, but as Foote sat alone on New Year's Eve, the music once again filled the apartment. The club was open that night until four for New Year's Eve, and the band kept playing the same songs—

"I'm in the Mood for Love," "Dream a Little Dream of Me," "I'll Get By," and "Red Sails in the Sunset." The last song had been in *The Provincetown Follies*.

Loneliness swept over him, and he finally bundled up against the cold and went outside, if only to get out of the apartment. As he came out of the building he looked across the street at the Province-town Playhouse, now closed and boarded up and looking forlorn and desolate, very much like Foote felt.

Foote walked around the block, and as he approached his front door he stopped and looked inside the nightclub. It was crowded with revelers, all of whom seemed to be having a good time. The band was playing loudly enough so that the music could be heard on the sidewalk, and Foote was tempted to go inside and buy himself a beer to celebrate the New Year. Then he thought he should prob-ably save his money, so he went upstairs to the apartment and spent the first hours of 1936 writing a letter to his parents, lying about what a wonderful Christmas he had spent with his friend John and how confident he was that he would get a job acting in a play soon.

It was in late January, as he was making his rounds, that Foote saw Rosamond Pinchot walking down Broadway. It had been a year since Foote had seen her in Pasadena, and he didn't know whether she would even remember him. Rosamond greeted him like a long-lost friend. She told him she was "studying with the Russians," and that she needed a scene partner for her class. She offered to pay his tuition for acting lessons if he would work on a scene from Shaw's *Candida* with her and perform it before her teacher. Foote, who was growing frustrated in his fruitless pursuit of acting jobs, read-ily agreed, although he was unsure exactly who "the Russians" were.

At the time, New York theater was in the grip of a great Russian invasion. Just as there was an influx of German writers, actors, and directors who had escaped the Nazis, there were also many Russian actors and directors who had fled Stalin's Soviet Union to avoid the cultural purges that had landed some writers and artists in prison or Siberia. They brought with them the new approach to acting taught by the Russian director Constantin Stanislavski, which later became known in America simply as "the method." Stanislavski's book *An Actor Prepares* became a sort of bible for aspiring actors, and the method would come to dominate American acting for the rest of the twentieth century and beyond. At the time, however, it was practiced only by some avant-garde companies like the Group Theatre.

Tamara Daykarhanova was one of the expatriate Russian refugees from the Moscow Art Theatre, and she had opened a studio on West Fifty-sixth Street, between Fifth and Sixth Avenues. Among the other teachers on her staff were Vera Soloviova and her husband, Andrius Jilinsky, both of whom were also veterans of the Moscow Art Theatre and had first come to New York with the Michael Chekhov company. Chekhov, a nephew of the Russian playwright, was considered one of Russia's finest actors. When his company disbanded, most of its members decided not to return to the Soviet Union for fear of persecution, and some of them, needing to find a way to make a living, began teaching.

Daykarhanova held classes on Tuesdays and Fridays for two hours in the afternoon. The next class was the following day and Rosamond asked Foote if he could be there. He said he would.

When he arrived, Rosamond took him to an office for him to enroll. A woman began to ask him some routine questions, but when it came out that he had first met Rosamond at the Pasadena Playhouse and that he had studied there himself, his interviewer frowned and asked, "Does Madame know this?" Foote said he had no idea.

The woman left the room and returned with an attractive woman in her midfifties. She had short, dark hair and wore a tailored skirt and silk blouse. She was introduced as Madame Daykarhanova. The woman who had been interviewing him explained that Foote had met Rosamond in Pasadena, adding ominously, "at the Playhouse."

"Ah, Pasadena," Daykarhanova said in heavily accented English. "You studied there?"

"Yes, ma'am," Foote replied.

"How old are you?"

"Nineteen."

"Well, and you want to study with me?"

"Yes, I do."

"Good," Madame said. "You know we don't teach here like at Pasadena Playhouse. Here we are strict. Very, very strict. Are you willing to work hard?"

"Yes, ma'am."

"You understand you will have to forget everything you learned at Pasadena Playhouse school. You are willing to do this?"

"Yes, I am," Foote replied, not really knowing how he would do that.

"Good," Daykarhanova said. "Is not always easy, you know, getting rid of old ways. Class is in ten minutes."

Throughout the following week, Foote and Rosamond worked on the scene she wanted to do from *Candida*, and they were scheduled to present it to the class the following Friday. When Foote arrived at the studio, however, Madame Daykarhanova called him into her office.

"Horton, I just had a call from Rosamond," Madame said. "She is leaving today for Hollywood. She is very distressed she is deserting you and promises she will be back soon. She has paid for your tuition, however, and if you want to continue studying here I will be happy to have you."

"Thank you," Foote replied. "I'd like to."

Thus began Foote's years of study with "the Russians," an experience that did not make him a great actor but had a deep influence on his approach to the theater when he began to write.

As it turned out, Rosamond did not return from California at all that year, and with the paucity of acting jobs, the scene-study classes with Madame Daykarhanova and another in technique taught by Jilinsky constituted Foote's one tether to the theater through most of that year.

John Forsht had already given up on getting an acting job and for some weeks had been looking for any kind of employment so he could stay in New York. When he still had not found work by late spring, he returned to Pennsylvania. Foote and Joe Anthony decided the MacDougal Street apartment was too expensive for just the two of them, so each moved into a rooming house.

Throughout the spring, Foote worked on various scenes with different partners, including one from *Ah, Wilderness!*, a sort of rite of passage for acting students of a certain age. He was partnered in it with Betty Goddard, who lived on Park Avenue and whose mother was close friends with Arthur Hopkins, a major producer, and played bridge with Pauline Lord, then one of the reigning lights on Broadway.

Another scene he did in class was from *The No 'Count Boy*, the play he and John Forsht had done the previous summer on Martha's Vineyard. He was partnered with Perry Wilson, and when they presented it in class, both Madame Daykarhanova and Madame Soloviova were much taken with it and told them they should do it for the studio's recital at the end of the semester. Foote was greatly attracted to Perry, and they went out together a few times. But she was also seeing Joe Anthony, and that turned serious. When Anthony and Wilson eventually married, Foote was best man at their wedding.

The final recital was an important event for the students since many agents, directors, and producers attended to get a look at the young crop of actors. After Foote did his scene with Perry, a talent scout from Warner Brothers who was in the audience came up to Foote and told him the studio would be producing plays on Broadway the next season and there might be something for him.

At the beginning of the summer Foote returned to Martha's Vineyard, but he was there only a few weeks when he got a call from Warner Brothers asking if he could come to New York to start rehearsals for a play called *Swing Your Lady*. When he arrived at the theater he learned that the show had been in rehearsal for several weeks, but they had avoided bringing in actors for smaller parts until the end so they could save money. Foote also learned that he was expected to rehearse for five days without pay, and that only then would he be given a contract.

In the afternoon, the stage manager gave him his sides and told him to enter from downstage, make his mark, and read his lines. Foote, who had not even seen his lines at that point, asked if he could rehearse it once. The stage manager told him the small roles didn't get a rehearsal.

When the time came for his scene, Foote was so nervous that his hands were shaking and he could barely hold his sides, let alone read them. He was struck for the first time with stage fright, and when he walked to his mark he just stood onstage for a few moments, unable to say a word. When he finally got the lines out, he was sure no one could hear him beyond the first row. He was hardly surprised when an assistant stage manager came to him afterward and told him they would not be needing him. It was small comfort that when the show opened ten days later, it got terrible reviews and closed after two performances.

In the fall, Foote returned to Madame Daykarhanova's. The technique classes with Jilinsky were an hour long every day, and the scene-study classes met for two hours twice a week. He worked hard for the classes at the studio, and about a month into the term, the work paid off.

Benjamin Zemach, a director and producer, had been attending some of the classes as an observer and one day he came up to Foote and told him he was doing the choreography for a show called *The Eternal Road*, a sort of pageant about the wanderings of the Jews throughout history, that would be directed by Max Reinhardt. Would Foote like to join the company? The pay was twenty-five dollars a week. Foote was elated. He wished he could tell Jody Schwartzberg that he would be working for Reinhardt and see her face. Foote also learned that Rosamond Pinchot would be playing Bathsheba in the show.

Reinhardt, the Austrian-born director of the Deutsches Theater in Berlin, had immigrated to New York, and *The Eternal Road* was being staged partly as a response to Hitler's persecution of the Jews in Nazi Germany.

Foote was to be in eight scenes, all small parts, sometimes playing Hebrews and sometimes playing Egyptians. When the ensemble actors left their rehearsal hall to join the rest of the cast at the Manhattan Theater on Thirty-fourth Street, Foote sat in the auditorium and looked around for Reinhardt, whom he felt he would recognize from the photographs Jody used to carry around with her in Pasadena. He finally saw him at the back of the theater talking intensely in German to another man. He asked one of the other actors whom Reinhardt was talking to and was told it was Kurt Weill, another refugee from Hitler's Germany. Weill was writing the music for the show.

Foote had not seen or heard from Rosamond since she left abruptly for Hollywood the previous year, but when he saw her one day at rehearsal she greeted him effusively and promised to introduce him to Reinhardt. She also told him that as soon as the show was up and running, they should have dinner. She even talked about returning to Daykarhanova's studio and working on scenes with him. But Foote rarely saw her again during rehearsals. As a member of the ensemble, Foote worked with an assistant director and was only called onstage to work with the principals when a scene involved him.

The show opened on New Year's Day 1937, to mixed reviews. Zemach assured the cast, however, that the producers were committed to keeping it open through the spring, so Foote would have a job during the winter. Toward the end of the run, Foote was leaving the theater one night at the same time as Rosamond. She grabbed him by the arm and apologized for not being in closer touch. She told him there was someone she wanted him to meet and led him out the stage door and introduced him to Jed Harris, one of Broadway's hot young directors. Harris, who the following year would direct Thornton Wilder's *Our Town* on Broadway, said little. As Rosamond left with Harris, she again told Foote they must get together soon. It was the last time he saw her.

The following January, Madame Daykarhanova called him into her office one day when he arrived for class.

"Horton," the Russian said, "I have something very sad to tell you. Rosamond Pinchot is dead."

She handed Foote a copy of the *New York Times* and pointed to a story on the front page. It was brief account of her death, saying that she had committed suicide. She was thirty-three years old and had been working on the sound effects for *Our Town*, which had been trying out on the road, under Jed Harris's direction.

"All that beauty," Daykarhanova said. "So young. All that beauty. And talent. Much more than she ever realized. Much more."

As summer approached, Mary Hunter, one of the students at

Daykarhanova's studio, announced she was going to start an acting company with several of the actors from the class. She asked Foote to join, and he jumped at the offer. The plan was to spend the summer rehearsing a play out of town and then bring it to New York in the fall.

In the end, fourteen students joined Mary Hunter's company. Among them were Joe Anthony and John Forsht, who had returned from Pennsylvania. Other members of the company included Mildred Dunnock, Perry Wilson, Betty Goddard, Frances Anderson, Mary Virginia Palmer, and Lucy Kroll.

The group named itself the American Actors Company and took over a house in Croton-on-Hudson that had belonged to Raymond Duncan, Isadora Duncan's brother, and had a large barn that served as a rehearsal studio. Everybody except Foote and John Forsht contributed three hundred dollars to the start-up for the company and to help pay expenses during the summer while they rehearsed. With such a large cast of women, Mary Hunter chose *The Trojan Women* for their first play, an ambitious undertaking.

Mildred Dunnock was cast as Hecuba, Perry Wilson as Cassandra, Frances Anderson as Andromache, and Mary Virginia Palmer as Helen of Troy. Foote and Forsht were both in small roles as soldiers. As the summer ended and the company prepared to move to New York, everyone was confident they would have a great success.

The critics, however, were savage. One said that if Helen of Troy was anything like the one presented by the new American Actors Company, there would never have been a Trojan War. Everybody came under withering criticism except for Foote and Forsht, whose small parts kept them out of the critics' scrutiny. Foote was certain that the devastating reviews would mean the end of Mary Hunter's attempt at starting a theater.

After conferring with Madame Daykarhanova, however, she decided to keep going. Mary had a regular job on a radio program called *Easy Aces* that provided enough income to mount another production. The free room and board that Foote had enjoyed in Croton-on-Hudson during the summer, however, came to an end and he began looking for work outside the theater.

He got a job as an usher in a movie theater—cinemas in those days had ushers to show patrons to their seats—while continuing his classes at the studio and making the daily rounds looking for work as an actor.

Mary Hunter decided the group should concentrate on American plays rather than classics—it was called the American Actors Company, after all—and she persuaded her friend Lynn Riggs to let her direct his play *Sump'n Like Wings.* They rented a space over a parking garage on West Sixty-ninth Street that had room enough to build a stage at one end and about thirty seats at the other. They rehearsed it for four weeks, then invited critics. None came, possibly because they remembered the fiasco of *The Trojan Women.* But the show ran for several weeks, and the actors were encouraged by the audiences' reception. In the spring, they put on an evening of one-act plays. Again, critics were invited. Again, none came. The company disbanded for the summer.

Foote spent the summer of 1938 working at the Maverick Theatre in Woodstock, New York. He appeared in two plays—as Mio in Maxwell Anderson's *Winterset,* and as Mister Mister in Marc Blitzstein's *The Cradle Will Rock.* At the end of the run, one of the owners of the Maverick told Foote that *One Act Play Magazine* was going to produce a season of short plays in New York and asked if he would be interested in joining. As part of his agreement with Mary and the American Actors Company, Foote was committed to being available for any production it might stage. Foote asked Mary about his offer, and she told him she would not start rehearsals on their next show until January, so he could take the job.

Foote was cast in two plays by the One Act Repertory Theater—*Coggerers* by Paul Vincent Carroll and *The Red Velvet Goat* by Josephina Niggli, a Mexican playwright who was just beginning her career. Several well-known Broadway actors were also in the plays and they opened at the Hudson Theater to high expectations. They were soon dashed. The critics hated all the plays except for *Coggerers,* and the show closed after five performances. Once again, Foote faced the prospect of having to find a job to pay his rent. But this time, the wait between jobs did not last long.

The New York World's Fair was scheduled to open in the spring of 1939 in Flushing Meadows, and one of the shows being prepared for it was a spectacle called *Railroads on Parade*, a celebration in song, dance, and scenes depicting the history of the Iron Horse in America. One of the producers who had seen Foote in the one-act plays came to him and asked if he would like to join the company. Since the show would begin in late spring and run through the summer, there was no conflict with his commitment to the American Actors Company and Foote signed on.

But before rehearsals began, an acting exercise and a chance conversation with Agnes de Mille would change Foote's life forever.

Mary Hunter had decided to stage another evening of one-act plays for the spring offering of the American Actors Company. As part of the rehearsal process, she had the actors stand up and do some improvisations. Since everyone in the cast was from different parts of the country, she suggested they perform something based on where they grew up. Foote did a total of five improvisations about life in a small Texas town.

After the last one, he went back into the theater and sat next to de Mille, who had agreed to choreograph some dances for a revue of scenes with music and dance to be called *American Legend*. Foote and de Mille had become friendly, and she had enjoyed his improvisations about Wharton. As he sat down, she leaned over and asked him, "Have you ever thought about writing?"

"No," Foote replied.

De Mille suggested he should try writing a play. Stunned, as the idea had never occurred to him, Foote asked what on earth he should write about. She gave him the blunt and eternal advice given every beginning playwright: "Write about what you know."

Foote went home to his rooming house, took out some paper and a pencil, and spent the entire night writing a one-act play based on one of the improvisations he had done. He used the names of people he knew and he wrote the lead part for himself. He called it *Wharton Dance*.

The next day he took the play to Mary, told her about his conversation with Agnes, and gave her the fruits of his all-night labor.

Mary took it home that night to read. The following morning, she told Foote she wanted to direct it herself and, along with two other one-acts by Thornton Wilder, stage it for the company's spring production.

Although it was only one act, *Wharton Dance* had a cast of fifteen and took place at the weekly Friday night dance that Foote knew so well. Three young couples are outside the dance hall, waiting for a fourth couple who are meeting clandestinely because the girl's parents had forbidden her to see the young man. They all have been drinking beer and are worried that someone might tell their parents. A cross section of the town passes by on their way to the dance—the town tough, a young widow looking for an old boyfriend, the disapproving mother of a high school acquaintance, and others.

On the surface, the play might seem slight, but bubbling just beneath are the small conflicts that make drama out of the mundane. Critics again were invited, and this time Robert Coleman of the *New York Mirror* came. Coleman was especially effusive in his praise of *Wharton Dance*. The evening of one-acts had a respectable run, but at the time Foote gave no thought to writing a follow-up play.

As soon as the show closed, Foote went into rehearsal for *Railroads on Parade*. It was a huge spectacle with horses, wagons, trains, and bicycles. It had parts for cowboys, Indians, and the Chinese laborers who built the American railroads. Foote was in a total of eight scenes and had twenty-four costume changes. They did three shows a day.

The money Foote earned that summer from *Railroads on Parade* allowed him to leave his rooming house and move in with six other young people in a large apartment on the Upper West Side of Manhattan. Foote thought that maybe his work in the World's Fair pageant would open some acting doors for him, and it was not long before the break he had been waiting for seemed to come.

One of his new roommates, Philip Lewis, an actor who wanted to be a playwright, had been hired by the Theater Guild for a small part in an upcoming production of Ernest Hemingway's play *The Fifth Column*. One Saturday, he called Foote and said one of the actors had just left the show and Foote should get down to the theater immediately.

Lee Strasberg was directing the play, and Franchot Tone and Lee J. Cobb were the two male leads. When Foote arrived, the stage manager took him straight to see the director, who was involved in a conversation with Tone. Strasberg looked him up and down and asked his name.

"Horton Foote."

"Have you trained anyplace?" Strasberg asked.

"What do you mean, sir?"

Tone interrupted and explained, not unkindly, "He means have you studied acting with anyone?" He smiled encouragingly.

"Yes, sir," Foote replied. "Daykarhanova's School for the Stage. I did scenes in her class. And I studied technique with Jilinsky."

Strasberg looked him up and down again for a few moments, then turned to Tone. "Okay, Franchot?"

"Okay with me," Tone replied.

Foote was in one scene only, playing a Spanish man who had been falsely arrested as a spy. Rehearsals began the following day. The play, which was set in 1935 and concerned the Spanish Civil War, during which Hitler had aided Generalissimo Francisco Franco's forces, took on added political resonance for American audiences in the winter of 1939–40. Momentous events were taking place in Europe. The previous year, Nazi Germany had annexed Austria and seized the Sudetenland in Czechoslovakia. The British prime minister, Neville Chamberlain, had met Hitler in Munich and reached a presumed agreement that Germany would cease its territorial claims in Europe. On September 1, 1939, however, the Nazis invaded Poland, and Britain and France declared war on Germany. In the United States, the question on everyone's mind was whether America would also join the war against Germany or stay neutral.

When *The Fifth Column* went to New Haven for its first tryouts, everyone was nervous. After the first performance before an audience, Strasberg brought the company together and explained that some scenes were going to be rewritten and some others trimmed.

Foote's one scene, however, was unchanged. When the play moved on to Philadelphia for a two-week run in the second round of out-of-town tryouts, the tension was even greater. This time critics would be seeing the show. On the morning after the Philadelphia opening, Wendell Phillips, one of the other actors in the cast, came to Foote's room carrying the local newspapers. He was not smiling.

"Are they bad?"

"Not bad. Just disappointing. They say we need work. We're too long."

The last stop before the show went to Broadway was Boston. By this time, the company that had been a close-knit group at the start of rehearsals had become querulous and depressed. Every day during the Philadelphia run there were more changes to the play, with actors having to learn new lines and blocking. On the Friday night of the last week before the play was to move, the stage manager came to Foote's dressing room.

"I have some bad news for you," he said. "You won't be going to Boston with us. They're cutting your scene out of the play. Strasberg says to thank you and it has nothing to do with your acting. He thinks you are very good, it's just the scene seems to be extraneous now."

"Yes, sir," Foote said. "Thank you."

Foote rode the train with the rest of the company when they left the next day for Boston, but he got off in New York. Foote spent the rest of the winter taking lessons with the Russians and making the rounds of casting offices. Money was tight until rehearsals began in the spring for the second season of *Railroads on Parade.*

The war in Europe was the biggest news throughout that summer. The Nazis had begun the air attacks on London that would become known as the Battle of Britain. There were sharply divided feelings in the company about the war and whether the United States should join the fighting. Foote was strongly in favor of an Allied position, while others believed America should stay out of the war altogether.

Foote saved as much money as he could from the World's Fair show, and in the fall he decided he would spend some of it and return to Wharton to visit his parents. He had been thinking of the experience of *Wharton Dance*, and he began to toy with the idea of writing another play. He hoped his trip home would provide inspiration for one.

On the train, he sat up all night thinking of possible ideas. As soon as he arrived home, Foote was bombarded with invitations for lunch or dinner from relatives and friends. But he announced at the start of his visit that he would not have time for socializing. He had come home, he told his parents, to write a play.

CHAPTER 4

New York:
The Writer Emerges

Foote wrote *Texas Town* in five weeks. He set it in a drugstore in a place he called Richmond, which was the name of not only a town between Wharton and Houston but also the street his grandmother lived on.

If *Wharton Dance*, with its cast of fifteen, seemed expansive, *Texas Town* was even larger. The play had twenty-three characters and, apart from being a much broader canvas, it also addressed bigger themes, questions that are confronted by every new generation in every town, big or small, in America. There are enough plots and subplots in the play for a Shakespearean tragedy, yet there is an economy to the writing that keeps the drama tight and focused and brings each of the characters to life.

The action takes place on a single day in which the governor of Texas is scheduled to make a campaign appearance in the town of Richmond. Based on Texas's real-life governor at the time, a former hillbilly radio singer named Pappy O'Daniel, Foote's fictitious governor has the town divided.

Foote introduces nearly all the major characters within the first ten minutes of the play. It opens with Hannah, an old black sharecropper, coming in to ask the young owner of the drugstore, Maner, for credit for fifty cents' worth of medicine for his sick wife. Maner refuses to give it to him, but Doc, an elderly physician with a fondness for whiskey, vouches for him. Then, in quick succession, a string of locals enter the store, each bringing a thread to the tapestry of small-town life that Foote weaves. First there are Digger and Pap, two farmers facing the economic hardships of the Depression and the vagaries of that year's cotton crop. Then there is Carrie, an attractive young woman who has been dating Maner but, uncertain what she wants from life, has so far refused to marry him. She no sooner arrives than Maner renews his proposal, promising her a honeymoon in New Orleans and an annual trip to Dallas if she will be his wife. Carrie, whose mother has been urging her to accept the security offered by Maner, says she will give him an answer that evening.

Carrie's old boyfriend, Ray Case, comes in. Ray has been working with a local oil drilling crew and is trying to save enough money to pay off his mother's mortgage, erect a headstone for the grave of his father—a recurring motivation in several of Foote's plays—and buy a one-way ticket out of town.

The parade of characters continues with the arrival of Fannie Belle, a young woman who is trapped in a loveless marriage and whose relationship with a single man is fodder for gossip among other women in town. A landowner named Damon, who holds a mortgage on Digger's small acreage, also shows up. Oil wildcatters are drilling on his property.

With each new arrival, complications multiply: Damon forecloses on Digger, which means that Hannah, the sharecropper with the sick wife, will be evicted; Ray is fired from his job, and his mother, trying to keep him in Richmond, thwarts his chances for another one that would take him out of town; Fannie Belle becomes ostracized; Doc sinks deeper into an alcoholic haze and sees his days stretching into endless sameness.

The main story line running through the play is that of Ray and Carrie, who are trapped in a life neither wants. They were high school sweethearts who broke up because of their families, but they still love each other. Ray is convinced he will never find happiness if he stays in the town. As Ray tells Doc, who has become a sort of surrogate father: "I sit and listen to trains passing through the night. I think about my Pa. We used to lie awake at night and listen. Sometimes he'd talk about the places he'd been—places he was gonna take me to. But he never did."

But there is more than youthful wanderlust behind Ray's yearnings. As he tries to explain to Carrie, "The things I've been hating wasn't one kind of job or another kind. It was the things that make people turn good into ugliness."

Carrie, who is more ready to come to terms with whatever life hands her, argues that one has to accept compromises and live with change. "There were things we thought we had to have, and we're learning we can get along without 'em," she tells Ray. "I know it isn't like it used to be, but this is how it is now. We've got to accept it."

Carrie is torn between her mother's insistence that she marry Maner, who will give her financial security and a respected position in town, and following her heart. In the end, a piece of casual advice from Fannie Belle makes up her mind. "Don't ever do it," Fannie Belle says. "It isn't worth it. Die an old maid, but don't marry a man you don't love . . . and stay in a small town."

Underneath the mundane concerns of daily life—foreclosures, jobs, affairs, and other human frailties—*Texas Town* explores issues that would recur throughout Foote's plays for the next seventy years: the inevitability of change and loss and the struggle to maintain one's dignity in the face of it.

The conflict between Ray and his mother is essentially that of one generation trying to hold on to the past and the next trying to break away from it. The family of Ray's mother had once been prominent in the town, and she clings desperately to the fantasy that Ray can restore the family to its proper place. In a scene that foreshadows one between Carrie Watts and her son, Ludie, that Foote would write for *The Trip to Bountiful* a dozen years later—and that Tennessee Williams would write in *The Glass Menagerie* and *A Streetcar Named Desire*—Ray's mother remembers the large white house of her girlhood, with servants in the hallways, and its big front lawn covered with trees. Ray, however, sees only the charred foundation where the house once stood, the land gone to waste, and the weeds growing everywhere.

Foote had few distractions as he wrote the play in the front parlor of his parents' home. His brother Tom Brooks was in college in Iowa and his younger brother was at school. Foote wrote during the

day, then spent the evenings visiting with his parents and other relatives. Conversation mostly centered on the war. The fighting was
going badly for Britain, and his father was worried that England
might lose. He couldn't understand why America wasn't doing more
to help. The day Foote finished writing the play, he told his mother
and father that he would have to get back to New York. His mother
asked him when he planned to leave, and he said the next day.

Foote had written the play in longhand on loose sheets of paper.
He had only one copy of it, which he kept on him throughout the
train ride back to New York. On the night he arrived, he went to a
party at Agnes de Mille's apartment. Mary Hunter was also there,
and when he told her about the play, she said she was eager to read
it. When she learned the only copy was in Foote's handwriting,
she told him to take it to a typing service and the American Actors
Company would pay to have six copies made. When the typist took
a look at the manuscript, she told him she would have to charge
extra because his handwriting was so bad. The morning after Mary
read the play she called Foote and told him she wanted to direct it
and that he would play Ray Case.

The play was planned for the spring. Because of the size of the
cast, Mary told Foote they would have to do it somewhere other
than the company's stage above the garage on Sixty-ninth Street,
which was too small. They finally arranged to rent the Humphrey-
Weidman school, downtown on Sixteenth Street. Doris Humphrey
and Charles Weidman ran a dance school in the space and gave
recitals twice a year. They also rented out the theater in the school
to other companies for various events.

Rehearsals for *Texas Town* began in March at the company's studio, then transferred downtown for the final week before opening.
Mary sent out invitations, and to everyone's surprise, Brooks Atkinson of the *New York Times* came to review it. He was the first New
York critic to see one of the company's productions in more than a
year, since Richard Coleman had seen *Wharton Dance*.

There were some other theater luminaries in the audience. Florence Odets, who had been working on another project with Mary,

came with her brother Clifford, and Lee and Paula Strasberg came with them. Opening night was the first time the cast had performed the play before an audience, and everyone was nervous. Foote had so many stage jitters about playing Ray that he almost forgot he was also the playwright.

Backstage after the performance, Florence Odets reported that her brother and the Strasbergs had been very impressed by the play and the acting. Other friends oohed and aahed and were genuinely enthusiastic. But as the actors adjourned to a nearby bar to celebrate, the one opinion that counted was still being written.

In those days, critics still went straight from the theater to their newspaper offices to write their reviews on deadline. The *New York Times* would not be on the streets until about three that morning, so the cast party collectively held its breath until about two thirty, when someone went out to buy the early edition of the paper. The bar grew quiet as Atkinson's review was read aloud:

> Even in real life virtue is occasionally rewarded, and "Texas Town" is a case in point. As acted last evening in an informal theater at 108 West Sixteenth Street, it does considerable honor to a group of tenacious players dubbed the American Actors Company. For four years they have held together, industriously rehearsing in a loft over a garage. Three years ago this correspondent happened to see them in a dismal production of Edith Hamilton's "The Trojan Women." To put it mildly that episode was not encouraging.
>
> But now they are acting a simply written narrative play by Horton Foote, who is one of their own actors, and it suits them admirably. In a general sort of way it is the drama of a young man who tries desperately to leave a small town in Texas and find some work—any work to do. But that is only the thread of a narrative that runs through an engrossing portrait of small town life. It is set in a drugstore where old and young people naturally congregate for gossip and relaxation. Although Mr. Foote has no particular ax to grind, his play gives a real and languid impression of a

town changing in its relation to the world—the old stock drifting down the economic and social scale, the young people at loose ends in an organization that does not employ them.

If "Texas Town" does not derive from Mr. Foote's personal experiences and observations, he is remarkably inventive. For none of the parts is stock theater, except perhaps the part he plays himself without much talent and with no originality. And it is impossible not to believe absolutely in the reality of his characters. The melancholy doctor who drinks in the back room, the hearty judge and his cronies, the bored wife who is looking for excitement, the chattering girls, the bumptious boys, the sharp edges of bad feeling that cut through the neighborhood leisure, the quick impulses of emotion, the sense of drifting without purpose or direction—these are truths of small town life that Mr. Foote has not invented.

Generally the good works of groups like the American Actors Company appeal to a reviewer's good-will more than to his happiness. But Mr. Foote's quiet play is an able evocation of a part of life in America, and most of the acting is interesting and thoughtful.

Atkinson went on to single out several of the performances for special praise, with the caution that some of the acting was "over-accented with detail." He concluded the review by saying:

> It is something to walk in out of Sixteenth Street in New York into the waiting and idle atmosphere of a small town in Texas. Mr. Foote and the American Actors Company have performed that feat of magic. If they do not feel encouraged, this department does.

Foote himself, however, did not feel very encouraged. The review left him with highly mixed emotions. He was glad Atkinson had liked his play, but he was crushed over what he had said about his performance as Ray. The rest of the company, however, was elated. Atkinson's review gave the company new life, but Foote himself felt like a failure.

The day after Atkinson's review ran, Foote had a call from the Shubert Organization asking to see a copy of the play. They kept it for a week, then took an option for a possible Broadway production. The Shuberts, however, wanted some changes. The offer nonetheless helped salve the wound Foote still felt from Atkinson's comments on his performance.

When Foote ran into de Mille at the theater the next day, he told her about the Shuberts' option. She just rolled her eyes and said, "Be careful." She had choreographed a musical for them and did not think very highly of their commitment to art.

The main change the Shuberts wanted was a different ending. In the original draft of *Texas Town*, Foote had the character Ray leave town, hitchhiking his way to Houston. Word comes from offstage at the end that he has been killed in an automobile accident. It was not satisfying to Foote at the time he wrote it, and he was not averse to trying to find a different ending. Over the next few weeks he wrote another two or three drafts, also taking into account some other changes the Shuberts discussed with him.

Meanwhile, the American Actors Company was preparing for its next production, *American Legend*, the show combining dance, music, and words that de Mille had been working on. The company rehearsed in the Sixty-ninth Street studio but staged the show at the Humphrey-Weidman space downtown. Once again, Brooks Atkinson came and gave the company a favorable review, citing de Mille for her "excellent choreographic ideas." Atkinson even mentioned *Texas Town* again in his review of *American Legend*, recalling that it had been the company's previous production and that it had been performed to "general satisfaction."

It was with a sense they were finally moving on the right track that the company disbanded for the summer after the run of *American Legend*, and the actors went their separate ways. Foote had agreed to spend the summer at the Montowese Playhouse in Montowese, Connecticut. The theater was operated by a hotel, but the hotel had been unhappy with the management and had asked Mary and her American Actors Company to take it over that season.

The first show was a production of George Abbott's *Broadway*, and the second offering put Foote and Joe Anthony together in James Thurber's *The Male Animal*. Anthony got a call from Metro-Goldwyn-Mayer during the brief run of that show, and he left immediately for California to appear in a movie. Foote acted in eight plays during the summer at Montowese, and it was during the rehearsals for one of them that the desire to act left him as abruptly as it had seized him as a boy in Wharton, and an obsession to write replaced it.

Foote would never be able to say what triggered it, but he woke up one morning that summer with an epiphanic certainty that he didn't care if he never acted again, and that he wanted to do nothing more in life than to write plays. He began work on a new one immediately.

As if to confirm the correctness of his conviction, when he returned to New York in the fall and told Mary and other friends of his decision, no one tried to talk him out of it. Unfortunately, his new career as a writer did not soar any faster than his career as an actor had when he first arrived in New York. The Shuberts were still not happy with the changes he had made to *Texas Town*, and the Dramatists Play Service, a publishing house to which he had submitted a copy of the play, rejected it outright.

Foote also soon learned that a starving writer gets just as hungry as a starving actor, and he again had to take an outside job to pay the rent and keep food on the table. On top of the basic necessities of life for himself, Foote suddenly felt partly responsible for someone else as well: his brother Tom had arrived in New York and was staying with him and Joe Anthony. Foote and Anthony had become roommates again after Anthony returned from making the movie in California. Tom had left Iowa State after one year and had decided he, too, wanted to be an actor.

Foote finished his new play in the fall of 1941 and showed it to Mary. It was called *Out of My House*, a quartet of linked one-acts that Foote subtitled *A Play in Four Parts*. Each part had its own title: *Night After Night, Celebration, The Girls*, and *Behold, a Cry*. Mary made plans to stage them shortly after the New Year.

The New York theater, just like the rest of the country, was in a state of confusion that fall of 1941, with most Americans' attention focused on the war in Europe. Germany had attacked the Soviet Union that summer, and the major topic of discussion in the United States was whether the country should join the fighting against Hitler. Japan was about to answer the question for them.

Foote was sitting in Mary Hunter's kitchen on Sunday morning, December 7, 1941, drinking a cup of coffee and discussing the casting of his new play and rehearsal schedules. The telephone rang and when Mary returned from answering it, she went straight to the radio and turned it on. An announcer was giving what few details he had of a Japanese air attack on a U.S. naval base at Pearl Harbor.

They were silent for several moments, then Foote said that America couldn't stay out of the war now. They talked a bit more, and Foote left.

The United States declared war against Japan and Germany the day after the attack on Pearl Harbor, and in the weeks to come Foote and his circle talked about little else. All of the actors, writers, directors, and choreographers that Foote knew put their careers on hold while waiting for the draft notices that would induct them into the army.

But life, even in wartime, carries on, and the production of *Out of My House* opened in January 1942. Once again Brooks Atkinson came from the *New York Times*. He had been so impressed with *Texas Town* that he was beginning to follow the career of the fledgling writer. He wrote:

> In case anyone asks Horton Foote, "How's your last act?" he can reply, "Stunning." Mr. Foote is the young man who disturbed the calm of last spring with an interesting play titled "Texas Town." Since then he has been in Texas long enough to gather the material for a sort of successor, "Out of My House," which the American Actors Company put on last evening at the Studio, 108 West Sixteenth Street. The new play, written in four parts, is loosely-contrived, and sometimes seems to be a footless variety show. But after he has portrayed the decadence of "certain levels," as the program calls them, of a Southern cotton town, Mr. Foote pulls

himself together in a vibrant and glowing last act that is compact and bitterly realistic and also remarkably well played. Although "Texas Town" was a better play than "Out of My House," none of "Texas Town" was so good as this last act.

In the few months since they had been living together in New York, Horton and Tom Brooks had become quite close. Foote introduced his younger brother to the Russians, as well as to Mary Hunter and his other friends. Tom Brooks had been taking acting lessons and had appeared in two of the four plays that comprised *Out of My House* at the American Actors Company. He had been favorably mentioned in the reviews of his brother's play, and during the run of that show he received an offer of a studio contract from Warner Brothers. It was for six months at fifty dollars a week.

The day before he was scheduled to go to the Warner Brothers offices in New York to sign the contract, Tom Brooks received his draft notice in the mail. He had to cancel the signing, and the following week he went to take his physical. He passed, and within a month he had left for training camp.

Foote expected to receive his draft notice any day. He spent the next three weeks giving away what little furniture he owned. He even gave away some of his clothes, and he entrusted a new play he had been working on to a friend for safekeeping while he was off fighting in the war.

Foote and Joe Anthony, who apart from being roommates had become close friends, received their notices on the same day. They went down to the draft board office together to take their physical exam. Once inside the induction center, however, they were separated and directed to different lines to await their turn with one of the doctors.

When his time came, Foote was ushered into a small office. After being examined, the doctor told him to report to an officer in an adjacent room. Foote stood there in his underwear, holding his bundle of clothes, waiting for the officer to sign his induction papers. To his surprise, however, the officer stamped his papers REJECTED and told him to get dressed and go home. The examining doctor had found that Foote had a hernia, which Foote had not even known about, and it disqualified him for military service. As he was leaving, Foote saw Anthony across the room. Joe had been accepted and he was departing immediately for the army. They waved to each other, and Joe went off with the other new recruits while Foote walked out onto a bustling Manhattan street.

The first thing Foote did after leaving the induction center was to call Mary Hunter and tell her what had happened. He was in a daze and felt disappointed. Not only was Broadway rejecting him, but the army didn't want him either. Apart from that, Foote had long believed America should join the struggle against the Nazis, and now he was told he wouldn't be part of it. He didn't know what to do. Mary told him to come over to her apartment. Her advice was that he should get back to work on his new play. She also loaned him some money until he could find a job, since he had given away most of his clothes and other belongings in anticipation of going into the army.

Foote retrieved the draft of the play and got a job running an elevator in an apartment building on Park Avenue to pay his rent, which he would have to shoulder alone now that both his brother and Joe Anthony had been drafted. He worked five nights a week, from six in the evening until six in the morning. Since most of the tenants in the building were home by midnight, he could spend much of the night writing.

Foote worked on the play through the summer, and by fall he showed a completed version to Mary. She wanted to do it right away, and she wanted to direct it. Foote called the play *Mamie Borden*. It had only six characters, a relief to Mary because finding good actors was difficult since so many had been drafted into the army. In the end, Mary used only one actor from her company. Hilda Vaughn played what was originally the title role, but she hated Foote's title, saying audiences would confuse it with Lizzie Borden and think the play was about the little girl who gave her parents forty whacks with an ax. She suggested the title *Only the Heart*, and Foote reluctantly agreed.

The play once again explored the theme of youthful restlessness and yearning, and the mirage of security that comes with money—and once again it was set in a small Texas town called Richmond and centered on a mother-daughter relationship. Mamie Borden is a conniving matriarchal character who runs her daughter's life, forcing the daughter, Julia, to break up with Less, the boyfriend she loves, and marry Albert, a man with better financial prospects. Mamie takes Albert as her partner in running the farms that she rents out to sharecroppers. But Mamie wants more. Oil is replacing cotton as the backbone of the economy, and the lure of wealth that only oil can bring convinces her to allow wildcatters to drill on her land, even though it will displace the farmers who work it.

"How would you like it if we had a few oil wells?" she asks Albert at one point, then answers the question herself. "I reckon we could stand it. I reckon we could stand anything if we had a few oil wells. Yes, sir, I just guess we could now."

In their obsession with finding oil on their land, Mamie and Albert fail to notice how restive Julia is becoming. Only Mamie's spinster sister, India, and Julia's father, a free spirit who lives with another woman but comes home to meals, notice that Julia is pining to break free of the cloistered existence her mother has created for her. When Julia's old boyfriend Less returns to town, her suppressed longings begin to stir, and Mamie's world is threatened with collapse.

The domineering Mamie is something of a cross between Regina in *The Little Foxes* and Amanda in *The Glass Menagerie*. But in the end Mamie proves to be no match for her daughter. Ibsen had been a strong influence on Foote since he first saw Eva Le Gallienne in three of his plays in Pasadena, and there is more than a little of Nora in *A Doll's House* in Julia.

The play opened in December. The Humphrey-Weidman Studio was not available, and rather than wait until it was free, Mary rented the Provincetown Playhouse. This time, all the New York papers sent critics. Brooks Atkinson, however, had relinquished his job as chief drama critic at the *Times* to become a war correspondent. His replacement was Lewis Nichols, and whether as a gesture to show his independence from Atkinson, who had championed Foote's plays, or because he was genuinely not that impressed, his was the only review with any reservations. All the others were raves.

With such uniformly good reviews, Foote had a flood of calls from Broadway producers asking to see the play. Two days after the opening, Helen Thompson, a former member of the Group Theatre and one of the producers at the Provincetown Playhouse, told Foote that Luther Green, a major Broadway producer, had seen the play and wanted to stage it on the Great White Way if Pauline Lord could be persuaded to play the part of Mamie. She said that Miss Lord was coming to see the play that night.

Foote was very excited. He had admired Pauline Lord almost to the point of idolatry since he had seen her in *Ethan Frome*. Even Mmes Daykarhanova and Soloviova had often spoken of her in class and said that Stanislavski thought she and Laurette Taylor were America's greatest actresses. Foote had made up his mind that any producer who wanted to transfer the play to Broadway would have to keep Mary on as director.

"What about Mary directing?" he asked Helen.

"We can discuss that after Miss Lord has seen the play," Helen replied.

The following morning, Foote received a call from Luther Green's office saying that he should call on Miss Lord at her hotel at two p.m. the next afternoon. Foote barely slept that night and was at the hotel half an hour early. He walked around the block several times, then walked up to the hotel desk at two o'clock on the dot.

"I'm here to see Miss Lord," he said, barely above a whisper.

"Who?" the clerk asked.

"Miss Pauline Lord," Foote said.

"What's your name?"

"Horton Foote."

The clerk picked up the phone, spoke quietly into it, then turned back to him, looking him up and down. "She's expecting you," he said with a trace of disbelief, and gave him the room number.

Foote had rehearsed several speeches he planned to say when he first saw her, but as he stepped off the elevator and walked down the corridor he could remember none of them. He had a momentary panic attack as he stood in front of the door and an impulse to flee back to the elevator and lobby and into the street. Then he told himself, *She's already seen the play. She either likes it or doesn't.* He knocked on the door.

She was simply but elegantly dressed, much smaller than he'd thought, and she smiled at him and asked him to come in and have a seat, and suddenly all his fear left him. "You are very talented, Mr. Foote," she said as she indicated a sofa for him.

Foote managed to get out that he had seen her in *Ethan Frome* and that it was the most moving performance he had ever seen on a stage. She smiled again and thanked him and began to tell him how difficult it was to find parts that were right for her. She said really good plays were rare, and those with parts right for her even rarer.

She then began to tell him that she had spent a restless night since seeing his play, which she thought was a very good play. She mentioned that Luther Green believed it was a perfect part for her, and she valued his opinion; but after long consideration, she felt that it was not. "I don't like playing strong women," she said. She said it was only because she liked the play itself so much that she wanted to tell him her decision in person.

Foote was crestfallen, and he tried to think of an argument to convince her that she was wrong. But the more she explained her reasons, the more she convinced Foote that as much as he was disappointed to hear it, she was probably right.

Despite its good run at the Provincetown Playhouse and all the good reviews, none of the prospective producers wanted to move it to Broadway without a star in the role of Mamie. After the play closed downtown, Foote was again out of work and very nearly out of money. The only thing he knew to do was to start writing another play.

Foote had met another young playwright at a party the previous year, and they had hit it off from the start. His name was Tom Williams, but everyone called him Tennessee. Both young men had been born in the South and were roughly the same age. Williams, who was born in Mississippi two years before Foote, had moved with his parents to St. Louis as a young child and had grown up there. In their conversations, they discovered they both had loved hearing old family stories when they were young. More than geographical or generational affinities, however, they shared a passionate love of the theater.

Williams, who traveled frequently and often seemed to have no fixed abode, was in New York throughout that winter and he and Foote saw each other often. Both were broke. Each was working on a new play. Foote gave his the working title of "Michael Strachen." Williams called his "The Gentleman Caller," and told Foote he would be perfect for one of the parts if he was still interested in acting.

Williams came up with the idea that both he and Foote should take jobs on a farm that summer somewhere in upstate New York. They could work in the fields during the day and write at night. "That would give us some money," Williams said, "and it would help the war effort." Because so many men had been drafted into the army, there was a shortage in the national work force, and any job that helped provide basic necessities was considered to be helping the war effort. Foote agreed with the plan and promised to scout summer jobs on farms while Williams visited his home in St. Louis at the end of winter.

One of the crazes that swept New York theater in the late 1930s and early '40s involved combining dance, music, and the spoken word into what was touted as the ultimate theatrical experience. At the vanguard of this movement were the new choreographers of modern dance, and they were to dominate all of dance for decades to come. Anyone who dared venture a defense of classical ballet at a cocktail party or over a dinner table was immediately labeled a relic from the past who was clearly out of step with the times, and therefore disregarded.

Foote, in part because of the influence of Charlotte Sturges at the Pasadena Playhouse and her devotion to Mary Wigman, was a strong proponent of modern dance, and at the time agreed with those who thought the theater of the future would combine all elements of word, music, and movement.

When the American Actors Company rehearsed at the Humphrey-

Weidman Studio on Sixteenth Street, Foote would often seek out Doris Humphrey in the theater and ask about her theories on modern dance. Humphrey was regarded, along with Martha Graham, as one of the great modern dance choreographers. Both had been trained by Ruth St. Denis and were by this time fierce rivals. Just as there was a plethora of conflicting theories on Stanislavski and his "method" acting, every modern dance choreographer had his or her disciples, and what might begin as a polite discussion at a bar or a party over who was the greatest modern dancer often ended in a raging row.

Foote was close friends with de Mille, and he got to know Humphrey during the time American Actors Company used her space for its plays. He had also met other young dancers around town, including Jerome Robbins, Erick Hawkins, and Nona Sherman. Foote and Robbins spent a good deal of time together that winter. Foote was matinee-idol handsome, but if Robbins entertained any hopes their friendship would become anything more, he was disappointed. It was Sherman who enlisted Foote in a project that ended up playing a large part in his immediate future.

Sherman was a dancer with the Humphrey-Weidman company, and she was preparing a solo performance of her own that would, according to the growing fashion, combine music and words with her own modern dance. The text for her piece was Carl Sandburg's poem "The People, Yes." She knew Foote had been an actor, and she asked him if he would read the poem during her dance. He happily agreed.

The performance was at the YMHA, whose Sunday afternoon cultural programs were a springboard for many aspiring artists at that time. It paid nothing, but gave dancers, musicians, and actors a chance to be seen and heard. For Foote, it started a snowball rolling that would not come to rest for several years.

In the audience that afternoon was Pearl Primus, a young black dancer who was beginning to make a name for herself. She came backstage afterward and asked Foote if he would read the poem "Strange Fruit" for a dance she was choreographing, to be performed a couple of weeks later.

On the Sunday Pearl Primus gave her concert, Valerie Bettis was in that audience. Afterward, *she* came backstage and asked Foote if he would be willing to work with her on a project. Although none of these appearances reading for dance recitals earned any money, Foote had nothing better to do, so he agreed to meet with her.

Foote had first met Valerie Bettis when they both appeared in *Railroads on Parade* at the World's Fair. She was another young dancer with impressive training credentials. She had studied with Hanya Holm, a German who had been a protégé of Mary Wigman. Valerie asked Foote to read the poem "The Desperate Heart" for a concert piece she was planning. Moreover, Valerie had plans for a series of theater pieces that combined words, music, and dance, and asked Foote if he had any plays that had not been produced. He showed her a one-act called *Daisy Lee*, which he had written a short time earlier. She liked it and began to work on a dance to go with it.

Foote's immersion into the world of modern dance that spring eventually led him to Martha Graham, albeit through a back door. Since he was at loose ends, with no paying job, Mary Hunter prevailed on him to act as producer on a play that Sanford Meisner was directing at the Neighborhood Playhouse called *The Playboy of Newark*. Meisner and Hunter were friends and the American Actors Company and the Neighborhood Playhouse occasionally worked together on projects, especially now that money was so tight because of the war. During this assignment, Foote became acquainted with Rita Morgenthau, who ran the school at the Neighborhood Playhouse.

Each year the Playhouse school commissioned an original work that would be presented at the end of the year. Morgenthau had seen Foote's work at the American Actors Company and knew of his avid interest in dance, so she asked him to write the play for that spring. Louis Horst agreed to compose the music, and Martha Graham would choreograph the dance for it.

Foote wrote a play he called *The Lonely* and showed it to Morgenthau. She liked it and sent it on to Graham, who also responded favorably. Foote met Graham at the first reading of the play. She sat next to Foote, listening intently. On the first day of rehearsals, as Graham began to give instructions to the actors on where and how to move, she turned to Foote and said, "Don't let me do too much. I have a tendency to overdo."

Foote was spellbound by Graham. They both lived in Greenwich Village, and like every other artist, dancer, musician, actor, and writer Foote knew at the time, both were perpetually broke and saved every nickel they could. At the time, Graham even sewed her own costumes to save money and could afford to work on only one project at a time. After rehearsals Foote and Graham often rode home together on the bus, talking about modern dance and how it would transform the theater.

It was only after Graham completed her choreography that Louis Horst came in to look at the show and compose the music that would go with it. Horst was devoted to Graham, and he and Foote also became friends during the time they worked on the play. Horst was also the editor of the *Dance Observer*, and he enlisted Foote to write several articles for the magazine.

Throughout the winter, despite all the initial enthusiasm for moving *Only the Heart* to Broadway, there had been no progress on finding a leading lady who would satisfy producers' insistence on a star in the role of Mamie Borden. After Pauline Lord turned down the play, Luther Green's interest had waned. And no one seemed to have any ideas for the right star for the role. Then, at the beginning of spring, Foote received a note from Jacques Therie asking him to come to lunch.

Therie was a French producer who liked to call himself the George Kaufman of Paris. He told Foote over lunch that he admired his work and wanted to stage *Only the Heart* on Broadway. He added, however, that he thought the play needed work, and he invited Foote to come to California that summer to do some rewrites while Therie worked on a film in Hollywood with Charles Boyer.

With all the work he had been doing with modern dancers, Foote had forgotten about his task of finding a summer job on a farm for himself and Tennessee Williams, until one day in early April when he had a letter from St. Louis. Williams, addressing Foote with the Russian word for "comrade," was still excited about their plans:

Tovarich,

How are you going on our Back-to-the-Farm movement? I am relying on you to get the ball rolling as the more I think of a bucolic summer the more it intrigues me. Let us if possible find one in the vicinity of a summer play-house and a beach and let us determine to work on one big problem (that is, one each) and not a lot of little pieces so that when the summer is over we shall have something significant completed.

I am taking it easy here, not writing at all since I got here. Reading a lot of Lawrence, his letters and novels, and absorbing my Grandparents' stories. I have no friends here, see nobody, but every afternoon about five thirty or six I go down on the river-front and have a beer and listen to a juke-box in one of the dusky old bars that face the railroad tracks and the levee. That is the only part of St. Louis which has any charm. I feel much calmer. I want to continue this sort of life—quiet and contemplative, I mean—for about five months. By that time I should know what I want to do with my life from now on and have the resolution to do it.

Drifting is no good!

Write me—

Always, Tenn.

Foote felt miserable and knew he had to tell Williams about his offer from Therie to go to California to work on *Only the Heart.* In fact, he felt so guilty about disappointing Williams, he delayed writing. He was relieved when he received another letter from Williams a couple of weeks later, telling Foote that he should grab any summer job that came along, even if it was just for one. The thrust of the letter was that Williams wasn't sure whether he would be able to spend the summer working on a farm as they planned. Williams asked Foote about his new play, asked to read it, and added:

I have been working with tigerish fury on "The Gentleman Caller," it has become a fully-developed play almost of usual length. It has at least one part in it for you and maybe two, if you can imagine such a thing. . . . We must remember that a new theater is coming after the war with a completely new criticism, thank God. The singular figures always stand a good chance when there are sweeping changes.

As it turned out, Williams had received an offer from Metro-Goldwyn-Mayer for a six-month contract as a studio writer in Hollywood, and both he and Foote spent the summer in Los Angeles. Although neither had a car, they managed to see each other frequently and spent a lot of their time together complaining about their respective jobs.

Foote had traveled to Los Angeles with Therie, and he and the Frenchman spent most of the train trip talking about the play. Foote realized almost at once that the changes Therie wanted were not going to make the play better. Therie kept telling Foote he wanted Dorothy Gish to play the role of Mamie, and that if Foote would make the right changes to the script, he would get Dorothy Gish to read it.

Foote was installed in a guesthouse at Therie's home in Laurel Canyon and spent most of his days working on the play. Therie spent his days at the studio working on the film with Boyer, then at night would look over the changes Foote had made. Foote was being paid a weekly salary while he was working on rewrites for Therie, and he saved as much as he could for when he got back to New York. Foote resisted most of the changes Therie wanted in the play, but after several weeks of work, he produced a script that both he and the Frenchman approved.

True to his word, Therie invited Dorothy Gish and Louis Calhern, with whom she was living, to come to his house for tea. It was the first time Foote had met either of the Gish sisters, although Lillian Gish would later play an important part in his career. Therie gave a copy of the reworked play to Dorothy, and she promised to read it.

When she called a couple of days later and said it wasn't something she wanted to do, Therie lost interest in the play, and Foote returned to New York.

Williams was having an equally miserable time at MGM. One night shortly before Foote left, Williams invited him to a party in Hollywood and introduced him to a young woman named Margo Jones. Jones was a fellow Texan and she and Foote hit it off immediately. She had enormous eyes and talked like a machine gun, but

Foote was captivated by her. Jones was a devoted fan of Williams and spent the evening talking about her plans to start a theater in Dallas that would do all new plays, including those of Williams and Foote. The postwar theater would not be centered in New York, Jones argued, but in cities around the country, in theaters more interested in art than in money.

When he arrived back in New York, Foote showed the revised version of *Only the Heart* to Mary Hunter and Helen Thompson, both of whom still believed in the play. Helen suggested Stella Adler for the part of Mamie, and they sent her a copy of the script. Adler, who had been a member of the Group Theatre, read the play and called and asked Foote to come around to see her. Both Helen and Foote thought that a good sign.

When Foote rang the bell on Stella Adler's apartment door the next day, a glamorous young woman, dressed to the nines, opened it, stared at him, and said, "Do I look like a bitter, frustrated woman?" Foote laughed and had to admit she didn't. Adler invited him in, and they spent a couple of hours talking about Foote's play, the theater in general, the demise of the Group, the current state of acting. Like Pauline Lord, Adler said she liked the play but didn't feel the part was right for her. It was a response Foote was getting tired of hearing.

Foote had just about decided that all hopes for getting *Only the Heart* on Broadway had run into a dead end. Helen had been working on lining up backing, but it still hinged on finding the right leading lady. Foote was at loose ends, and he began to spend a lot of time with Valerie Bettis. Bettis was also a native Texan, and Foote enjoyed her company. At the time, she was living with Bernardo Segall, a Brazilian concert pianist, and Foote visited their apartment almost daily. He had been working on a new play called *In My Beginning*, and Bettis wanted to do it with dance and original music.

Bettis and Segall entertained most evenings, and Foote met several other young artists there—dancers, composers, writers—and they argued and discussed the future of the theater until the small hours. Among them were John Cage, Merce Cunningham, Hanya Holm, Louis Horst, and even Alma Mahler, the composer's widow.

Another habitué of the Bettis-Segall salon was Harry Holzman, who was the executor of the artist Piet Mondrian's estate, and who shocked everyone by saying he thought Martha Graham was passé. All agreed, however, that the realistic theater was dead, and that the future would be a fusion of dance, music, and words. Foote joined in the attacks on the current state of Broadway, and even wrote some articles about it for the *Dance Observer.* At the time, he vowed never to write another realistic play.

When they weren't arguing over the future of theater and dance, they were discussing the war. There were rumors of an impending invasion of France by Allied forces, and fighting was raging in Italy and on the Eastern front with the Soviet Union.

There was a surge of sympathy, especially among the young, liberal intellectuals and artists in New York, with the hardships the Soviets were going through as they fought the Nazis. At one point, Foote even attended an American Communist Party meeting with some friends, but he was greatly disappointed. Rather than discuss politics and ways to help the Russians in their struggle against the Nazis, the American comrades began arguing over the decadent bourgeois modern art forms. At one point, one got up and began a vehement attack on Martha Graham, saying her dancing sowed the seeds of Fascism. It so infuriated Foote, he left and never went back.

As the year drew to a close, Helen finally got all the backing she needed to mount a Broadway production of *Only the Heart.* She had raised about eighteen thousand dollars, which seemed like a fortune at the time, especially to stage a play that originally had been produced for less than three thousand. Only the casting remained to be settled.

In the end, June Walker agreed to play the role of Mamie. If she was not exactly an A-list star at that point, she had the credentials to win the support of some producers. Walker had starred in *The Farmer Takes a Wife* with Henry Fonda and in *Green Grow the Lilacs* with Franchot Tone, and both had been Broadway successes. Mildred Dunnock, at that time a rising young actress, was signed to play the role of Mamie's daughter, Julia, and the producers agreed that Mary Hunter should direct.

Since his brother Tom's induction into the army, Foote had corresponded regularly with him. In a postcard from Salt Lake City in August 1943, Tom reported he had finished training there and had been assigned to a Flying Fortress as a radio-gunner and would start combat training at another base, but he didn't know which one. From then on, because of military censorship, Foote was never quite sure where his brother was. Foote had to write him in care of his squadron to an APO box in New York.

In a letter dated January 9, 1944, Tom said he had been in Casablanca, Tunis, Sicily, and Naples and was now at a forward base in Italy. He had already been on two missions over Germany and was flying out on a third the next day. He wrote that because they had arrived at the base before the supplies, he and his squadron had slept in a tent. It had been so cold and wet, Tom said, they made a stove out of an old oil drum. They had no electricity, or even candles, but they made a lantern out of an old wine bottle, using fuel oil and a sock for a wick. He said he wouldn't object to receiving a box of chocolates and signed off by saying he needed to get to bed since he had to get up early the next day for the mission.

Foote wrote back the day he received the letter, saying that rehearsals were about to begin for *Only the Heart*, and passing on news and gossip about their friends in New York. He told Tom about going to a show starring Zasu Pitts with Bunny Wallen, a girl Foote had been dating since the fall. The show wasn't very good, he said, but Zasu had been funny. He added that Bunny's mother planned to send him some candy. He also told Tom about going to the opera for only the second time in his life, but liking it very much, and seeing a revival of *The Cherry Orchard* and a production of *Our Town* at the new City Center.

Rehearsals for the play began shortly after the New Year, and they had been going on for only a week when Foote got a letter from his parents telling him that Tom Brooks had been reported missing in action over Germany. Foote called his mother and father as soon as he read the letter and said he would come home immediately. They insisted he stay with the play, however, since there was nothing he could do there. Also, his parents were hopeful that

Tom had been taken prisoner. They recalled the experiences of two other families in Wharton whose sons had been reported missing, and both had turned up in German prisoner-of-war camps months later. Foote agreed to stay in New York, and he sat down immediately that night and wrote a letter to his brother, which he sent to the only address he had for him. It was a short letter, telling him that rehearsals finally had begun on *Only the Heart* and asking him to keep his fingers crossed.

"I haven't forgotten our pact, and that this, my brother, is part yours." He ends by telling Tom the theater "will be needing you more than ever when your present job is finished, and hope together we can do some really fine things."

When the announcements of the play's opening were printed, Foote sent one to his brother with a note saying he wished Tom could be there for it, but "we'll have many, many more to share together— yours as well as mine." All three of Foote's last letters to Tom were returned with the word "Missing" written on the envelope.

During the rehearsals for the play, Foote had been nervous. He was still uneasy about some of the changes he had made in the script at Therie's urging the previous summer, and there had been a last-minute change in the casting that Foote was dubious about. At one of the final previews, Arthur Hopkins came to see the play. He was enthusiastic and optimistic, however, and Foote began to think that maybe his doubts had been wrong.

The play opened at the Bijou Theatre on West Forty-fifth Street on April 4, 1944. The reviews were terrible. Only one, in the *New York World-Telegram*, found it "absorbingly interesting and satisfying." Foote took Valerie Bettis with him to the opening night. After they had seen the papers, Foote and Bettis went to an all-night diner for a cup of coffee. Bettis told him he was wasting his talent on these kinds of plays. Foote was torn. Part of him agreed that there was no future in narrative drama, but part of him was loyal to *Only the Heart* and to Mary Hunter.

Dorothy Willard, who had been one of the backers of the original Group Theatre, put some more money into the production to keep it going. Foote deferred his royalties, and the cast took a pay cut.

The show ran for six more weeks, then closed. Foote was crushed. He was also broke. Despite the fact that he had a play on Broadway, he was not making any money from it and he had no prospects of earning any from his writing. He decided he would have to take an outside job just to pay his rent.

Foote had been reading a lot of Faulkner in his spare time, and he knew that Faulkner had once worked in a bookstore to support himself while he was writing. He heard about an opening at the Doubleday store in Penn Station, and went in to apply. He was hired as a clerk, and within a couple of weeks he was promoted to night manager.

He had been working at that job about a month when a young woman came in looking for a summer job. She was wearing a gray Mexican peasant-style blouse and a blue peasant skirt. Her name was Lillian Vallish. She was a senior at Radcliffe and was hoping to go into publishing, so she was looking for a job in a bookstore. Foote was smitten. He hired her on the spot.

At the time, Foote was still seeing Madeline Wallen, aka Bunny, who was a secretary to the Broadway producer Alfred de Largo Allegre. Through his early years in New York, Foote's social and romantic life was at best a sometime thing, dictated by the status of his financial situation at any given time. When he first saw Lillian, however, Foote was swept off his feet. As he later wrote to his parents, she was not only beautiful, but she was smart as well.

That first evening, as he was getting ready to close the store, Foote asked his new employee if she would like to go for a walk along the river that evening. Miss Vallish politely refused him. Months later, she told him that she had been worried that he might be some sort of strangler. Her fears, however, were quickly overcome. The following day, as they were closing the store, Foote again asked her if she would like to take a walk along the river after work. This time, she accepted.

Thus began the courtship of Lillian Vallish by Horton Foote. Their first date was the proffered stroll along the Hudson River. Neither had much money, and although they occasionally went to a movie or dinner, they mostly just walked and talked. Lillian liked

Mexican food, as did her Texan suitor, and they sometimes ate at a Mexican restaurant on Forty-eighth Street. They talked about poetry and novels and discovered they liked the same writers. As it turned out, Miss Vallish had actually seen Foote in *Railroads on Parade* at the World's Fair four years earlier, although she did not remember him specifically.

Foote wanted to spend all his time with her. He occasionally took her to a party or a movie. But mostly he wanted to be alone with her. They never seemed to run out of things to say. And when they did, each seemed content to be with the other in silence. Foote knew he had met his life's mate. One afternoon Joe Anthony, who had ended up being assigned to U.S. Army intelligence during the war and was home on leave, came into the store. Foote pointed to Lillian, who was standing behind the counter across the store, and said, "Joe, that's the girl I'm going to marry."

It was only six weeks before Foote proposed. The summer was moving on, and Lillian would be leaving soon to go back to college. It was on one of their frequent walks along the river that Foote asked her to marry him. Lillian at first demurred. She had only just turned twenty, and she had another year of college to go. Foote agreed they should wait until she got her degree. She said that her mother, especially, would not approve, but Foote told her that didn't matter. Still, she hesitated.

Foote was nothing if not persistent. Just as he had done when asking her out for a walk, Foote proposed again. The second time, Lillian accepted.

CHAPTER 5

Lillian

LILLIAN ROSELLA VALLISH was born July 18, 1923, in Mount Carmel, Pennsylvania, one of seven children of Walter and Barbara Vallish. Two brothers died in infancy, and she was the youngest of five daughters who survived.

Walter Vallish had immigrated to the United States from Poland as a young man. Although he had a college degree, the only work he could find in the New World was in a Pennsylvania coal mine. Walter's marriage to Barbara was an arranged one, and although she had little formal education, it was Barbara who was the brighter and more ambitious of the two. She opened a small grocery store to serve the miners' families in the town, and took the profits from that and opened a furniture store.

As the furniture enterprise prospered, she rented a four-story brick building in the middle of town. The family lived on the top floor, and the other three floors served as showrooms. The furniture business thrived, and the Vallishes became quite wealthy and a prominent family in the town. One economic disaster, however, nearly wiped out all their success and became the source of a rancorous dispute that lasted for years. Mrs. Vallish had begun to invest in stock in the late 1920s, and she once gave her husband a check for twenty-five thousand dollars that she had saved and told him to invest it in a certain stock. When her husband got to the bank, the manager talked him into investing it all in a railroad instead. The railroad went bust in the Wall Street crash, and the Vallishes lost all their savings.

It was Barbara Vallish who pushed her daughters to go to college. Lillian's two older sisters eventually quit, but Rita, the sister

to whom she was closest, attended Radcliffe. When Lillian graduated from high school, she first went to the University of Pennsylvania, but she didn't like it, and she, too, ended up at Radcliffe. Rita
had since married George Mayberry, who was the book editor at the
New Republic magazine.

After she started dating Foote, Lillian took him to meet Rita.
The Mayberrys lived in a large apartment in an old brownstone on
East Seventy-sixth Street in Manhattan. Through the rest of that
summer, Foote and Lillian were frequent guests there for dinners
and parties.

Toward the end of summer, Lillian took Foote home to meet her
parents. Although her father seemed amenable enough, he stayed
mostly in the background. Mrs. Vallish, however, took an instant
dislike to Lillian's fiancé. She had even looked up his name in Dun
& Bradstreet and discovered that although Foote had had a play
produced on Broadway, he was basically penniless.

Mrs. Vallish found other reasons to object to the proposed marriage. For one thing, she was a devout Catholic. Rita and Lillian
had attended Catholic boarding schools as girls, although Lillian
had hated it and eventually returned home and went to Mount Carmel public schools. Foote had been raised a Methodist. There was
also the age difference—Foote was eight years older than Lillian,
and Mrs. Vallish still thought of her youngest daughter as a little girl. Finally, there was the inevitable question of money. How
would Foote support Lillian? He had a job in a bookstore, true, but
he insisted on pursuing a career as a writer. Writers, Mrs. Vallish
observed, didn't make a lot of money.

Still, when Lillian returned for her final year at Radcliffe that
September, she and Foote were firm in their plans to marry when
she graduated the following spring. The fall and winter of 1944–45
was a restless time for Foote, however. It was the first time since
their engagement that they were apart. Foote missed Lillian terribly and would become uneasy if he didn't hear from her every two
or three days. They wrote frequently; but like anyone who has had
to rely on the U.S. Postal Service to keep the flame of passion alive,
neither found it the most satisfactory way to carry on a romance.

Their letters were filled with news and gossip about friends, shop talk from the bookstore, politics (it was a presidential election year and Foote was worried that Thomas Dewey might beat Roosevelt, who was running for a fourth term), the books each was reading, and plans for their marriage.

In addition to Foote's other anxieties, there was always the question of money. At the time, Foote was living in a furnished apartment in Greenwich Village, but he knew that once he and Lillian were married, they would need a bigger apartment. Foote thought Lillian's mother might give them some furniture from her store, but Mrs. Vallish was still adamantly opposed to the marriage and Foote wasn't sure she would ever change her mind. In one of his first letters to Lillian after she left New York at the end of summer, Foote urged her to "get close to your mother and family again. We know that bitterness and resentment never accomplish anything."

In one letter, Foote told Lillian that Jerome Robbins, with whom both had become friendly the previous year, was going to California the following spring and had offered to let them stay in his apartment until they could find a place of their own.

That fall, Foote plunged back into a play he had been working on at the beginning of the summer. At the end of September he wrote Lillian that he had been looking it over and that he "liked it and got to working on it and got a whole section done. It so happens that it's turning out very well."

He also received an offer to direct a one-act play at the Neighborhood Playhouse. It would provide almost a month of work for which he would be paid a flat fee of $175. Although that worked out to less than $6 a day, he needed every nickel he could save.

The Neighborhood Playhouse was a descendant of the pioneering theater founded by Alice and Irene Lewisohn. Originally located on Grand Street on the Lower East Side as an adjunct to the Henry Street Settlement, it had over the years been a venue that attracted such lights as Ellen Terry and Ethel Barrymore and had been a springboard for Martha Graham. It had spawned the Neighborhood Playhouse School of the Theatre, which was directed by Sanford Meisner.

Meisner had taken a job to direct a play on Broadway, and Rita Morgenthau, who ran the Playhouse, asked Foote to direct Meisner's advanced acting class in a one-act play. The offer coincided with the return of Tennessee Williams to New York. The day after he arrived back in town, Williams went to see Foote at the bookstore. Williams said he had finally finished his play, which he described as "uncommercial" and which he now called *The Glass Menagerie*. Foote asked if he could read it, and Williams gave him a copy.

Foote was enthusiastic about the play and asked Williams if he could direct the "gentleman caller" sequence as a one-act for Meisner's class at the Neighborhood Playhouse. "Sure," Williams said.

Foote was already in rehearsals when Williams got word that his agent, Audrey Wood, had sold the play to Eddie Dowling for a production in Chicago at the end of the year, with a possible transfer to Broadway the following spring. Foote was afraid he would have to cancel the production that was already in rehearsal and find another play on short notice. But Williams and Foote talked with Audrey and she agreed to let the Neighborhood Playhouse class production go forward.

It was also during rehearsals for the Playhouse show that Lillian paid her first visit to New York since she and Horton had parted at the end of the summer, and each looked forward to it as much as any long-parted lovers. In the end, however, what Lillian hoped would be a romantic interlude almost derailed their engagement.

As she often did when she visited New York, Lillian stayed with her sister Rita and her husband, George, in their apartment on East Seventy-sixth Street. It was a long way from Foote's apartment on East Tenth Street in Greenwich Village, and between rehearsals at the Neighborhood Playhouse and seeing Lillian he spent a lot of time on the subway.

Foote was determined to show his fiancée a good time, introduce her around, and impress her with the social swirl of New York literati. He took her to two rehearsals at the Playhouse, where she saw for the first time a different side to the mild-mannered, easygoing Texas gentleman she had met in the summer. There were late dinners with friends at downtown restaurants at which the future of the theater and dance and literature would be argued into the small hours.

One night he took her to a party at Jacques Therie's apartment. Foote was still bitter over the way Therie had treated him over *Only the Heart* the previous summer, but the Theries gave elegant parties, and he thought Lillian might enjoy it. In fact, she hated it and was repulsed by what she regarded as a room full of people trying only to impress one another with their erudition.

Throughout the week, Lillian had begun to withdraw into herself. She and Foote had little time alone, and the stream of dinners, rehearsals, and parties only depressed her. In addition, Rita had joined Mrs. Vallish in opposing the marriage. The sisters quarreled and, in the end, Lillian ended up cutting short her visit, returning to Radcliffe two days early.

Foote was troubled by the turn of events and wrote asking her what was wrong. It was several days before she replied that "New York and I certainly didn't jibe this time." She went on:

Horton, something's gone wrong—aside from my little tiff with Rita. You've been growing restless and a little annoyed with me. Wednesday night at the restaurant you seemed so unsympathetic and harsh towards me. God knows I've tried so hard to block out certain thoughts and emotions, but I don't seem to be very successful. This is a very difficult period for me and I was wrong to depend on someone else for support. I do want independence, but I don't seem ready yet for out and out defiance. Although I may give the impression of maturity, I'm still adolescent in my indecision and fear. And, Horton, I don't believe it's a problem of family interference. I felt that you were growing apart from me before that—especially at the Playhouse rehearsal and at Jacques'. Maybe it put things in a new perspective and I saw how the land really lay. I felt like an intruder—the one who doesn't seem to belong. Your friends have all been sweet and kind to me, but I've only been accepted because of you. Before I felt happy and secure to the point of smugness and now all my confidence is gone. Maybe my analysis is all wrong. Tell me what you think Horton and please be straightforward and frank. We said there were never to be any secrets between us. If you don't love me as you did before, come out with it and let me know. A marriage can't be successful if this barrier persists.

Foote had written her twice the day after she abruptly left New York, but he didn't respond to this letter for two days. When he did, he addressed her family concerns first, then tried to assuage her fears over their relationship.

First of all, if I knew the basic answers to the basic things you propose in your letter I would be at once the wisest man in the world and the greatest writer. For back of it all is fear and insecurity—those two things that plague us seemingly interminably. Second, Lillian, I cannot, must not, I will not allow myself to advise you over things you must do and decide for yourself. I would no more take on my shoulders the responsibility of advising you or telling you what and what not to do with your family than fly to the moon. But there is one thing I do rather resent, dearest, and that is having any friction that might have gone on between us raised to such gigantic proportions in retrospect, and reducing two cases of nervous hysteria to "that little tiff with Rita." To my way of thinking they were two God-damned very distressing scenes with Rita and I personally, in spite of them, think you and I managed to get along very well. Now about us I can only say that I am shocked, perplexed and upset that you felt anything like you described and also a little angry with myself for being so insensitive. I thought you were really enjoying yourself. Use your head a little, dearest. Did you ever see me at a rehearsal before? Such a play demands full concentration. It's a very exhausting experience, but if I were bored with you why did I ask you twice. And as for Jacques, did I seem congenial with them? Good God. As a matter of fact, listening to his prattle, I never felt so fine being away with you before. It gave me such a wonderful feeling to say to myself "Lillian and I needn't ever have people like that around us. She doesn't like them any more than I do." . . . As for your getting afraid and frightened dearest, I'm sorry. I wish it was me writing ten years ago and then I'd tell you I'd take you in my arms and they'd vanish, but I can't with an honest

heart tell you that—I fight them—all of us should fight them more.
Anyway, I do want to take you in my arms for I love you very much.
I need you here badly. Believe me the next few months will be no eas-
ier for you than for me. But they can be lots easier if we don't give in
to despair. I really want to lick the dragons as they appear. I love you.

Whatever doubts may have lingered about their marriage disappeared over the next couple of months. Rita wrote Lillian a peace letter, explaining that the misgivings she had expressed about the marriage during Lillian's visit had been influenced by their mother—and by the fact that she had always felt she had married too young herself and had been tied down by it, and she didn't want Lillian to make the same mistake.

Even with Lillian back at college, the Mayberrys often asked Foote to parties at their apartment and began to treat him already like a member of the family. For all the paucity of work that was coming his way that fall, Foote's social schedule was full. He shuttled between gatherings at the Bettis-Segalls downtown and parties at the Mayberrys uptown, mingling with different but equally fascinating groups of guests.

At George and Rita's, the talk was usually about writers and artists, almost never about music or dance. It was at one of their parties that Foote met Robert Motherwell, who was just beginning to be known as a painter. Among other frequent guests were Albert Erskine, who had been married to Katherine Anne Porter; Malcolm Cowley, the critic; and Agnes Smedley, the war correspondent. Everyone held strong opinions about the young writers of the day. George had just reviewed for the *New Republic* a first novel by a young writer named Saul Bellow and was full of praise for him. The only time Foote recalled dance being mentioned was one evening when Erskine said he hated all modern dance, and Martha Graham in particular, because he thought it was ugly.

Inspired by the talk at the Mayberrys, and with ample free time on his hands and a shop full of books at his disposal, Foote read voraciously throughout the fall. He had always been an avid reader, but the years of acting and writing and trying to make ends meet had curtailed one of his favorite pastimes for the past few years. He had always been a fan of Faulkner, and he began to reread him. He also plunged into poetry, devouring T. S. Eliot, Ezra Pound, W. H. Auden, William Carlos Williams, Marianne Moore, and Wallace Stevens. He also read James Joyce, Evelyn Waugh, Flannery O'Connor, Eudora Welty, and, as he had met her former husband, Katherine Anne Porter. He was particularly taken with *Pale Horse, Pale Rider* and in years to come would cite it as a major influence on his own work.

By contrast, the conversation at Valerie and Bernardo's almost always centered on music and dance, rarely on art or writing, which by this time was considered to be subservient to the other disciplines anyway.

The 1944 presidential election occupied a good deal of talk at both salons. Foote was anxious about Roosevelt's chances for a fourth term against his Republican challenger, the former governor of New York Thomas E. Dewey. Election Day coincided with the opening night of the one-acts Foote had directed for the Neighborhood Playhouse. Foote wrote Lillian that he stayed up until five the following morning listening to the election returns on the radio, and when it became clear Roosevelt had won, he went to an all-night diner and had scrambled eggs to celebrate. "I was really joyous when I thought Claire Booth Luce was heartbroken," he wrote.

Rita Morgenthau had been impressed by the one-acts Foote had directed at the Neighborhood Playhouse and wrote him a note saying, "You fit into N.P.'s point of view and attitude so perfectly that I somehow think of you as a member. We shall call upon you constantly."

By December, however, there were no new theater jobs on the horizon, either at the Neighborhood Playhouse or anywhere else, and the realities of his economic situation were becoming dire. He pawned his wristwatch, and at the beginning of the month he wrote Lillian asking about her plans for Christmas, explaining that he didn't have enough money to come to Boston. Lillian replied that she had decided to stay at Radcliffe over the holidays and work on her thesis. By not returning home, she said, she could avoid another confrontation with her mother over their engagement.

Although he had been offered a promotion by Doubleday to be manager of the Fifth Avenue store, Foote was ambivalent about it. He certainly could use the extra money it would bring. He was trying to save enough to get his watch out of hock and to pay for a ticket home to Texas. The new job would ease another worry that was at the back of his mind. When he had only his own welfare to consider, the lack of money was not such a big deal. But now that he had to consider supporting a wife, it was a real issue. On the other hand, his great fear was that he would become trapped into a job that would take him away from writing, and he felt the new job offer at Doubleday's flagship store threatened that. Also, he was beginning to have doubts about his talents as a writer.

In one letter to Lillian just after Christmas, he raised the age-old question that every writer faces: How does one create? "There is only one answer to that stupid question," he wrote. "And that is to create. I hope I will never forget that and that you won't let me." He went on to explain the underlying fear that he believed was blocking his writing. "There has always been a dark hidden dread in me of change of any kind," he wrote. "But these feelings are all excess baggage."

By the New Year, he had managed to save seventy dollars, just the amount he needed to redeem his watch and pay for a train ticket home. He had not been home in a long while, and he felt the need not only to see his parents but to replenish the creative inspiration that always came with a visit to Texas. In addition, there still had been no news of Tom Brooks, and it had by now been many months. Foote's father had become convinced that his middle son was dead, although his mother still held out hope that he was in a German prison camp somewhere.

From the moment he arrived in Texas in early January, Foote wrote Lillian almost every other day. In his first letter, he wrote that he and his family "were having a fine time together—mostly talking and catching up on the past, dissecting and rattling around the family skeletons."

In a second letter, he wrote: "Last night I went 'honky-tonking' or 'juking,' as it is called here, which means visiting the beer joints on the highway. They are considered sinful places but after the Village dives seem quite tame—rather sad and futile." In another, he told Lillian that he described her to all his relatives as resembling Ingrid Bergman, and they all went to the local cinema to see Bergman's latest movie so they would know what his fiancée looked like. He wrote another time that he went to services at the Methodist church to sing hymns, a joy that he had not experienced since he was a child. In yet another, he mentioned that he found a complete set of Hawthorne's novels published in 1880 in the family bookcase, and that his mother promised to give them to him. At one point, some of his old high school friends gave a party in his honor, and he wrote Lillian: "I keep finding myself thinking of them as they were. I'm afraid I prefer them that way." In one letter that he wrote late at night, he noted: "There is a dog howling outside. Negroes say a man dies when a dog howls. I feel very close to their legends once again."

To his growing concern, however, Lillian wrote rarely and sparingly while he was in Texas. In one letter, he complained, "I haven't heard from you and wonder why." After a week and still no letter, he began imploring her to write, saying that he was "in a lover's agony" waiting for word from her and worrying that her silence had more sinister meanings. Later in his stay, he complained that he had received only one letter a week.

As the visit came to a close, however, Foote stopped chastising her about the paucity of her correspondence and wrote her about his feelings about his hometown and his family, and what they meant to him and his work. If nothing else, the trip had rejuvenated his creative energies and restored his confidence. The "family skeletons" that he had been "dissecting and rattling around" during his visit had come to life. In a final letter to Lillian before he was to return to New York, Foote wrote:

I've been filling myself with stories of the past years. You know I know nearly everyone here and it's like filling in the missing chapters. No matter where I am or go, I carry this world around with me. I think if only I could be surrounded by this seemingly simple and pastoral existence, how well I could work and write. But then I hear the tales *and get reports of the inner lives. I see them unmask themselves and I know that whatever that inner thing that seeks to destroy and flay people is at work here. But I have an impersonal feeling about it all that I've never had before. I have in mind my next two plays.*

No sooner was Foote back in New York than the problems he had fled to Texas to avoid began to crowd in upon him again. He received a call from the Prentice Hall publishing house, asking him to come in to interview for a job as an editor. As strapped as he was for money, he knew it was a temptation that would lead him away from writing. Margo Jones approached him about coming to spend a year at her new theater, and at one point he wrote Lillian to say they might spend the first year of their married life in Dallas. The Pasadena Playhouse was looking to take on a playwright-in-residence, and he was told he might get the job if he applied. But that would only take him away from New York, which was still the center of American theater. He also had an argument with Mary Hunter over the future of the American Actors Company. The company was in financial straits as well, and Mary was talking of abandoning it. Finally, she offered to renew his connection with the company at thirty-five dollars a week for a forty-week minimum and the promise of doing two of his plays there. He grabbed it.

On top of it all, in February, two weeks after his return from Texas, Lillian wrote to him asking that they postpone their marriage. She said she had been under "terrific stress this term—emotional, mental and physical," and that she "would like to recuperate somewhat before assuming the many obligations that marriage carries with it." She said it would mean waiting only a few months.

Foote could hear Lillian's mother in almost every sentence she'd written. The whole experience was beginning to resemble a scenario from one of his own plays. He knew that Lillian's reticence stemmed only from her mother's opposition to the marriage, and he replied calmly to her letter, refuting her arguments one by one. But he didn't refuse her request for a delay.

At one point, Lillian left Radcliffe and returned home to Mount Carmel for a few days to try to win her mother's blessing. "I want to talk to mother about us and see what I can do," she wrote. "At times I become depressed. There seem to be so many obstacles ahead of us."

Toward the end of March, Williams came to visit Foote at the bookstore again. *The Glass Menagerie*, which had been a huge success in Chicago, was opening that night on Broadway and Williams asked Foote if he would like to come see it. Foote eagerly accepted. Williams arranged for Foote to meet him outside the Playhouse Theatre fifteen minutes before the curtain.

When Foote arrived, he found Tennessee standing alone by the entrance. "Come with me," Williams said and led Foote down an alleyway to the stage door. Eddie Dowling was outside, smoking a cigarette. Dowling, who had bought the rights to the play as a vehicle for himself, was coproducer (with Louis J. Singer), codirector (with Margo Jones), and one of the stars, playing the part of Tom, the play's narrator. Dowling was old-school Broadway, the kind of guy who always had a smile and a handshake and who called every male acquaintance "laddie."

"Eddie," Tennessee called out and introduced Foote. "Eddie, can you get him a seat for tonight?"

"Laddie, it's all sold out," Dowling said, smiling. "Not a seat to be had." Then he turned to Foote. "Laddie, would you mind standing?"

"No, sir," Foote replied.

Dowling put out his cigarette and disappeared inside the theater. He came out a couple of minutes later. "I've arranged it," he said. "Tennessee, tell them at the front to let him in. He's to stand."

"Thank you, sir," Foote replied. "And good luck tonight."

"Thank you, laddie," Dowling said and went back inside the theater.

Foote watched the opening night of *The Glass Menagerie* standing at the back of the theater. Like critics and everyone else who saw it, he was mesmerized, especially by Laurette Taylor's performance in the role of Amanda. He saw Margo Jones at intermission, and she asked him to come by her room at the Royalton Hotel for a party after the show. She said Tennessee and some other friends would be there.

After the final curtain, Foote saw Tennessee outside the theater.

He waved and told him he would see him later at Margo's. Williams, however, was swamped by admirers, surrounded by people, none of whom Foote knew, and he wasn't sure Williams heard him. Foote went to Jones's hotel and joined in the opening-night celebration. Jones kept telling him, "It's just the beginning, baby," and said her theater in Dallas was going to do Foote's plays, Tennessee's plays, and everybody else's plays that she believed in. Foote stayed until about two in the morning, but Tennessee never appeared. He didn't see him again for nearly six years.

Throughout the spring, Foote countered the objections Lillian's mother kept making to their marriage. He was confident of Lillian's love, but he knew she was torn over her mother's opposition. In an effort to overcome one of the obstacles Mrs. Vallish raised, Foote began to take instruction in the Roman Catholic Church. None of their efforts, however, held any sway with Lillian's mother, and in the end, Foote and Lillian made plans for the wedding on their own.

They were married on June 4, 1945, at the St. Jean Baptiste Church in New York. Only Rita and her husband, George, were present from either family. They did not even tell Mrs. Vallish about the wedding in advance. A few close friends attended. There was no honeymoon trip, and the newlyweds moved into the small apartment that Foote had been living in most recently at 148 West Tenth Street in the Village.

It was left to Rita and George to break the news to Mrs. Vallish, and it was George's parents who brought the whole family together a couple of weeks after the wedding. The Mayberrys organized a reception for the newlyweds at their house in New Jersey and invited Mr. and Mrs. Vallish to come.

Foote kept thinking of the story of his own parents' marriage, and how his grandmother and grandfather didn't speak to his mother for nearly a year after she married his father, until just before Foote was born. He took some comfort in the fact that all had ended well with his parents. His grandmother, Baboo, had grown to admire his father and rely on him after Foote's grandfather had died. He felt confident it would turn out all right in the long run with him and Lillian, if he had the patience.

At the time of the Mayberrys' party, however, feelings were running high. When Lillian's mother arrived she was dressed entirely in black, as though she were going to a funeral rather than a wedding reception for her youngest daughter, and went around weeping as though she were at a wake.

It was Mrs. Mayberry, George's mother, who finally called her aside and said in no uncertain terms, "Barbara, you've got to stop this. He's a very nice boy."

Over the years, Foote became her favorite son-in-law.

The war in Europe had ended in May, and although the fighting still raged against Japan in the Pacific, many soldiers were coming home from military service. Foote had a call in the summer from a returning veteran who said he had been the pilot of the plane Tom Brooks was on when it was shot down over Germany. The man said he had immediately been taken prisoner by German soldiers. As he was marched off he saw Foote's brother slumped over the radio controls, bleeding. He said it was possible that Tom had only been wounded and had been taken prisoner as well.

Foote called his parents with this news, which—reflecting his parents' personalities and outlooks on life—only strengthened Foote's father's opinion that Tom Brooks was dead while bolstering his mother's hopes that her middle son was still alive.

Among the returning soldiers there was also a large number of actors, directors, and writers, all trying to find work in the theater. The New York theater, however, was rapidly changing, and perhaps the biggest change was the advent of the agent as the sine qua non for getting just about any job in the theater. There had long been theatrical agents, of course. In the past, however, it was mostly only the big stars who had them. Suddenly, there was a proliferation of agents. The old routine of making the rounds of theatrical offices was abandoned, if not overnight, at least over the summer. Now if an actor or writer didn't have an agent, the chances of getting an audition were slim, and there was no way your play would be read.

One of the first to recognize this trend was Lucy Kroll, a former member of the American Actors Company. She had given up on pursuing an acting career herself and had become an agent with the Sam Jaffe Agency. She and Foote had become friends during their time at the acting company, and she asked him if he had an agent. When he replied he didn't, she signed him up as her first client. She soon broke away and formed her own agency and acquired an impressive stable that included Helen Hayes, Lillian Gish, James Earl Jones, and Uta Hagen. Foote remained with her throughout her life.

In August, Foote took Lillian to Texas. He was eager to introduce his bride to his family, and she, in turn, to meet them. He was confident they would get along beautifully, and he was right. Lillian felt immediately at home in Wharton and was embraced by all of Foote's extended family. Before leaving for Texas, Foote had given Lucy Kroll two plays that he had been working on for the past year—*Marcus Strachen* and another titled *People in the Show*—to send out to Broadway producers.

Marcus Strachen, which progresses in a succession of small scenes, almost vignettes, is about a man who comes to a small Texas town after the Civil War with a modest stake, but who makes his way fast. He marries the boss's daughter, gets rich, keeps a Negro mistress, abuses his wife, and is finally undone by a man craftier and smarter than he. He abandons his wife, his mistress, and the town and moves on to try his fortune in another place, having learned nothing.

Kroll first sent *Marcus Strachen* to the Theater Guild, which was run at the time by John Gassner. It was assigned to one of the Guild's readers, Molly Thatcher. In rejecting it in her report to the Guild, Thatcher complained that the play was too grim, too cold, too gray, and lacked "attractiveness of whatever kind." In a letter she wrote personally to Foote, Thatcher lectured him on what was missing in his play and said he needed to take "more account of audience reactions." She advised him to work harder at writing plays that "will attract, will give pleasure . . . or a belly laugh."

Forwarding the report to him in Texas, in a letter dated August 10, 1945, and addressed simply "Horton Foote, Wharton, Texas," Kroll did not even mention the rejection, but was full of hope and promise for the future. She wrote, "Everything is simply wonderful in this world of ours now that the Pacific War seems to be coming to its end, I hope, sometime today." Japan unconditionally surrendered that same day, formally ending World War II.

People in the Show was the play that Foote had completed writing while he was in Texas at the beginning of the year. It was based on his experiences acting in the *Railroads on Parade* pageant at the New York World's Fair. It's a large panorama—three acts and a prologue—that takes place during the run of a fictitious pageant, called *Century of Progress*, at a World's Fair. It is a backstage drama with a large cast and several stock characters—the drunken actor; has-been thespians living on memories; a married star having an affair with a younger man; a veteran actress secretly in love with the married star's cuckolded husband. But the play also addressed some social issues current at the time and was the most overtly political play Foote had ever written.

One of those issues was the war itself. Set in May 1940, at the time of the German invasion of France, the company in the fictitious pageant is divided over whether America should become involved in the war or stay neutral, and the major concern for many of the characters is whether the war will force the show to close and cause them to lose their paychecks.

"War is good for show business," one says. "Look at the last one." That line was a reference to the patriotic musicals that thrived on Broadway during America's brief involvement in World War I.

Foote also explored the issue of racial friction among blacks. Two of the characters in the play (and in the imaginary pageant) are Negro actors who loathe each other—one, named Stilwell, is a Communist and civil rights activist; the other one, called Stetsie, is content with the status quo and is branded an "Uncle Tom" by Stilwell. Stilwell ends up being fired when she protests not being served a cup of coffee in the theater's canteen.

But the biggest issue running through the play is the anti-Semitism that was rife in America before World War II, and the Fascist sentiments that some Americans harbored. The male lead in the play is a Jewish actor named Sam who is having a romance with a Gentile character named Irene. Some of the characters express outright anti-Semitic feelings, and the play ends with the death of the Jewish protagonist in a fight with one of the other actors.

It was a bold play, told in broad, sweeping strokes. But backstage drama has always been difficult for playwrights to capture. With some notable exceptions, theater people do not make good theater. It also indulged in some melodramatic affectations. There is, for example, a trio of aging actresses who have bit parts in the fictitious show and who form a sort of chorus of harpies in Foote's play, lamenting, among other things, the death of the theater. It's almost as though Foote borrowed Shakespeare's three witches from *Macbeth* to provide a running commentary on all that occurs onstage.

The rejections Kroll received for both plays were indicative of the problems Foote and other playwrights faced in the fall of 1945. Producers believed that after a decade of the Great Depression, followed by four years of war, audiences mainly wanted to be entertained.

In the end, Mary Hunter mounted a production of *Marcus Strachen* at the American Actors Company, but it was only a half-hearted effort, and Foote himself was dissatisfied with the result. The company did not have the money for the large cast in *People in the Show*, and Mary herself had lost interest in trying to keep the company going. She had become involved with a new project called the American Theatre Wing, through which she was starting to offer acting, directing, and writing classes for returning veterans. In the fall, the American Actors Company quietly dissolved.

Another problem for playwrights in New York immediately after the war was that producers were mainly looking for vehicles for known stars, actors whom people would pay money to go to see. There were few accepted box-office writers. Since his success with *The Glass Menagerie*, Tennessee Williams was considered a bankable writer, and he was working on a new play he at first called "The Card Game" but later titled *A Streetcar Named Desire*. Arthur Miller had had one play on Broadway, but like Foote's *Only the Heart*, it had been poorly received.

The economic and creative malaise of the immediate postwar theater in New York helped convince Foote that the eulogies for narrative drama that he had been hearing were correct. As much as he loved storytelling, Foote felt more certain than ever that those who believed the future of theater was in the fusion of dance, music, and words were right. The plays that were being produced on Broadway were mainly British imports, mostly comedies (for a "belly laugh"), and almost always had a star. This flagrant commercialism led Foote and his circle of friends to the conclusion that serious theater in postwar America would no longer be centered in New York.

A month after the war in Japan ended, the last hope that Tom Brooks was still alive evaporated. The Footes received word that his body had been found buried in Germany. Foote, like his father, had feared the worst, but the final confirmation that his brother had been killed only added to his conviction that he wanted to begin something new, and that he would have to leave New York to pursue it. It was Valerie Bettis and her husband, Bernardo Segall, who found him an exit.

Segall, whose concert career was waning, had taken a job teaching piano once a week at the King-Smith School in Washington, D.C. The institution had been an elite finishing school for young ladies, mostly from the South; but during the war it too had fallen on hard times and was now a boardinghouse for young women working in Washington, mostly in government jobs. In an effort to maintain its reputation as a cultured establishment, it offered evening classes for its residents in art, music, and literature.

With the advent of the GI Bill, the King-Smith directors decided to reestablish a full-time school with day classes as well as those at night and to expand the curriculum to include dance and theater. On one of her trips to Washington with her husband, Bettis had talked to the school about teaching dance there and expounded on her theme of the new theater. The school was receptive to the idea and promised her a performance space if she would come to Washington and find someone to run the theater.

Back in New York, Valerie began her sales pitch to Foote. This was the chance for him to do the kind of work they had been talking about. Broadway and New York were dead ends, the future was in the new multimedia theater, and the King-Smith School could be the springboard for them. He would have a free hand to do whatever he wanted.

Foote was intrigued by the opportunity, but he was daunted by the prospect of teaching classes and trying to administer the theater at the same time. He wasn't sure he would have any time left to write. Still, he was now a married man with the responsibility of providing for his young bride, and he had no prospects of advancing his writing career in New York.

One of the thousands of returning soldiers who descended on New York that fall was a former radio actor named Vincent Donehue. Foote had known Donehue at the American Actors Company, and when he returned from military service, Donehue looked Foote up. When Foote asked him if he would like to go to Washington and help run an acting school and a theater, Donehue quickly accepted.

Within a month, Foote, Lillian, and Donehue had moved to Washington. The plan was that they would go down as the vanguard to get the school started, and Valerie and her husband would join them later. The latter never happened. Bettis and Segall came down once a week for a while, but they never moved to Washington. Segall began to get some more recitals, and Bettis landed a role in a Broadway musical. It wasn't long before they stopped coming to Washington altogether. Foote and Lillian and Donehue ended up staying four years.

Lillian, who had had no training in running either a school or a theater, took over most of the administrative duties for both at King-Smith, which was located on New Hampshire Avenue. With the influx of veterans returning from the war, the school had a healthy enrollment, but the tuition was not high and Foote found himself in the usual position of being strapped for money to stage new productions. Still, he and Donehue managed to have a show running most of the time, and although they charged only a small admission, it augmented the school's income.

They also discovered that, unlike New York, the nation's capital, which was just across the river from the heart of the Confederacy, was still very much a Jim Crow town. Even in the years immediately following the war, and despite efforts led by Eleanor Roosevelt, public places in Washington were still racially segregated. Foote, without fanfare, opened the school's and theater's doors to all races, and thus held the first public shows for an integrated audience in Washington.

With Lillian taking care of the day-to-day affairs of the school and the theater, Foote threw all his energy into writing pieces that would accompany modern dance and music. He wrote and directed one new play each year he was in Washington. *Good-bye to Richmond* had a score composed by Gerald Cook and choreography by Angela Kennedy, who had been a member of Martha Graham's company. *Themes and Variations* and *The Return* both had music by Robert Evett and choreography by Kennedy.

In addition, Foote directed at least one other play each year, and Donehue directed one or two productions a season. Sometimes, outside directors were invited to stage a production at the theater. Mary Hunter, with whom Foote had patched things up, came down to direct Sartre's *No Exit*, a seminal play in the Existentialist movement that was already being touted as the next "theater of the future" that would supplant the short-lived infatuation with the fusion of words, music, and dance.

Sartre was mainly a philosopher and novelist, but his plays, which he began writing in a Nazi prisoner-of-war camp, were groundbreaking and a forerunner of Beckett and the theater of the absurd. Foote was always enthusiastic about new voices in the theater, and his production of Sartre's drama of three disparate characters who suddenly find themselves alone in hell, bound together for eternity, was one of the first in America.

In Foote's last season at King-Smith, Donehue directed a production of *People in the Show*. Although they had little money to work with, they could offer actors a small stipend and room and board, and Donehue persuaded two rising young actors named Eli Wallach and Jean Stapleton to come to Washington to play the backstage lovers.

The theater at King-Smith was too small to accommodate the large cast the play required, so it was staged in a rented theater in

Virginia. Marlon Brando, who had just had his first big Broadway success, came to see it and created quite a stir, not least because he arrived at the theater barefoot.

Whether it was the good audience reception *People in the Show* received, or the fact that after four years he had become tired of trying to bend his talents to other disciplines, Foote decided in the late spring of 1949 that he wanted to return to New York, and to full-time writing.

Foote had been rereading a lot of Chekhov that spring, and Treplev's speech in the last scene of *The Seagull* struck a chord with him. Chekhov's character says: "I'm coming more and more to the conclusion that it's a matter not of old forms and not of new forms, but that a man writes, not thinking at all of what form to choose, because it comes pouring out from his soul."

Having experimented with other forms, Foote had come to the decision that he wanted to go back to his earlier way of writing. He was first and foremost a storyteller, and he wanted to write plays simply and directly, plays that came pouring out of his soul.

He met with Lillian and Vincent and told them how he felt. He had enjoyed the time in Washington and was grateful for the chance it gave him to experiment, but he thought it was time he went back to New York. They both agreed. Vincent returned to New York, while Foote and Lillian went to stay with his wife's parents in Pennsylvania. Mrs. Vallish by this time had amended her first impression of Foote and had grown extremely fond of him, not least because Lillian was now pregnant and Foote and her daughter were about to make her a grandmother.

They stayed in Pennsylvania through the summer, and Foote spent the time working on a new play he called *The Chase*. It was a dark drama involving an escaped convict, a double-crossing best friend, infidelity, vengeance, and an honest sheriff who is tired of the life of violence that surrounds him. Like his earlier plays, it was set in a small town in Texas, again called Richmond.

When he finished it, Foote sent it to his friend Harold Clurman in New York with the idea of getting it produced. Clurman wrote back that he liked the play but thought it needed work, that it struck him as too bleak. "Black on black is not an aesthetic," Clurman advised.

When they arrived back in New York, Foote and Lillian stayed at a friend's apartment in Chelsea while they looked for a place of their own. They needed to find a place with at least two bedrooms to accommodate the baby, which was expected in March. As always, money was an issue. But they had sold the car they bought while they were in Washington and had enough for a decent apartment, at least for a while.

Lucy Kroll had sent *The Chase* around to several producers. She also submitted it for a prize, for the best new American play, that carried a substantial monetary award. Herman Shumlin, a producer and director who had brought Lillian Hellman's *The Children's Hour* and *The Little Foxes* to Broadway, was one of the judges on the committee that would decide the winner. When he read the play, Shumlin told Lucy not only that it would almost certainly win the prize, but that he would like to produce it himself on Broadway. The problem was that it would be unethical for him, as a committee judge, to take an option on a play in the competition. He persuaded Kroll and Foote to withdraw *The Chase* from consideration for the prize. They complied with his request, and Shumlin took an option. In the end, however, Shumlin himself backed out, and Foote had neither the prize money nor a Broadway production.

Foote was beginning to wonder if it had been a mistake to leave Washington. He had a play that was attracting a lot of interest, but nobody was writing any checks to put it in a theater. The money from the sale of their car was running out, and there was little prospect for any more coming in anytime soon.

Knowing he needed some sort of income, Mary Hunter hired Foote to teach a class at the American Theatre Wing, but that job did not pay the sort of wages on which one could raise a family.

The money situation became more critical in the early spring of 1950 with the arrival of a baby girl, delivered on March 31 at the French Hospital in New York. They named her Barbara Hallie, after Lillian's and Foote's mothers.

Since his own return to New York that summer, Vincent Donehue had run into an old friend named Fred Coe with whom he had once worked in summer stock. After returning from military service, Coe had taken a job in the new medium of television, and he was now beginning to make a name for himself as a producer.

Before the war, television had belonged to the realm of science fiction. It was at best a clunky contraption, available only to the very rich, and with limited possibilities for reaching a large audience. Directors had to frame the action within the lens of only one camera, a huge and stationary device that was simply pointed at the image they wanted to convey through space, and that was it.

But toward the end of the 1940s, television had become much more advanced. For starters, several cameras could be used and a director could switch between them to give several views of the same scene. The cameras, still large, were by now also mobile. They could be turned and swiveled to follow an actor moving across a set, or from one set to another. Most important, however, more and more American households had television sets. Within a few short years, it was predicted that every American home would have one—that television not only would become as ubiquitous as radio, it might even replace it. Some even speculated that it would replace Hollywood.

There were great hopes and expectations for television in its early days. It would bring culture, including great American drama, right into people's homes and it would also provide a source of learning and education for the nation's youth, much like radio had done with programs such as *Mr. President.*

Fred Coe had been hired by Martin Stone, one of television's pioneers, to produce a half-hour show, aimed mostly at kids, that would stage reenactments of important moments in American history. Coe hired Donehue to be his director. Jerome Coopersmith had signed on as a writer for the show, and Donehue suggested his friend Horton Foote be added to the team as a cowriter. Coe agreed, and Foote, who needed the money, jumped at the opportunity.

Stone had created a popular children's puppet show called *Howdy Doody* and was regarded as an expert in kids' programming. He had already lined up Gabby Hayes, a cowboy film star who played Roy

Rogers's sidekick in the movies, as the narrator for the show. The collaboration between Foote and Coopersmith turned out to work very well. Coopersmith did most of the research for each of the episodes, and Foote did most of the writing.

The program, originally known as *The Quaker Oats Show*, had its debut on October 15, 1950. The opening credits, which ran over the sponsor's jingle, said: "The Quaker Oats Show. Starring Gabby Hayes. Written by Horton Foote and Jerome Coopersmith. Produced and Directed by Vincent J. Donehue. A Martin Stone Production."

A teleplay from one of the first programs shows the level of sophistication the program aimed for.

ANNOUNCER: The Quaker Oats Show . . . starring Gabby Hayes.
(*Dissolve to close-up of Hayes, live; cut to commercial cards.*)
ANNOUNCER: Brought to you by Quaker Oats, Quaker Puffed Wheat, Quaker Puffed Rice. And Aunt Jemima Pancakes.
(*Dissolve to picture, Quaker Canyon*)
ANNOUNCER: And now to hear the stories that belong to all of America we go to Quaker Canyon, U.S.A., and listen to its favorite story-tellin' citizen—Gabby Hayes.
(*Scene: Front porch of a general store. Gabby is in the middle of a hair-raisin' yarn.*)
GABBY: They was comin' from the left, comin' from the right. Soldiers in front, soldiers in back—hundreds of 'em. Ridin' and shootin' and slashin'—hundreds of 'em against Terrible Tom.
JANE: Terrible Tom?
GABBY: That's what the British soldiers called him—Terrible Tom, and wouldn't you know it, he was a Hayes. Scared the livin' daylights out of every Redcoat in the War of 1812. He was the fastest-shootin', quickest-drawin', toughest hombre this side of Alberkerkee.
BUCK: What was he, Gabby?
GABBY: Well, it ain't nothin' we like to talk of, 'cause Terrible Tom was the black sheep o' the Hayeses.

In this particular episode, Terrible Tom was a pirate in Louisiana during the War of 1812, and the story segues into a slice of American history in which General Andrew Jackson made a truce with Lafitte in the Battle of New Orleans. Each episode had to have a link to some member of Gabby Hayes's fictitious family, and the writing had to be tailored to the star's homespun, cornpone, already familiar character. The show usually ended with a plug not only for the next week's show but also for the latest Roy Rogers movie.

Each show opened in the general store in "Quaker Canyon." If Gabby wasn't in the middle of telling a story, he might be sitting on a barrel, whittling and singing "Clementine" or some pioneer song. He was always surrounded by kids, and he had two sidekicks—Jane and Buck—who acted as straight men, asking questions to pull the story out of him.

It was formulaic writing, and because it was a live half-hour show a week, it occupied Foote nearly full-time. But it paid three hundred dollars a week, a comfortable sum in those days. There were no thirteen-week seasons in television then, and Foote and Coopersmith had to come up with a new episode every week. The first season ran through the fall, winter, and spring and ended in June 1951.

After a two-month summer break, the show started its next season on August 26 with a new name: *The Gabby Hayes Show*. It was also growing in popularity, and Foote continued to write for it through that summer and fall. But as the year drew to a close, Foote saw an opportunity to break free of the rut of writing a weekly kids show and return to writing drama. The last installment of *The Gabby Hayes Show* written by Foote and Coopersmith was aired on December 23. Over the two seasons, they had written a total of fifty-four episodes.

During his time with *The Gabby Hayes Show*, Foote had gotten to know Coe fairly well. One of the more hopeful directions television was taking in the early 1950s was the production of new dramas for the home screen, and Coe was a chief promoter of doing original plays for TV audiences.

There were two competing schools of thought about the direction TV drama should take—toward Hollywood and the movies or toward Broadway and the theater. Foote supported the latter, and at that time he had an ally in Coe. In those days, television shows were broadcast live. Once a performance began, it couldn't be stopped, and in that respect it was more like the stage than film.

Coe began producing straight plays for television, and toward the end of 1951, during the final months he was working on *The Gabby Hayes Show*, Foote wrote a teleplay and showed it to Coe. It was called *Ludie Brooks*. Coe liked it and it was aired on the program *Lamp Unto My Feet* in February 1952. Coe hired Foote to write another TV drama, called *The Old Beginning*, that was shown on November 23, 1952, on the *Goodyear Television Playhouse*. It was the first time that Foote used a fictional town named Harrison for his setting. Another teleplay titled *The Travelers* was produced shortly afterward, and Coe then signed Foote to a contract to write nine more TV dramas. Foote was paid a thousand dollars for each one.

Coe did not like to read scripts. He wanted writers to give him a one-page synopsis. Foote had another play in mind, but when he tried to write out a summary of it, he found it impossible to reduce to one page. He asked Coe if he could just come in and tell him about it—a sort of forerunner of what would become the Hollywood pitch.

In a very short time, Foote had become Coe's favorite writer. Coe had a habit of developing a crush on certain writers, and Foote was by now his latest pet. The producer agreed to let Foote give him a verbal description of his next play. But Foote still wasn't sure how Coe would react to it.

He went to Coe's office and sat down across from him.

"This is a story about an old lady who wants to go back home," Foote said.

Coe waited for him to go on, but he didn't.

"That's all?" Coe asked.

"That's all," Foote replied.

"Okay," Coe said. "I trust you."

CHAPTER 6

Golden Age of Television

Foote gave the woman the name Carrie Watts, and the home she wanted to return to was in a small Texas town he called Bountiful. Carrie Watts is a woman in her sixties for whom life has been a series of disappointments. As a girl, she had been in love with a man of whom her father disapproved, and she ended up marrying another. She lost two babies, and only her son, Ludie, survived. She is now living in a small apartment with Ludie and his wife in Houston, signing over her monthly pension check to help pay for the small room she occupies, enduring her stepdaughter's carping criticism, and pining to return to the place of her birth for one last visit.

Carrie Watts, however, is quietly one of the most determined and indomitable spirits ever written for the American theater. When we first meet her, Carrie is sitting in a rocking chair, looking out the window of her son's apartment at a full moon and quietly singing an old hymn. By the end, she has carried the audience on a journey to visit the graveyard of the American dream and is returning to reality, not with bitterness and rancor, but in wistful mourning for a time when everything seemed possible. When she finally reaches her hometown, she discovers it no longer exists. Bountiful has been kept alive only in her memory.

Foote reached as far back into his own memory as he could for the inspiration for *The Trip to Bountiful*. One of his few recollections of his grandfather was of riding around the countryside with him when Papa, as he called him, would visit his farms scattered around the county. As they drove through small towns on their rounds, young Horton was always struck by one town that had been totally abandoned. Though it had once been a prosperous little community, only seven uninhabited houses and an empty general store were still standing. All that remained was the cemetery.

That memory itself was perhaps spawned by Foote's own reading at the time he wrote the play. He had been immersed in poetry, and some lines in Robert Frost's "Directive" struck him:

> *There is a house that is no more a house*
> *Upon a farm that is no more a farm*
> *And in a town that is no more a town.*

Foote also drew on several of the stories he had heard growing up: the aunt whose beau, forbidden by her father to visit, used to walk down her street every day at the same time, just so he could see her sitting on her front porch; another woman who had to sign over her pension check every month to ungrateful relatives; yet another who became bitter over not being able to bear children; even the old superstition that a dog howling means a person has died. He also borrowed something his mother-in-law once said to him, when Carrie tells the young girl Thelma on the bus, "I wasn't in love with my husband."

In fact, Foote began trying to write the play from the beginning of Carrie's story, with her love for Ray John Murray, who is mentioned only in passing in the final script, being thwarted by her father because of a feud he had with Murray's father. However, the story became too cumbersome, especially in attempting to work in Murray's futile daily walk past Carrie's house. Finally, he decided to focus the play on Carrie as an old woman, longing to return home.

The show aired on March 1, 1953, on *The Philco Television Playhouse* on NBC. Lillian Gish played Carrie Watts, and Vincent Donehue directed. Within minutes of the end of the show, the network's switchboard was flooded with calls from viewers. The head of the rival CBS network saw the show and telephoned the head of NBC to congratulate him. "Television came of age tonight," he said. The response was such to convince Fred Coe that he wanted to move the play to Broadway.

Over the course of its various incarnations as a television drama, a Broadway play, and a motion picture, Foote made various alterations to adapt it for each new format. For example, the hymn that Carrie is singing in the opening scene changed. In the stage version, she is singing "There's not a friend like the lowly Jesus." In the movie version, she is singing "Softly and tenderly, Jesus is calling." Perhaps the biggest change came during the transition from the original TV script to the stage version, when Foote added some dialogue to the closing scene.

Because of strict time considerations, television dramas had to be tailored to fit a one-hour time slot. With commercials thrown in, that meant that Foote's teleplay had about forty-eight to fifty minutes of playing time at most. When Coe decided to produce a stage version, the text needed to be filled out to make a full evening of theater. The format for all plays in the 1950s called for three acts with two intermissions. That meant that a play originally written to be performed without interruption now had to have two. Also, some additional material was written to flesh out the characters. Foote wrote one new speech for Carrie's son, Ludie, and it is one of the most poignant in the entire play.

In it, Foote drew on his own recollection of his grandfather's death, as Ludie recounts being taken into the room where his grandfather was laid out in a coffin with his grandmother sitting at the side, crying. Ludie also confesses to his mother that he shares her memories of walks she took him on when there was a full moon, and of their time in Bountiful, although he had been denying that he had. As they are about to leave, Carrie asks her son if he remembers his grandfather at all.

No, ma'am. Not too well. I was only ten when he died, Mama. I remember the day he died. I heard about it as I was coming home from school. Lee Weems told me. I thought he was joking and I called him a liar. I remember you takin' me into the front room there the day of the funeral to say good-bye to him. I remember the coffin and the people sitting in the room. Old man Joe Weems took me up on his knee and told me that Grandpapa was his best friend and that his life was a real example for me to follow. I remember Grandmama sitting by the coffin crying and she made me promise that when I had a son of my own I'd name it after Grandpapa. I would have, too. I've never forgotten that promise. Well, I didn't have a son. Or a daughter. . . . Oh Mama. I lied to you. I do remember. I remember so much. This house. The life here. The night you woke me up and dressed me and took me for a walk when there was a full moon and I cried because I was afraid and you comforted me. Mama, I want to stop remembering. . . . It doesn't do any good to remember.

But it is Carrie who delivers a sort of requiem for the land and for the past combined with a prophecy for the future. As she and Ludie stand outside the abandoned and dilapidated house that had once been her childhood home, she looks around at the weeds and wildflowers, the sagging roof, and rotting steps to the front porch.

MRS. WATTS: Ludie, Ludie. What's happened to us? Why have we come to this?

LUDIE: I don't know, Mama.

MRS. WATTS: Pretty soon it'll all be gone. Ten years . . . twenty . . . this house . . . me . . . you.

LUDIE: I know, Mama.

MRS. WATTS: But the river will be here. The fields. The woods. The smell of the Gulf. That's what I always took my strength from, Ludie. Not from houses, not from people. It's so quiet. It's so eternally quiet. I had forgotten the peace. The quiet. And it's given me strength once more, Ludie. To go on and do what I have to do. I've found my dignity and my strength.

LUDIE: I'm glad, Mama.

MRS. WATTS: . . . Do you remember how my Papa always had that field over there planted in cotton?

LUDIE: Yes, ma'am.

MRS. WATTS: See, it's all woods now. But I expect some day people will come again and cut down the trees and plant the cotton and maybe even wear out the land again and then their children will sell it and go to the cities and then the trees will come up again.

LUDIE: I expect so, Mama.

MRS. WATTS: We're part of all this. We left it, but we can never lose what it has given us.

The stage version of *The Trip to Bountiful* opened in the fall of 1953 at Henry Miller's Theatre. Lillian Gish reprised her role as Carrie Watts. Jo Van Fleet played her stepdaughter, Jessie Mae, and a young Eva Marie Saint played Thelma, the young girl who befriends Carrie on her trip home. Gene Lyons played Ludie.

There were problems almost from the start. Gish and Van Fleet took an instant dislike to each other. Van Fleet thought the play was about her character, not the mother, and the two actresses sniped at each other throughout rehearsals. It was a feud that carried on for the rest of their lives. Thirty years later, as the movie version was being planned, Van Fleet sent Foote a note asking for a part in it. "I read that you were going to do *Trip to Bountiful*," she said. "If that's true I suppose you've already hired someone for the mother. Probably Lillian Gish again."

In addition, Foote was apprehensive about interrupting the flow of the story for lengthy intermissions. As it turned out, he had reason to be concerned. Critics gave it mixed reviews, and much of the criticism focused on what Walter Kerr, writing in the *New York Herald Tribune*, called a lack of "sustained vitality." It was exactly the problem Foote had foreseen. By breaking the narrative twice for intermissions, the buildup of tension in Carrie's drive to reach Bountiful is lost. One unreserved rave, from William Hawkins in the *New York World-Telegram and Sun*, however, said the evening provided "an indelible memory" and said the play was an emotional chase, filled with "suspense and tense excitement."

Hawkins proved to be the prophet. If the stage version did not exactly sweep Broadway off its feet—it ran through the winter and closed in the spring—it has certainly had legs. The movie version, finally filmed in 1984, won an Oscar for Geraldine Page in the role of Carrie. And of all of Foote's plays, *The Trip to Bountiful* has probably been produced more than any other.

More than half a century later, in December 2005, a revival directed by Harris Yulin presented the play as it was intended, as a long one-act. That production cast Lois Smith as Carrie, the playwright's daughter Hallie Foote as Jessie Mae, and Devon Abner, his son-in-law, as Ludie, and it played a sold-out extended run at the Signature Theatre in New York. Extra tickets were sold to people willing to sit on the steps in the aisles, and they were snapped up within minutes. Audiences of young and old alike were in tears, on their feet for standing ovations night after night. The New York staging was reprised intact two years later at the Goodman Theatre in Chicago, again to sold-out houses.

On opening night of the original Broadway production, Foote was surprised to see Tennessee Williams standing in the lobby during the second intermission. They embraced like old friends, and Williams told Foote he thought it was the best thing he had written. They promised to keep in touch.

Williams and Foote's relationship was a complicated one. As young writers, before either found success, they had formed a sort of mutual admiration society. They explored similar themes, such as domineering mothers and the urge of youth to break free of familial moorings. But they viewed this psychic landscape from different perspectives: Williams dwelled on the despair, while Foote saw a faint glimmer of light. Williams saw only the dark side, lives trapped in dead ends with no way out; Foote, on the other hand, looked for escape routes. Foote believed, like Faulkner, that while there was life, there was the possibility of redemption—that mankind, to borrow words from Faulkner's Nobel speech, "will not merely endure, he will prevail."

Perhaps the divergence of their points of view can be traced to their childhoods. While Williams grew up with an absent father and overbearing mother, Foote had the benefit of a loving and supportive family. Whatever the reason, it eventually led Williams to regard Foote with a certain ambivalence. In a letter to Donald Windham during the summer they were together in California, Williams once recounted spending the entire day with Foote and complained that he was full of "sweetness and light, which has such a withering effect upon my spirit." Yet he added that Foote "probably believes in his sentiments more than I do."

There was also a measure of jealousy in Williams's attitude toward Foote. Williams, for example, was a great admirer of Mary Hunter, who he once said was "the most intelligent woman I have ever met." Yet he perceived that Hunter preferred Foote's work to his. (Hunter once passed on directing Williams's play *You Touched Me* to direct one of Foote's plays.) He also once wrote to his agent, Audrey Wood, that he regretted ever introducing Margo Jones to Foote, because he believed she liked Foote's plays better than his.

However difficult their relationship was, the fact of the matter was that their careers were taking them in separate directions, and their meeting in the lobby after the opening of *The Trip to Bountiful* was the last time they saw each other for a long time.

During the time Foote was writing the television version of *Bountiful*, he had not given up hope for getting *The Chase*, the play he had written the previous summer, to Broadway. The lure of the Great White Way remained the grail for which every playwright strove. Foote still believed that whatever success he might have on television, it would take a smash Broadway hit to validate his talent as a writer, in his own eyes as well as others'.

Ever since Herman Shumlin had backed out of producing *The Chase*, Lucy Kroll had been sending the play to other producers and had received some interest. The play represented a marked departure for Foote, not only in theme but also in characterization. For one thing, there are few out-and-out villains in Foote's entire canon. One of the hallmarks of his plays, and what makes actors eager to perform in them, is the human element to all his characters. There may be men and women who behave badly, even despicably—drunkards, liars, scoundrels, tyrants, cheats, and crooks. But there is nearly always some redeeming quality that will enable an actor to embrace the character. There was, however, very little good to be found in the character of Bubber Reeves as Foote created him.

The play opens in the office of Sheriff Hawes, a name taken from a well-known family in Wharton. Hawes is the kind of small-town sheriff who is on call twenty-four hours a day to solve everyone's problems, listen to their complaints, break up fistfights, settle disputes, and get kittens down from trees. He also captured and sent to prison a local delinquent named Bubber Reeves, who had turned to robbery and killing.

Hawes has decided he wants to quit being the sheriff. His wife, Ruby, is pregnant and he wants a peaceful life for his family. Hawes no sooner informs the town's leading citizen of his decision than he learns that Bubber has escaped from the state prison and is heading toward Richmond to kill him. Many of the town's residents, fearful of having a murderer on the loose, push Hawes to go after Bubber and kill him, while Bubber's mother pleads with the sheriff to spare her son and send him back to prison.

Over nine scenes and three acts, Foote examines civic, social, and ethical questions: How much does a civil servant owe his community against the obligations he has to his family? At what moral price can peace of mind and a sense of security be bought? And to what extent should the wife, mother, and best friend of a murderer protect him, knowing that he is intent on killing again?

One of the more intriguing possibilities for staging the play came from an unlikely source. Foote had showed a copy to his friend Mildred Dunnock, and she, in turn, had given it to her friend Patricia Neal. At the time, Neal was romantically involved with Gary Cooper and she showed him the script. One day Foote had a call out of the blue from Cooper, asking if he would see him.

Cooper came to Foote's apartment and told him he liked the play very much and wanted to do it. The main character was not unlike the sheriff Cooper had just finished playing in the movie *High Noon*, and it was a character Cooper felt he understood and could do well. With a star name like Gary Cooper, producers would fall over one another to get it staged. But Cooper said there was one big drawback. He suffered terribly from stage fright. The camera didn't bother him, but the thought of going onstage made him physically ill. In the end, Cooper did not do the play.

Meanwhile, two producers were competing to stage *The Chase*.

One was Jean Dalrymple, who had plans to cast Franchot Tone in the role of Sheriff Hawes. The other was José Ferrer, who had star status as an actor from his performances in *Cyrano de Bergerac* and *Golden Boy*, and who seemed the more likely of the two to get financial backing for a Broadway production. Ferrer, who would also direct, wanted John Hodiak to play the lead. He also wanted Foote to make some changes in the script.

Foote preferred Tone for the role, and the actor wanted to do the play. Also, Dalrymple had been first in contacting Lucy Kroll about producing it. Kroll, however, wanted to go with Ferrer. In a decision that Foote said later he always regretted, he agreed to a request from Lucy not to answer the phone when Dalrymple called with her offer, and Ferrer became producer by default.

The changes Ferrer wanted had to do with a personal matter. At the time, he and his wife had been trying to have a child, but there were complications. Ferrer wanted the issue of the inability to conceive introduced in some way into the play. Foote had no problem with that and inserted some dialogue indicating that the sheriff and Ruby had been trying for some time to conceive a child before succeeding with her present pregnancy. By odd coincidence, it was during the rehearsals for *The Chase* that Lillian learned she was once again pregnant herself.

The biggest surprise for Foote, however, came in a meeting he had with Ferrer shortly before rehearsals began. Ferrer told Foote that he had a hands-off approach to directing, and that he, Foote, should take over the day-to-day running of the rehearsals, and that he, Ferrer, would come in at the end and give his approval or make suggestions. For all intents and purposes, Foote ended up directing the play himself, although Ferrer was listed as director.

Kim Hunter, who had just had a major success in Tennessee Williams's *A Streetcar Named Desire*, was signed to play the part of the sheriff's wife, Ruby. For some of the other roles, Foote had a free hand with the casting. Lillian had seen a production of Federico García Lorca's *House of Bernarda Alba* and had been much taken with the performance of a young actress named Kim Stanley as one of the daughters. Foote auditioned her and signed her to play the difficult part of Anna Reeves, the killer's young wife. It was the beginning of a lifelong friendship.

The Chase opened on April 15, 1952, at the Playhouse Theatre. The reviews were mixed, but overall not promising, especially as Brooks Atkinson, who was back as chief drama critic at the *New York Times*, did not favor it with a good notice. The play ran for several weeks, then quietly closed.

Foote had little time to nurse his wounds. If the neon lights of Broadway were dim and flickering for Foote at that time, the little light on the TV camera was glowing brightly. He plunged back into work on the dramas for television for which he was contracted, and for once he did not have to worry about money following the closing of a stage play.

With their second child on the way, he and Lillian decided they had to find a bigger apartment. They found one in an elevator building on the Upper West Side, at Broadway and Eighty-ninth Street. It had a separate living room and dining room; two large bedrooms and one smaller bedroom, which could be used as a nursery; and a maid's room at the back. They had already moved in when Albert Horton Foote III was born on November 7, 1952, in French Hospital, the same place where Barbara Hallie had been delivered.

The success of the original television production of *The Trip to Bountiful* had made Foote, if not exactly a household name, a writer who had caught the attention of producers on both coasts. Over the next two years, Foote spent most of his time writing the nine television dramas he had contracted to write, all produced by Coe and most directed by Donehue, for either the Philco or the Goodyear playhouse programs.

The taut, hour-long format that TV required suited Foote very well during this period. He had been rereading a lot of short stories—Chekhov, Porter, and Faulkner, in particular—and he learned to build drama with the economy of language and scenes that the new medium required. Foote, along with Paddy Chayefsky and Tad Mosel, set a high standard for drama on the home screen that has never been equaled and that led to the 1950s being called "the golden age of television."

Just a month after *The Trip to Bountiful* was aired, *A Young Lady of Property* was presented on *The Philco Television Playhouse* and was well received by critics and audiences alike. The two back-to-back successes established Foote as a major voice in the new medium. Every couple of months there was a new Foote play on one of the networks' drama programs, including *The Death of the Old Man*, *The Midnight Caller*, *Expectant Relations*, *The Tears of My Sister*, *John Turner Davis*, *The Dancers*, and *The Oil Well*. Foote revisited some of these TV dramas in later years for material for other plays, and some, like *Bountiful* and *A Young Lady of Property*, had a later life on the stage.

Despite his heavy commitment to Coe for the television plays, the siren call of Broadway kept echoing in Foote's ears, and in the spring of 1954 he began work on a new stage play. It was called *The Traveling Lady*, and, like *The Chase*, it had to do with a prisoner getting out of jail.

The play opens with Georgette Thomas arriving in town with her small daughter, looking for a place for her and her husband, a native of the town, to live when he gets out of prison the following week. Henry Thomas had been a local ne'er-do-well who was raised by a woman named Kate Dawkins who beat him as a child in an effort to break his unruly will. Thomas, whose ambition was to be a country singer, turned to drink, stabbed a man, and ended up in the state penitentiary in Huntsville. Most of the action takes place on the day of the Dawkins woman's funeral.

Georgette thinks her husband is getting out of prison the following week, but in fact he was released several weeks earlier and is already back in Richmond, staying with a Mrs. Tillman, a local woman who has a hobby of saving drunks and reprobates, and working for her as a handyman. When Thomas learns his wife is in town, he goes on a bender, robs Mrs. Tillman of her silverware, and desecrates Dawkins's grave.

As usual with Foote plays, there are several subplots, and one involves a man named Slim whose fiancée has died and who helps Georgette and her daughter. Slim is about to leave for a trip along the Gulf Coast to try to forget his grief, and in a speech that echoes Ray in *Texas Town*, Georgette says she has always wanted to travel:

My idea of heaven would be to travel. I used to lie in bed at night back in Tyler and not be able to sleep and listen to the trains. I always feel so lonely when I hear a train whistle.

Unlike he did with Bubber Reeves in *The Chase*, however, Foote gave Henry Thomas some saving graces, chief among them a genuine desire to reform. Although Henry admits he had no intention of returning to his wife and daughter after leaving prison, he is ashamed of the fact, and in a tearful, agonized confession that ends Act Two, Henry tells Slim:

I want to do right. I swear to my Maker I want to do right, but I'm weak. I'm just plain weak. . . . I was gonna desert her. I never intended gettin' in touch with her or the baby. . . . What kind of man would act like that? I'm just not worth killing.

The Traveling Lady opened at the Playhouse Theatre in New York on October 27, 1954, with Kim Stanley in the role of Georgette, Jack Lord as Slim, and Lonny Chapman as Henry. Vincent Donehue directed. The critics were not enthusiastic. The reviews mostly were mixed, with a couple of outright negative notices. None embraced the play wholeheartedly. It ran for five weeks.

Brooks Atkinson, who was back reviewing for the *Times*, said there were "genuine and very poignant scenes in this play" and it was a pleasure to see characters behave like "normal human beings." Atkinson also praised the writing as being "wonderfully honest," but complained that overall the play lacked strength. Walter Kerr, writing in the *Herald Tribune*, concurred with that assessment, saying it had little "theatrical vitality."

Foote reworked *The Traveling Lady* several times, and it had various incarnations—as a television drama two and a half years after the Broadway production, and eight years after that as a movie, with the title changed to *Baby, the Rain Must Fall*. There were even several drafts of the stage version before it landed on Broadway. The first version set the play in "Richmond," the name Foote used as his surrogate hometown for Wharton in most of his early work. By the time the play reached Broadway, the town's name was changed to "Harrison," the name he had used in some of the television dramas and the one he would use in all his later plays.

If the critics could not easily find the thread of human drama in Foote's early Broadway plays, he had no shortage of admirers from producers, directors, actors, and book publishers. The success of his television plays prompted Harcourt Brace to bring out an edition of them under the title *Harrison, Texas: Eight Television Plays*. And an editor at Rinehart & Company convinced him to turn *The Chase* into a novel, which was published in 1956.

In the spring of 1955, Lillian learned that she was again pregnant. Barbara Hallie turned five about the same time, and the Footes began to think about leaving the city. They wanted the children to grow up in a house in a small town, like they had done, rather than an apartment in the big city. They also wanted to find a good school system. They finally settled on Nyack, New York, a bucolic town within easy reach of the city and one where several theater people had homes.

Walter Vallish Foote was born on December 4, 1955, and a few months later Horton and Lillian moved to Nyack, first to a rented house and later to their own home. During that time, Foote continued to write plays for the home screen, including *The Roads to Home*, *Flight*, and *A Member of the Family*.

Writing television drama came naturally to Foote, who was an avid admirer of the short story form in fiction, and he relished the freedom of being able to move the action from place to place and not be tied to a single set. In an article he wrote for the *New York Times* in 1952, Foote talked about the freedom that television afforded.

When I first began to write for the medium I found myself wanting to go every place, into set after set, for the sheer joy of moving around. I soon found that such freedom is meaningless unless you have a real need to change locale. Whether using one set or ten sets, there has to be a need in terms of your characters and your story or else the use of numerous locales simply clutters and confuses. When there is a need, however, how wonderful to be able to go directly to the place most effective for your action.

It was also an asset that Foote could write on deadline. He wrote profusely and he wrote fast, another factor that made him much in demand for television. The time constraint was one of the draw-backs of television for many serious writers. But Foote had learned a valuable lesson during his days with *The Gabby Hayes Show*, when writers wanting to rework a particular piece of dialogue, make a change to the script, or add a scene were rebuffed with the stock excuse "There's not enough time." In the early days of television, a show was rehearsed for a week, or ten days at most, then performed live, broken only briefly for a few minutes for commercials. The actors moved from set to set in a studio, with the camera following them. In the same article for the *New York Times*, Foote wrote:

> There is an extraordinary feeling you get when you sit in the control room, look up at the clock, and see the hands getting nearer and nearer to the time when your teleplay begins. There are three minutes left, and then two, and then silence, silence like no other in the world, and then the music and the impersonally assured voice of the announcer. Suddenly you realize that nothing can stop the ticking of the clock, that for good or bad you have had your inning for ten days, or a week, or however long you have rehearsed the show. . . . Of course, you want to take it back and work on it some more, see it rehearsed some more, but there's no time. . . . In the theater there is time, in motion pictures there is time, in television, there isn't.

At the start of Foote's television career, Fred Coe had told him that he would have to make peace with the little box, meaning its limi-tations. Foote made his peace with the TV camera, but he often wished for more time and space to develop his characters and sto-ries. Technology would soon give it to him.

CHAPTER 7

Adaptations

B<small>Y THE LATE</small> 1950s, the tug-of-war between the East Coast and
the West Coast for the future of television, including the ideologi-
cal battle of whether the black box would be a child of the stage or
the movies, was slowly being won by the West. While the networks'
corporate offices remained in Manhattan, production of the shows
that would be sent to homes across America was shifting to Hollywood.

Fred Coe had moved his production company to Los Angeles,
and the invention of a new technology called videotape meant that
the days of live television drama were numbered. Although television programs were still aired only from dawn to midnight, and
there were only the three main networks, demand for new material
to fill the airwaves was increasing. Producers and directors searching for stories began to think of adaptations as well as original teleplays.

Coe, who was a native of Mississippi, shared with Foote a great
admiration for Faulkner, especially the short stories. Although
Faulkner had won the Nobel Prize in Literature in 1950, his early
work was still not widely known among the American reading public, and Coe believed he could remedy that oversight by bringing
the author's stories into living rooms through television. Coe called
Foote, who he knew had a great affinity with Faulkner, and asked if
he was familiar with the novella *Old Man*. Foote was, and Coe asked
him to think about adapting it for television.

While he had reworked many of his own plays from one medium
to another, Foote had never dramatized another writer's stories

before. He was very wary of it, but because he so greatly admired Faulkner, he reread the story several times.

The old man of the title is the Mississippi River, and most of Faulkner's story takes place on it during a flood. Prison inmates have been enlisted to help rescue people stranded by the flood-waters, and the story focuses on two such convicts who are sent out in a boat to find people on farms along the river. One prisoner falls overboard, and the other, now alone, finds a pregnant woman sitting in a tree. He takes her aboard the boat and sets out to get her to safety before her baby is born.

Foote loved the story and was taken with the characters. The situation was not alien to him. Although he grew up in South Texas rather than Mississippi, the river in Wharton flooded almost like clockwork every two years, and he was familiar with the hardships a flood imposed.

Coe had told him that John Frankenheimer, one of the leading television directors of the day and who would soon become one of Hollywood's top filmmakers with movies like *Birdman of Alcatraz*, *Seven Days in May*, and *The Manchurian Candidate*, had been signed to direct the show. Coe said Frankenheimer wanted to do the show live, acted in sequence, the way television dramas had always been done. Foote could not envision how they could re-create a Mississippi River flood live on a TV soundstage. The house in which Foote and Lillian lived in Nyack was along the banks of the Hudson, and he spent several days walking along the river, trying to imagine it in flood.

Foote finally decided it was a technical problem, and one that he didn't have to worry about. It would be for Coe and Frankenheimer to work out. He called Coe and said he would take on the project.

Faulkner's novella is a sprawling work that moves up and down the Mississippi, stopping at various points as the convict tries to get the pregnant woman to safety; he loses his way in the churning floodwaters, spends some time in a Cajun's deserted shack, then heads back into the roiling river.

Foote was fascinated by the characters—the prisoner, who, despite all his chances to escape in the flood, wanted only to get the woman to safety and return to serve out his sentence; and the woman, who did not judge the convict and who accepted all of life's hardships with humor and joy. Faulkner's story concentrated on the convict, but Foote wanted to flesh out the character of the woman; he made her a constant talker and created a detailed back history for her.

Foote also knew that most of the action would take place with the two main characters surrounded by water. He knew that the scenes on the river would be limited to what could be staged in a large tank in the studio, but he wrote the teleplay as though they would have the entire Mississippi at their disposal. As Faulkner's story moves up and down the river, the scenery is constantly changing. Foote also knew they would have only six or seven sets to work with on the CBS soundstage, an abundance compared with the early days of television in New York, but still restraining.

Foote wrote the first draft at home in Nyack and sent it to Coe in Los Angeles. Coe called as soon as he read it, saying they were all very pleased and excited and that Foote should come to California in two weeks for the start of rehearsals. There were a few suggestions for some minor changes to discuss and they wanted Foote on the set. It began a period of nearly seven years Foote spent as a bicoastal writer.

Foote took rooms at the Montecito, a residence hotel on Franklin Avenue in Hollywood. Several actors, writers, and directors from New York stayed there, as it was located not far from the studios. One of his neighbors in the Montecito on that first visit was Martin Balsam, and Foote wrote to Lillian that they took turns cooking dinner for each other.

It was the first time Foote had been away from Lillian for an extended time since they had married, and he wrote home nearly every day. Several changes had been taking place in Foote's life since he and Lillian moved to Nyack. For one thing, he had to learn to drive a car. Growing up in Wharton, his family had not owned a car, and his father never learned to drive one. His mother sometimes drove one of his grandparents' cars, but without a car in the family, Foote himself had never learned.

More important, however, Foote had received letters from his mother telling him that she and Baboo had been attending services at a Christian Science church. The Methodist church in Wharton had moved two miles away to a shopping center, and Foote's mother and grandmother started going to a church that met in a tent on a vacant lot across the street.

Foote had been raised as a Methodist and Lillian as a Catholic, and they had not attended church regularly since their marriage. As a result of his mother's letters, however, Foote and Lillian went to a Christian Science service, and Foote had sought more information about the movement. He received in the mail a booklet titled "By-Laws of First Church of Christ, Scientist" in Nyack. Foote and Lillian became converts and faithful members, taking the children regularly to Sunday School. Although neither ever made an issue of their faith, and the religion never figured in any of Foote's writing, Lillian eventually became a Second Reader in the church. In one of his first letters home from California, Foote mentioned that he had attended a service there and visited a Reading Room.

In addition, some renovations had begun on the house in Nyack, and their letters were a mixture of family news, progress reports on the work on the house, gossip from the studios, and updates on how the rehearsals were going. They discussed kitchen cabinets and the color of the paint for an upstairs bedroom. Barbara Hallie had been inducted into the Brownies, and Foote regretted not being home for the ceremony. Lillian sent him pictures of the children, which he put on his desk at the Montecito, and he wrote back asking Barbara Hallie to take a snapshot of her mother so he would have a photo of Lillian.

Foote especially missed New England in the fall, and as Halloween approached he longed to be home to go trick-or-treating with the children. In one letter addressed to Barbara Hallie, Horton Jr., and Walter, he included three crisp dollar bills and wrote: "I wanted to buy you something here for Halloween, but I was afraid it would not get to you in time, so I am enclosing a dollar for each of you and I want you to get what you like for yourselves."

During the evenings and in his spare time on the set, Foote was reading *Madame Bovary*. After finishing it, he wrote Lillian, "The last twenty-five pages are the most profoundly stirring thing I've ever read."

Foote received what he called "a royal welcome" at the CBS studio in Hollywood. He was invited to the Frankenheimers' house for dinner and the director told him *Old Man* was the finest script he had ever worked with. Geraldine Page had been cast as the woman and Sterling Hayden as the convict who saves her and delivers her baby.

Foote was impressed with the performances, especially that of Page, and he wrote Lillian: "I can't wait to tell you about her. She is not at all like she seems. She is more aggressive than Valerie, Kim and Uta all in one. But she is very nice, and I like her."

Frankenheimer was still insisting he wanted to do the play live, with the actors moving from scene to scene in sequence. He had two enormous water tanks built, which he planned to use for the river scenes, but as the rehearsals moved from an empty soundstage to the sets, trouble began immediately.

Once they were filled with water, the tanks were so heavy that the foundation in the CBS studio cracked. Another day, as the technical crew was trying to follow the actors from one set to the water, a crew member fell into one of the tanks and nearly drowned. Frankenheimer finally accepted that he would have to use videotape and shoot the scenes out of sequence. He could not risk the possibility of someone drowning on live television. *Old Man* became the first TV drama to be so taped and, because of its instant success, did much to end the era of live television.

During the middle of Foote's stay in Hollywood, Lillian called him with the news that she was again pregnant. They had talked only a few times on the telephone, trying to save money for the remodeling of the house. But they called each other occasionally, and once Foote apologized for the extravagance, explaining in one letter, "I had an acute attack of loneliness." But Lillian did not want to write with the news about the baby. Foote hung up the phone and immediately wrote back: "I think it is wonderful about you know what. Every time an event like this has come to us we have been greatly blessed."

Foote was a doting father who always took a lively interest in whatever activity the children became involved in. Whether it was swimming or riding or basketball or soccer, he loved taking them to lessons or games, and when he was out of town he wrote to them often, asking for progress reports. His greatest agony over working in California was that it separated him from his family—both Lillian and the kids—and he missed having the children running in and out of the house, sitting down to a dinner table with them all around, or watching television with Lillian and him in the evenings.

As the taping on *Old Man* drew to a close, Foote splurged and took Geraldine Page and the Frankenheimers to dinner at the Brown Derby, partly to repay the latter for all the dinners they had given him at their house during his stay. When the show finally aired, it was an overnight sensation. CBS and Foote received sacks of mail and congratulatory telegrams. One was from Paul and Joanne Newman, addressed simply to "Horton c/o Playhouse 90" and which read simply: "You have did a classic." Foote was ebullient.

Everyone seemed happy with *Old Man*, and Foote was flying home on the weekend. In a final letter before leaving, he wrote his wife: "I have a million things to tell you, a million kisses to give you. I thank you for your love. It's my greatest treasure."

One of the million things Foote had to tell Lillian was that he would be going back to California in two months' time. His star was rising in Hollywood. Foote had been bombarded with offers not only from television but from movie studios. He also found he had enjoyed the adaptation process, and he was open for other offers, but only if the original material interested him. Toward the end of his stay, Warner Brothers asked him to write a screenplay based on Erskine Caldwell's novella *Claudelle Inglish*. It offered a lot of money, and it was that project that took him back to California in January 1959.

Foote had had one previous experience with a Hollywood movie studio a few years earlier, working on a screenplay called *Storm Fear*, which was based on a novel by Clinton Steely and was directed by its star, Cornel Wilde. On that project, Foote had been involved with the development of the movie on a daily basis, working with the director (and star) and producer as the shooting took place.

This time he was on his own, writing every day at the studio, but having little contact with any of the other people involved in the movie. When he first arrived on the lot, he didn't even know who was going to produce, direct, or act in the movie.

Foote once again stayed at the Montecito. This time Eileen Heckart was one of his neighbors at the apartment hotel. Heckart, a Broadway actress who had won an Academy Award nomination for *The Bad Seed* a couple of years earlier and would win an Oscar a few years later for *Butterflies Are Free*, was also pining for her family and she and Foote often had dinner together in the evenings. "She talks nonstop, but is very funny," Foote wrote Lillian, but that he liked her a lot.

His days consisted of going to the studio each morning, punching a time clock, then sitting in an office in a two-story building on the Warner Brothers lot and writing. Most of the offices in the building were empty. The studio provided him with a secretary, who greeted him on his first day, "Welcome to the graveyard." The secretary was fond of telling him stories about the old days, when all of the offices were filled with writers—Christopher Isherwood, Faulkner, and others—and the corridor would be filled with the sound of type-writers clacking away. The only other occupant in the entire build-ing when Foote arrived was Marion Hargrove, who was a writer on the *Maverick* TV series.

Foote would write pages, send them off by messenger to the studio head, and then wait for word back on whether they were accepted. He tried to find out who was the producer, director, or even the actors on the project, but his secretary, who was normally a font of information about studio politics, told him it still had not been decided.

Several people whom Foote had met during the making of *Old Man* called, and he went to dinner with them. John Frankenheimer, who was about to make a trip to New York, promised to telephone Lillian when he got there. Lillian wrote Foote about a week later saying the Frankenheimers were coming up to Nyack for din-ner, and Foote immediately wrote back saying John liked to drink Scotch, so she should buy a bottle to have for him.

One old friend who got in touch with Foote during his second stay in Hollywood was Joe Anthony. Anthony was in California working on a movie and was also separated from Perry and his family. He and Foote began to spend a lot of time together.

With little to do during the days while waiting on word about his script, Foote took excursions around Los Angeles with Anthony, who had a car. One day they drove over to Pasadena to see the Playhouse, but it was closed. No plays were being produced on its stages and the school itself was on its last legs. Gilmor Brown was ill, and when he died the following year, the theater and school went into bankruptcy. It remained dark for most of the next twenty-six years, until reopening in 1986. Foote and Anthony also drove by the rooming house where Foote had lived while studying there, but it had been torn down. Another day they went to the Huntington Library art galleries and gardens and spent the entire day there. On another excursion, they drove up to San Juan Capistrano, and Foote sent Lillian a postcard from the old mission.

As the assignment stretched into a second month, Foote was beginning to feel very lonely. He asked Lillian to try to write him every day, "even if only a few lines," because it so lifted his spirits just to receive a letter from home. "I feel quite like I did that time after the summer we first met and you went back to school," he said.

Toward the end of February, Lillian wrote that a revival of *The Trip to Bountiful* had been staged in an Off-Broadway theater and she had gone into the city to see it. She said she had mixed feelings about the new production and was having a problem letting go of the play. Foote wrote back:

> *We can and I think should think of it with confidence, if we want to. The difference in how I thought about it five years ago and now is this: then I worked for good notices, success etc.—all coming from the critics or a material source—now I know and feel with confidence the play is being blessed, and can only bless anyone who comes to hear it, and anyone who comes to hear it can only bless it. I have now such a deep confidence in these works and their final recognition.*

But recognition was not coming from Warner Brothers. The studio kept wanting revisions to the script, which extended Foote's stay by weeks. He was missing the family more and more and asked Lillian to have Barbara Hallie and Horton Jr., whom they now called "Brother" after Foote's uncle, write him letters. He even wanted to have their school homework papers forwarded to him so he could see how they were doing. He missed the children terribly and wrote separate letters to them. In one, he told them about a trip he and Joe Anthony had made to Knotts Berry Farm, and in another he described a visit he made to Marine Land on the Pacific Ocean, where he saw a porpoise, an octopus, and four whales. Lillian sent him a snapshot that she had taken of all three children together.

In late March, he was still working on rewrites. Joe Anthony came over for dinner one night at the Montecito, and after he left, Foote wrote Lillian about how at one point in the evening Anthony looked at all the pictures Foote had of her and the children around the apartment and said: "I have to confess something. I don't miss Perry or the children. I never think about them but once in a great while, and when I do I have a slight moment of thinking wouldn't it be nice to see them, but then it's over, and I get interested in what I'm doing and I never think about them again." Foote added, "Isn't that sad."

Finally the studio accepted a draft of the screenplay, and Foote flew home. Over the next few weeks, he heard that the studio had finally assigned the film to a producer, who brought in another writer, and then another producer, and yet another writer. A couple of months later, Foote heard that a third producer had been assigned to the picture. This producer sent Foote the screenplay as it then stood and wanted to put him back on salary to polish it. When the script arrived, Foote found it had none of his original work in it. He phoned back to thank the producer for thinking of him, but declined the offer. He turned to Lillian and said, "Well, that will be the end of my Hollywood career."

Daisy Brooks Foote was born on July 3, 1959. Foote was working on a new play that he hoped would be staged on Broadway, and he told Lillian that if it was a hit, perhaps he would never have to leave her and the children again. But if Foote believed he was finished with Hollywood, Hollywood was not finished with him. Once again, it was a story by Faulkner that lured him back to Los Angeles.

In the fall, Foote had a call from a producer at CBS named Herbert Brodkin. Brodkin was also a Faulkner admirer and he asked Foote if he had read a short story called "Tomorrow," which Faulkner originally wrote for the *Saturday Evening Post* magazine. A novella-length work, it was later included in a collection of "six mystery stories" under the overall title of *Knight's Gambit.* The stories had all been written in the 1930s and '40s and were linked by a single protagonist—Gavin Stevens, the erudite lawyer who returns to Yoknapatawpha County from an education at Harvard and Heidelberg to open a practice and eventually become county attorney. Unlike most mysteries, however, Faulkner's tales were not so much whodunits as psychological puzzles that Stevens solves with the aid of his young nephew, Charles, who plays Watson to Gavin's Holmes.

The tale that intrigued Brodkin concerned a backwoods man named Jackson Fentry. Fentry had once worked on a cotton farm, but at the time of the story he is employed by a sawmill and living in a shack in the woods. One day a pregnant woman shows up at his door, in flight from her abusive husband and his family, and he lets her stay. As he looks after the woman during the last weeks of her confinement, Fentry falls in love with her and asks her to marry him. "I can't marry you," she explains. "I already got a husband."

When she is about to give birth, Fentry goes to fetch a midwife, and during the delivery, it becomes clear to both mother and midwife that she may not survive. As she realizes she is about to die, the woman consents to marry Fentry, and he promises her that he will raise her son as his own, which he dutifully does for a few years, until the woman's husband and his brothers come and take the boy away. Years later, the boy, now grown and known around town as Buck, is killed in a fight, and Fentry ends up on the jury in the trial of the man accused of killing him. The sweet little boy whom Fentry had raised had grown into a bully of a young man with his biological father's family, and the defendant has a clear case for self-defense. But Fentry refuses to acquit his killer, and the trial ends in a hung jury.

At the time Brodkin called, Foote was unfamiliar with the story, but he read it and immediately agreed to adapt it for *Playhouse 90*. Faulkner's story, which is short—only twenty pages in a pocket-size paperback—concentrated on Stevens, who was defending Buck's killer, trying to figure out why that one juror, Fentry, refused to vote to acquit his client. Foote, however, was intrigued by the relationship between Fentry and the runaway woman he took in. The situation was not unlike that of the convict and the pregnant woman he rescues in *Old Man*, though *Tomorrow* has the added complication of Fentry falling in love with the woman and developing a bond with her son.

In the original story, Faulkner gives only a couple of paragraphs to the woman—he doesn't even give her a name. In the teleplay, Foote worked to expand on the relationship between Fentry and the woman. For Foote, the drama was in the quiet love that wells in the heart of a lonely, shy backwoods man for a woman he takes in, and then is transferred to the son she delivers just before dying. The woman, of course, is a central character in that drama. Foote named her Sarah and gave her a back history. He said later, "She became somebody I knew."

Foote wrote a draft in Nyack, then returned to Hollywood in February 1960 for final revisions and the taping. The original teleplay starred Richard Boone as Fentry and Kim Stanley as Sarah and was shown on March 7, 1960. When it aired, critics hailed *Tomorrow* as one of the best dramas ever produced for television, and the program was repeated a year later. Faulkner, who rarely talked about any of his work or voiced an opinion on the stage or film adaptations made of his novels and stories, said that he greatly admired Foote's version of *Tomorrow*, and he wrote Lucy Kroll with his permission for Foote to publish the teleplay and to share the copyright with him.

While Foote was in California working on *Tomorrow*, he and Lillian were in the process of buying a new house in Nyack. The closing took place while he was away, and when he returned, it was to the new address. More renovations were under way, but Foote stayed in Nyack only a month before he was back in California. With the success of *Tomorrow*, television producers were besieging him with offers.

In April, he flew to Los Angeles to begin work on another project for Fred Coe and *Playhouse 90,* a drama about the last fifteen years of Mark Twain's life, during which the author experienced the death of his wife and two daughters. The teleplay, which was adapted from Twain's letters from the time, was called *The Shape of the River* and starred Franchot Tone as Twain. This time Foote stayed at the Del Capri apartments on Wilshire Boulevard, and he wrote home every day, again appealing to Lillian for letters with news, "no matter how trivial," of the family and the work on the house.

After *The Shape of the River,* Foote turned down several offers for adaptations. He hated being away from Lillian and the children, and he wanted to work on a play he had in mind. But a call from David Suskind in the late summer, asking him if he would write an original teleplay for the *DuPont Show of the Month* on CBS, intrigued him. This, at least, afforded him the opportunity to stay in Nyack for a time and return to writing his own stories.

It was a story he had heard several times in his childhood that provided the inspiration—and it was the first germ of what would later become the nine-play *Orphans' Home Cycle.* The story was from his father's youth, when his father had lived briefly with his mother before she moved to Houston and remarried, leaving her son to live with her parents.

Foote's paternal grandmother and her sister had opened a boardinghouse for a time in an effort to make a living. Foote's father was just a young boy, and he was given some baby chicks to raise. His father doted on the chickens and would feed them from his hand every day after school. One day his father came home from school and found all his chickens had been killed. As times were hard, the mother and her sister had killed them for their boarders' supper.

The story was a true one, and Foote used it to build a delicate domestic drama. Daniel Petrie had been signed to direct the show, and when Foote finished writing it he asked Petrie to come up to Nyack to read it. He did, and the director was very excited about the script. They both assumed Suskind would share their enthusiasm. They couldn't have been more wrong. In fact, Suskind hated it.

Fortunately, there was another producer on his staff named Audrey Gellen who read the script and was excited by its possibilities. Suskind gave her a green light, and the project moved forward. Petrie put together an all-star cast that included Julie Harris, E. G. Marshall, Mildred Dunnock, Jo Van Fleet, and Fritz Weaver.

The only other problem with the production came in a dispute over the title. Foote originally called it "A Golden String," after a line in a Blake poem that reads: "I give you the end of a golden string / Only wind it into a ball, / It will lead you in at Heaven's gate, / Built in Jerusalem's wall."

By this time, advertisers were beginning to have a large say in the content of the shows they were sponsoring. The advertising agency that handled DuPont agreed with Suskind that the show was too depressing for television and insisted that it at least have a different title. Foote came up with "Roots in a Parched Ground." It also was taken from a poem, this one by William Carlos Williams. Both Petrie and Gellen liked it, but the advertising agency objected again. They finally settled on *The Night of the Storm*, a reference to the boy running away from home on a stormy night. Years later, when Foote rewrote the teleplay for the stage, he returned to the title of *Roots in a Parched Ground*.

Even after the taping was finished, the sponsors were nervous about the teleplay and wanted to cancel it. Suskind, despite whatever reservations he had about the script, fought to get it aired, and it was finally shown on March 21, 1961, to great audience and critical praise.

When Harcourt Brace published the play some time later, the critic Stark Young, an admirer of Foote's television plays, wrote in a preface that when he saw the show he was so touched by "the purity of tone, the precision of writing . . . that its tragedies are scarcely horrors in themselves at all. The little boy, Horace, is the gentlest and sweetest child I have ever encountered in a story."

Young urged Foote to write the story as a stage play, and Foote said he would think about it. However, it would be a dozen years before he came back to *Night of the Storm*.

Foote's telephone kept ringing and his mailbox was crammed

with offers to undertake adaptations or join various projects. Anthony Quinn wrote Foote from Spain, wanting him to write a vehicle, anything, for the actor to star in. Suskind, who, whatever he thought about *Night of the Storm*, was not one to ignore rave reviews, approached him about adapting James Agee's *A Death in the Family* for television. Nina Vance wrote Lucy Kroll saying she would like to premiere one of his plays at her Alley Theatre in Houston. Jean Stapleton, who had appeared in *People in the Show* in Washington years earlier, wrote him a note saying she had heard he was working on a movie and added: "Please think of me if there is anything I can do in it—even when you get to the point of thinking about understudies. It would be a joy, as it always has been in the past, to be associated with anything you do."

One proposal that interested him was to adapt Tennessee Williams's one-act play *This Property Is Condemned*. Williams wrote that he was excited about the prospect of Foote writing the screenplay, but in the end Foote did not take the assignment. A movie was eventually made, with Sydney Pollack directing Natalie Wood and Robert Redford, but a committee of writers made a hash of the script.

Foote did not take up any of the offers, and through the summer of 1961 he remained in Nyack, working on a play and enjoying being home. The children were growing, and he relished the trivia of daily life around them. They were all taking swimming lessons, and he and Lillian took turns driving them to the pool every day. The household now included a dog named Tony, two cats, a turtle, and a goldfish. It was the kind of life he grew up with and he loved it.

Toward the end of August he received a call from Alan Pakula, a producer he had met during his trips to Hollywood. Pakula had just taken an option on a new novel, and he wanted to send it to Foote to read with an eye to adapting it for a movie. Foote said he would look at it, although he had not heard of the author or the book, and he was not inclined to undertake yet another adaptation or spend more time in Los Angeles away from his family. A copy of the novel arrived a couple of days later in the mail, and Foote put it on a downstairs table and forgot about it.

Foote had taken over a room on the top floor of their new house as his writing room. One of the unwritten rules of the house was that when he was in there with the door closed, he was not to be disturbed, either by Lillian, the children, the dog, or the cats. He liked to write in the mornings, and he liked to write in his pajamas. He was working there one morning when Lillian rapped once on the door and came in. His wife had a determined look on her face that he recognized. She had picked up the novel Pakula had sent and had just finished it.

"Horton," she said. "I think you'd better read this book."

Foote had long trusted his wife's judgment in literary merit, and he could tell that she thought this was something special. "Okay," he said, and went downstairs to read the novel. He read it in one sitting, then called Pakula and said he wanted to do the screenplay.

The author's name was Harper Lee. It was her first novel, and it was titled *To Kill a Mockingbird*.

CHAPTER 8

Oscar and Disappointment

Fʀᴏᴍ ᴛʜᴇ sᴛᴀʀᴛ, there were problems getting *To Kill a Mockingbird* in front of the cameras. For one thing, none of the Universal studio brass were enthusiastic about the movie and believed that at best it would be a flop and at worst it could get the studio embroiled in a civil rights controversy, with pickets outside the gates and at theaters across the country. The evocative novel was told in the voice of a grown woman remembering her childhood in the Deep South during the Depression, focusing on the trial of a black man accused of raping a white woman.

Alan Pakula had already enlisted Robert Mulligan to direct the movie. Both men had been greatly moved by the novel and immediately thought of Gregory Peck for the role of Atticus Finch, the father of the girl, Jean Louise, aka Scout, and her brother, Jem. Finch is a widower and a lawyer, and it is he who undertakes the defense of Tom Robinson, the black man charged with rape. Rock Hudson, also a big Hollywood star at that time, had also read the book and told the studio that he wanted to play the part of Atticus. But Pakula and Mulligan were determined to try to get Peck for the role, and they sent him a copy of the book.

As soon as Peck read the book, he was committed to getting the movie made. Peck said the book, although set in rural Alabama, reminded him of his own childhood in La Jolla, California. Peck, who had trained as an actor at the Neighborhood Playhouse in New York under Sanford Meisner, recognized in Atticus Finch the role of a lifetime.

For Pakula and Mulligan there was no discussion about whom

139

they wanted to write the screenplay. Foote was their first, second, and third choice, and once he agreed to take the job, there was only one hurdle to cross.

When Foote called to accept the assignment, Pakula told him that while Lee did not want to write the screenplay herself, she did have approval over who would do the adaptation. Lee lived in New York, and the producer suggested that Foote invite her up to Nyack so they could size each other up over dinner.

From the moment they met, Foote and Lee were old friends. The author arrived with Pakula for dinner at the playwright's house one summer night, and by the end of the meal she was convinced that no one else should do the screenplay of her book.

"I don't want you to bother me until it's done," Lee told Foote as they were leaving.

In early September, Foote flew to California to conclude the deal and sign the contracts. By now, Foote was a seasoned traveler, and in his first letter home he boasted that he had been able to sleep on most of the flight to Los Angeles. He said he was sorry to have missed the kids' first day of school and was glad to hear that Horton Jr. and Hallie had set swimming records at the Field Club.

Foote returned to Nyack a week later and began work on the screenplay. He had planned to take the whole family to Texas to spend Christmas with his mother and father in Wharton, but he had to return to Los Angeles early in December and that trip forced a change in plans. Early in the month, he wrote his mother that he had to go to California "to continue my work on 'To Kill a Mockingbird' and cannot get to Texas before December 23rd or 24th, but know we will have a good visit when I do."

While he was in Los Angeles he had one letter from Lillian describing a snowstorm that had hit Nyack, and a snowman the children had built. She also reported that Barbara Hallie had begun taking horseback-riding lessons at the club, though she would have to interrupt them over the holidays.

Lillian and the children flew to Texas on December 16, and Foote joined them just before Christmas. In March, Foote returned to California. Mulligan, who had directed Foote's teleplays of *The*

Traveling Lady and *Tomorrow*, had become a close friend, and he had a deep respect not only for Foote's writing but for his instinct about actors. If Foote recommended an actor, Mulligan said, he knew he or she would be good.

Foote loathed theatricality in acting, and whether from his training by the Russians or by instinct, he could spot a natural talent from one interview. The director wanted Foote's advice in helping to complete the casting for the movie, especially for the roles of the locals who would be the supporting players.

Peck was the only name star signed for the movie, although Kim Stanley, who was now an above-the-title star in her own right, agreed as a favor to Foote to read the voice-over narration. It was a stroke of genius; Stanley's narration is one of the most moving parts of the film.

There had been a massive talent search to fill the children's roles, especially that of Scout, the young girl whose story is at the center of the novel. Mulligan was against using experienced child actors for Scout and her brother, Jem. He felt they would be too mannered; he wanted the spontaneity of children who had not been trained. He also was looking for Southern natives, since he did not want to have to deal with teaching young actors an accent.

There was an old-fashioned cattle call for children in Birmingham at a local theater, and the mother of a young girl named Mary Badham took her to it over the objections of the girl's father. Mary had never acted before, and at first she had mixed feelings about trying out for a part. There were hundreds of hopeful girls there, most of whom were trying their best to look like Shirley Temple. Mary, clearly something of a tomboy, like the girl she was auditioning to play, made the cut as one of the finalists and went to New York for a screen test.

Instead of having the children read or perform scenes for the screen test, Mulligan sat each child before a camera and simply interviewed them. He was looking for natural reactions and facial expressions. Mulligan said later he knew that Mary was his Scout almost from the first time he saw her. Phillip Alford was similarly chosen to play her brother, Jem. Only John Megna, who was cast as their friend Dill, had previous acting experience, and that had been on the stage.

Foote had recommended some actors whose work he knew for smaller roles—Graham Duncan as Mr. Cunningham and Frank Overton for Sheriff Tate—but they were still searching for someone to play Boo Radley, the small but crucial part of the recluse who lives down the street from the Finches. Although Boo does not actually appear on-screen until the final scenes, his unseen presence is a driving force in the story.

Foote and Lillian had earlier seen a production of the stage version of his teleplay *The Midnight Caller* at the Neighborhood Playhouse in New York. Sanford Meisner, who had directed the production, had sent Foote a note saying he should come into town and see the show if only for the performance of a young actor who appeared in it. The actor, a student at the Playhouse, was named Robert Duvall.

Foote and Lillian went with Kim Stanley, Mulligan, and his wife to see the production, and all five were stunned by Duvall's performance. They went backstage to congratulate him, and it was all they could talk about at dinner afterward. When Foote mentioned to Lillian in a phone call from California that they were at a loss in finding an actor to play Boo Radley, Lillian said, "What about that young man we saw in *Midnight Caller*?"

Foote nearly always heeded his wife's advice, and he suggested Duvall to Mulligan, who of course remembered the actor's performance as well. They immediately signed Duvall to his screen debut as Boo.

While he was in California to help Mulligan with the casting, Foote also became involved in a dispute over the set. For the Finch house, the designer had come up with a huge structure with pillars that looked like an antebellum mansion from *Gone With the Wind*. But Finch was a poor country lawyer and the town was struggling through the Depression. Work on the set had already begun when Foote saw the drawings for it. He raced to Pakula and Mulligan and told them the house that was being built was all wrong.

"I lived in a house like Atticus's," he told them. "Believe me, it doesn't have pillars."

They stopped construction immediately and Mulligan and Foote got in a car and went house hunting. They found an old bungalow in a run-down section of Pasadena that was being condemned to make way for a highway. Pakula persuaded Universal to pay to dismantle the entire house and move it to the studio back lot to use for exterior shots of the Finch home.

Foote stayed in California for a week, living this time at the Chateau Marmont on Sunset Boulevard. Even on so short a visit, he missed being at home and wrote letters to Lillian almost every day. Harper Lee was also in California at the time, staying at the Mulligans' house, and Foote got to know her better. "She is a very nice, gentle person," Foote wrote Lillian, and also reported he had "a nice time" at a dinner at the Peck house.

Foote had high hopes for the movie, though he knew from Pakula that the studio had been making difficulties, treating it like a low-budget film. For one thing, the studio made clear to Pakula that it would not pay for the screenwriter to be on the set for the duration of the filming, and neither Pakula nor Mulligan could convince the studio heads that Foote should be present.

In the end, Foote was just as happy not to have to stay in California. He wrote Lillian that he was "counting the days until I leave." When he returned to Nyack, Foote worked at finishing the screenplay. He would write a few pages, and Pakula, who was staying in New York, would come up on the train to read them over, offer a suggestion or two, then go back to the city. When Foote completed a workable draft, they sent the script to Mulligan and Peck in Los Angeles. When Peck finished reading it, he asked incredulously, "Is this a first draft?" To him, it seemed like a finished product.

By all accounts, the actual filming of *To Kill a Mockingbird* was one of those extremely rare instances where everyone on the set worked and got along well. Everyone involved in making the movie—from actors to cameramen to seamstresses to lighting technicians—spoke of it for years to come with nothing but fond memories coupled with the wish that all artistic endeavor should be so imbued with personal good will and higher purpose. Indeed, to hear cast and crew talk about it decades later, the back lot at Universal became a virtual lovefest during the shooting.

For starters, Peck forged a special bond with the children from day one, especially with Mary Badham. Mary's father had died unexpectedly, and Peck became almost a surrogate parent to her. During breaks in the shooting, she would often go over to him and climb into his lap. Peck, whose own personality bore a strong resemblance to the wise, mild-mannered character he was playing, sometimes read to her. Mary was a frequent guest at the Peck house on weekends, playing with Peck's children.

Peck had a more adult relationship with the slightly older Phillip Alford, who played Atticus's son, Jem. Peck taught Phillip to play chess during the filming, and man and boy would often play a match on the set between scenes.

About the only people who didn't share in the sense of excitement about the movie were the studio heads. After the filming began, they insisted on seeing the dailies and then pestered Pakula with grumbling notes almost every day. One, for example, complained that Peck "didn't look glamorous" in the scenes that had been filmed one particular day and suggested that the actor use more makeup.

The anxiety over the racial issues in *Mockingbird* spread beyond the studio. The Motion Picture Association of America, which was then Hollywood's main oversight body on moral and ethical content of movies, wrote two letters complaining that the screenplay they had been sent used the words "nigger" and "nigger lover" several times. They also objected to having Scout, a young girl, use the word "damn," and her brother, a young boy, use the word "hell." They strongly suggested all those words be cut and hinted that the MPAA's "final judgment" on the film would be withheld until the board saw the final version.

Everyone had been a bit nervous about the movie at the outset. Even Peck thought at the beginning that the name should be changed. Nobody, he thought, would go see a movie about killing birds. But when the novel won the Pulitzer Prize for Fiction and acquired a permanent place on the bestseller lists for more than a year, there was no further discussion about changing the title for the movie.

For the studio, the main problem with the movie—apart from the racial theme of the story—was that there was no action. It is nearly an hour into the movie before Atticus confronts a lynch mob and the trial of Tom Robinson actually begins. Up until that time, the most dramatic scene is one of Atticus visiting Robinson's wife and being spit upon by the racist father of the white woman Tom is accused of raping. Nothing happens, the studio screamed, pleading for the producer, director, and writer to come up with something to grab the audience's interest.

It's an old complaint. Stanislavski once made the same objection to Chekhov over *Three Sisters*. But like the Russian writer, Foote was a master storyteller, and like the novel he was adapting, he slowly drew his audience into the world of the children and the slow, lazy pace of life in a small Southern town during the Great Depression. It was a time and place Foote knew well. Maycomb, Alabama, where the novel is set, could easily be Wharton, Texas, or even Yoknapatawpha County, Mississippi, for that matter.

Foote was also familiar with Lee's characters. He knew and understood them as well as his own family and neighbors. Like Atticus, Foote's father had been held in high esteem by his hometown's black population. And like Atticus, he had grown up in a free-thinking Methodist family. Foote also knew firsthand the grim reality of redneck Southern justice—one of his older cousins had been the unwitting motivation for a lynching.

Foote certainly recognized the character of the mysterious reclusive neighbor. Every town and childhood has one—the seldom seen phantom about whom horrifying stories are told and who keeps the local children in such a state of perpetual fear that they run rather than walk past his house. In Foote's own case, it was the house of the man in Wharton who had been tarred and feathered.

The plot follows two story lines that don't come together until the final scenes and keeps the character of Boo Radley, the bogeyman who becomes the savior, in the imagination until the very end.

Foote took a rambling narrative that takes place over two years and faithfully condensed it into a cohesive drama that covers two consecutive summers. He had read a review of Lee's novel that compared it to Twain's *Huckleberry Finn,* and it convinced Foote that the main thrust of the movie should be exposure of hatred and hypocrisy in a small town through the eyes of the children.

As with his adaptations of Faulkner, Foote also added some original material of his own. For example, one of the most poignant scenes in the film—one that both Mary Badham and Mulligan said in later years was their favorite of the film—is pure Foote. The scene comes very early in the movie, and though brief, it quietly and simply establishes the entire relationship of the family and defines each of the characters. In it, Scout is being tucked into bed by Atticus. She is reading to her father, and when he takes out his pocket watch and tells her it is time to go to sleep, she closes the book and puts it on the nightstand.

SCOUT: What time is it?

ATTICUS: Eight-thirty.

SCOUT: May I see your watch? (*He gives it to her. She opens the case and reads the inscription.*) "To Atticus, my beloved husband." Atticus, Jem says this watch is going to belong to him some day.

ATTICUS: That's right.

SCOUT: Why?

ATTICUS: Well, it's customary for the boy to have his father's watch.

SCOUT: What are you going to give me?

ATTICUS: Well, I don't know that I have much else of value that belongs to me. But there's a pearl necklace . . . and there's a ring that belonged to your mother . . . and I've put them away . . . and they're to be yours.

(*Scout stretches her arms and smiles. Atticus kisses her cheek. He takes his watch and gets up. He covers her and puts out the lamp.*)

Good night, Scout.

The nighttime scene continues but the camera moves to Atticus outside the house, sitting in a swing on the front porch, where he overhears a conversation between Scout and Jem from inside the house.

SCOUT: Jem?
JEM: Yes?
SCOUT: How old was I when Mama died?
JEM: Two.
SCOUT: And how old were you?
JEM: Six.
SCOUT: Old as I am now?
JEM: Uh-huh.
SCOUT: Was Mama pretty?
JEM: Uh-huh.
SCOUT: Was Mama nice?
JEM: Uh-huh.
SCOUT: Did you love her?
JEM: Yes.
SCOUT: Did I love her?
JEM: Yes.
SCOUT: Do you miss her?
JEM: Uh-huh.

Even when the film was finished and Elmer Bernstein's haunting score was added, Universal was wary of the reception the movie would get. Studio executives wanted to market it as an "art film" and release it only in small theaters in large cities. However, Peck insisted the premiere be held at Radio City Music Hall in New York and exhibited in first-run commercial theaters.

The studio heads also wanted to make cuts in the final print of the movie once it was completed, and they would have taken out several scenes if they'd had their way. Once again, it was Peck who saved the movie. Peck, who had been a big star for so many years, was an old hand at studio politics and was very smart about how the system worked. Peck had insisted on a clause in his contract that gave the final cut to Pakula and Mulligan, so the studio couldn't touch the final version. Otherwise, the studio executives would have hacked the film up by cutting scenes they didn't like or thought slowed down the action, like the one between Scout and Jem talking about their mother. It was only after the film won several Oscar nominations that Universal studio executives got behind it and said they knew they had a hit all along.

Among the Academy Award nominations for *To Kill a Mockingbird* was one for Foote for Best Screenplay. He had been invited to go to Los Angeles for the ceremony, but since he had not been there for the filming, he decided to stay at home. He and everyone else expected *Lawrence of Arabia*, the big blockbuster film that year, to sweep the awards. It was a very competitive year, with other Best Screenplay nominations for the film adaptations of *The Miracle Worker* and *Sweet Bird of Youth* in contention.

Foote had little hope of actually winning the Oscar and was very gratified just to be among the nominees. He had thought Robert Bolt and Michael Wilson would win the writer's award for *Lawrence*. He watched the awards at home, dressed in his pajamas, with all the family gathered around the television set.

Peck won the Best Actor award over Paul Newman (*Sweet Bird of Youth*) and Peter O'Toole (*Lawrence of Arabia*); and when the time came for Best Screenplay, Bette Davis was the presenter for the award. Davis had long admired Foote's work and had once written him asking that he keep her in mind if he had a play she was right for. When she tore open the envelope and read the name Horton Foote . . . "for *To Kill a Mockingbird*" she almost shouted it out and held the Oscar over her head in triumph.

Foote, sitting at home, was stunned. Within two minutes, his front doorbell rang. His neighbors in Nyack descended on the house, and an impromptu party sprang up. Foote had to race upstairs and change out of his pajamas into street clothes. The phone kept ringing all night, and the celebration went on until the early hours.

Foote later recalled, "I thought I had been elected president of the United States. People I hadn't heard from in years called me."

If Western Union in Nyack hadn't known who Horton Foote was, or that he lived on Ferris Lane, they soon found out. By noon the following day, more than fifty telegrams arrived at Foote's home congratulating him on the award.

Two days later, he received two special delivery letters in the mail. One was from John Frankenheimer, saying, "For once the Academy gave an award to someone who really deserved it." The second was from Tad Mosel, a fellow writer who had also made his name in the Golden Age of Television, recounting a recent Hollywood party at which a man had come up to him and congratulated him on writing the screenplay and getting an Oscar nomination for *Mockingbird*. Mosel went on:

> *Had it been any other picture or any other writer he had in mind, I would probably have asserted myself. Do you mind if I accepted his compliment graciously? My conscience has been telling me to pass it on, with my own congratulations, and tonight (for it is just after the Awards), I can put it off no longer. What a beautiful picture and what a well-deserved award. I hope that man still thinks it was me.*

There were those, however, who tried to diminish Foote's achievement with the screenplay, suggesting that all he had done was take Harper Lee's novel and turn it into dialogue. Lee, who never gave interviews and rarely talked about her work, took the unusual step of writing a rebuttal in an essay for the magazine the *Mass Media*.

> Horton Foote's screenplay is a work of such quiet and unobtrusive excellence that many people have commented that the film's dialogue was lifted chapter and verse from the novel. This is simply not so. Scenes humorous, scenes tender, scenes terrifying, each with a definite purpose and value, blended so delicately with the original, created an illusion that these were Harper Lee's words. If the integrity of a film adaptation is measured by the degree to which the novelist's intent is preserved, Mr. Foote's screenplay should be studied as a classic.

The ultimate success of *Mockingbird* led to another movie collaboration with Pakula and Mulligan, only this time Foote was adapting one of his own works. The project was a film version of *The Traveling Lady*, the play that had been Foote's last on Broadway, nearly a decade earlier. Since its lukewarm reception on the Great White Way, Foote had reworked the story as a television drama. Mulligan also had directed the TV version, which was broadcast on *Studio One*. Kim Stanley again had starred as Georgette, the lady of the title, just as she had done on Broadway.

Pakula and Mulligan persuaded Foote to do some rewrites for the movie version. They wanted him to open up the action a bit more and tailor the parts for the two stars they signed for the lead roles—Steve McQueen as the singing convict, Henry Thomas, and Lee Remick as Georgette, the wife he deceives.

In turning the play into a movie, Foote also made several changes, slight but significant, in the story line and introduced a couple of new characters. He altered the names of some of the characters, and the story even got a new title that switched its focus from the traveling lady to her roving husband.

The title of the movie ended up as *Baby, the Rain Must Fall*, taken from a song Henry sings, but until its release, Pakula, Mulligan, Foote, and the studio heads back in Los Angeles pondered over different ones. At one point, Pakula wrote Robert Ferguson at Columbia Pictures, "We are still sweating out the title situation," and promised to let him know if there were "any further inspirations."

As he had done in *To Kill a Mockingbird*, Foote injected more social content in the screen adaptation than had been in the original stage version. If racial intolerance was a major theme of *Mockingbird*, the target in *Baby, the Rain Must Fall* was the pettiness and hatreds that can poison a small town and its inhabitants. Henry emerges as a more sympathetic character than he had been in the stage and television versions, and Foote uses his character's dreams of becoming a singer as a metaphor for the perils of greed. At one point Henry tells his young daughter he will one day become a rock star "like Elvis" and live in Hollywood and drive a white Cadillac.

Part of his inspiration for using pop music came from his brother

Horton Foote at age one, about the time his parents moved into the house built for them by his grandfather, and the one he would call home for the next ninety years.

DeGolyer Library, Southern Methodist University, Dallas, Texas, A1992.1810.

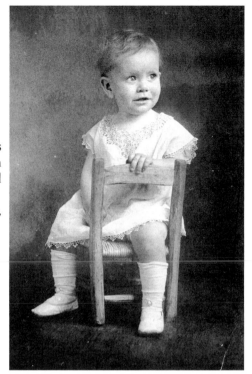

As was customary in Texas in the early twentieth century, little boys had their picture taken in cowboy outfits, as Foote is shown in this one, circa 1920.

DeGolyer Library, Southern Methodist University, Dallas, Texas, A1992.1810.

The Brookses, Foote's maternal grandparents, were among Wharton's wealthiest and most respected families, despite having three profligate sons. This photo was taken circa 1920. Seated, from left: Tom Brooks, Foote's grandfather, holding Foote's younger brother, also named Tom Brooks; Daisy Brooks, Foote's grandmother, whom he called Baboo; his uncle, Brother Brooks; another uncle, Speed Brooks; and his aunt Laurel, in chair with Foote. Standing from left: Foote's uncle Billy, his aunt Rosa; and his mother and father, Hallie and Horton Foote Sr.

DeGolyer Library, Southern Methodist University, Dallas, Texas, A1992.1810.

Foote had tried to break into acting in New York; he had matinee idol good looks and felt his left profile was his best side.

DeGolyer Library, Southern Methodist University, Dallas, Texas, A1992.1810.

Tom Brooks Foote followed his brother to New York and wanted to become an actor. An offer from a Hollywood movie studio was interrupted by his being drafted in 1942 to serve in the army in World War II. He was killed in action.

DeGolyer Library, Southern Methodist University, Dallas, Texas, A1992.1810.

Foote brought his young bride, Lillian, home to Wharton to meet his parents soon after they were married in 1945.

Barbara Hallie Foote and the Estate of Horton Foote.

Lillian came to love the small Texas town as much as her husband did.

DeGolyer Library, Southern Methodist University, Dallas, Texas, A1992.1810.

Foote and Lillian loved to dance, and they were the only couple on the floor at a party in the late 1940s.
Barbara Hallie Foote and the Estate of Horton Foote.

Foote and Lillian in the 1940s.
DeGolyer Library, Southern Methodist University, Dallas, Texas, A1992.1810.

Foote and Lillian on a romantic trip to the beach in the early 1950s.
DeGolyer Library, Southern Methodist University, Dallas, Texas, A1992.1810.

As their family grew, Foote and Lillian moved to the suburbs of Nyack, New York, in 1956. Foote is holding Horton Jr. while Barbara Hallie stands behind baby Walter and Lillian.
Barbara Hallie Foote and the Estate of Horton Foote.

Foote with Barbara Hallie on their way to Sunday School in Nyack in 1959, shortly after moving into a new house and three months before the birth of Daisy.
Barbara Hallie Foote and the Estate of Horton Foote.

Barbara Hallie held her infant sister Daisy in 1959. They became best friends and have remained so.
Barbara Hallie Foote and the Estate of Horton Foote.

With the new arrival of Daisy in 1959, the Foote children posed for a family snapshot in Nyack. Clockwise from top left: Barbara Hallie, Horton Jr., Walter, and Daisy.
Barbara Hallie Foote and the Estate of Horton Foote.

Foote and the author Harper Lee appeared together before the 1962 opening of Foote's film adaptation of her novel, *To Kill a Mockingbird*, for which he won his first Oscar.

Barbara Hallie Foote and the Estate of Horton Foote.

Foote posed in front of posters for several of his Broadway and other theatrical productions of his plays for a newspaper feature in 1962.

DeGolyer Library, Southern Methodist University, Dallas, Texas, A1992.1810.

With the first act of his career at its zenith, Foote was the subject of a photo essay in the old *Journal-News* newspaper in 1962 that included a picture of him at his writing desk in Nyack.

DeGolyer Library, Southern Methodist University, Dallas, Texas, A1992.1810.

The 1962 *Journal-News* newspaper photo essay included a posed picture of Foote's family looking at him adoringly as he stood by the mantle of their home in Nyack. From left: Barbara Hallie, Daisy, Lillian, Horton Jr., and Walter.

DeGolyer Library, Southern Methodist University, Dallas, Texas, A1992.1810.

Foote and Steve McQueen on the set of *Baby, the Rain Must Fall*, the 1965 film version of Foote's play *The Traveling Lady*, which was shot on location in Foote's hometown of Wharton, Texas.

Barbara Hallie Foote and the Estate of Horton Foote.

Foote with his children and assorted cats and dogs on the lawn of his house in New Hampshire. Standing, from left: Foote, Walter, and Daisy. Seated: Horton Jr. and Barbara Hallie.

DeGolyer Library, Southern Methodist University, Dallas, Texas, A1992.1810.

When Walter Foote joined the school basketball team, Foote and Lillian built a half-
court at their house in New Hampshire in
1970 so he could practice.

*DeGolyer Library, Southern Methodist University, Dallas,
Texas, A1992.1810.*

Horton Foote Jr. enlisted in the army in
1972 rather than take his chance on being
drafted and sent to Vietnam. He became an
MP and was posted to Germany.

*DeGolyer Library, Southern Methodist University, Dallas,
Texas, A1992.1810.*

Daisy Foote began taking riding lessons shortly after the family moved
to New Hampshire and by 1974 was competing in equestrian events.
Foote and Lillian built a barn on the property for her to house her
horse, Dude.

Barbara Hallie Foote and the Estate of Horton Foote.

As an actress, Hallie Foote became a chief interpreter of her father's work and was often directed by him.

DeGolyer Library, Southern Methodist University, Dallas, Texas, A1992.1810.

Foote no longer had to leave Lillian and the children to make a movie. The shootings of *1918* and *On Valentine's Day* in Waxahachie, Texas, in the mid-1980s became a sort of family reunion.

DeGolyer Library, Southern Methodist University, Dallas, Texas, A1992.1810.

Foote was happiest when, after the children were grown, Lillian could join him on the sets of movies. They became partners in their own production company to make independent films of his plays.

DeGolyer Library, Southern Methodist University, Dallas, Texas, A1992.1810.

On the set of the film version of *1918* in Waxa-hachie, Foote went over some script changes with Matthew Broderick, who played the part of Brother.

Photograph by Deana Newcomb. DeGolyer Library, Southern Methodist University, Dallas, Texas, A1992.1810.

Foote and Lillian clowned for the camera in their apartment on Horatio Street in New York City in the late 1980s.
DeGolyer Library, Southern Methodist University, Dallas, Texas, A1992.1810.

Foote with Lillian Gish and Fritz Weaver, 1985.
DeGolyer Library, Southern Methodist University, Dallas, Texas, A1992.1810.

During a break in the shooting of the film version of his play *Convicts* in Louisiana in 1990, Foote listened to blues music he wanted to use in the movie.

Photograph by Tad Hershorn. DeGolyer Library, Southern Methodist University, Dallas, Texas, A1992.1810.

Foote was one of the honorees at the American Academy in 2003, along with, from left, the poet J. D. McClatchy, and fellow playwrights Edward Albee and Arthur Miller.
© *Benjamin Dimmitt.*

Robert Duvall was not only a starring actor in many of Foote's plays and movies but also one of the playwright's best friends.

Barbara Hallie Foote and the Estate of Horton Foote.

Foote had a new play for the start of the new millennium. It was called *The Carpetbagger's Children*, and it played in Houston and Hartford before winding up at Lincoln Center in New York. Foote and the play's director, Michael Wilson, are standing with the cast (seated from left) of Jean Stapleton, Roberta Maxwell, and Hallie Foote.

Barbara Hallie Foote and the Estate of Horton Foote.

One of Foote's proudest awards was the National Medal of Arts, which he received from President Clinton in 2000. Daisy accompanied him to the ceremony at the White House.
Barbara Hallie Foote and the Estate of Horton Foote.

Foote and Estelle Parsons had reason to smile after the 2005 opening of *The Day Emily Married*, a play Foote had written more than twenty years earlier but didn't produce until the real-life people on whom it was based had died, earned rave reviews from New York critics.
Barbara Hallie Foote and the Estate of Horton Foote.

John Speed. Unlike Foote and Tom Brooks, the youngest of the Foote brothers had never been much interested in the theater. He had, however, a secret ambition to be a country singer. Although they occasionally exchanged letters, Foote had never been close to his youngest brother, mainly because of the difference in their ages. At the time Foote left home to pursue his acting career, John Speed was only eight years old, and as Foote had never returned home for an extended time, the brothers never got to know each other well.

John Speed had worked in the Wharton drugstore as a young man, and after serving in the marines during the war, he married and hoped to take over the same drugstore he had worked at as a young man. However, his wife, Betty, hated small-town life, and they soon moved to Houston, John Speed taking a job as a traveling salesman for a pharmaceutical company. During Foote's trips to Texas for *Baby, the Rain Must Fall*, he got to know his young brother better and discovered that he had long been a devotee of country music, and that his one secret dream had been to be a country and western singer.

Mulligan planned to shoot the movie in Wharton, which pleased Foote and created quite a stir in the town. The director also insisted that Foote be on the set for the duration of the filming. Foote went to Wharton in the spring of that year to help Mulligan scout for locations. In the end it was filmed entirely in Wharton except for the courthouse scenes, which were shot in nearby Columbia. Foote stayed with his parents at the start. Lillian, who had come to love Wharton almost as much as her husband, remained in Nyack with the children for the school year. Again, Foote wrote her nearly every day.

He was happy being back in Wharton, and in one letter he wrote that the back fence of the yard at his parents' house was covered with sweet peas and that the chinaberry trees were in flower, "the first time I've been here while they were in blossom since I was a child." Foote also visited the Wharton cemetery, since one key scene in the movie was to take place in a graveyard, and he drove out to look at the farms his grandmother had once owned.

As soon as school was out, Lillian and the children flew to Texas, and Foote rented a house for them all to stay in during the actual filming, which took most of the summer. By August, the summer heat in South Texas had grown unbearable, and Lillian returned to Nyack with Barbara Hallie, Walter, and Daisy. Horton Jr. stayed with his father for part of the month, then also returned to get ready for the start of school in September. In one letter after his wife's return, Foote reported that it had been 105 degrees in Wharton the previous day, that filming had been slowed, and that he was spending his free time working on a screenplay draft for *The Chase*, a project that the producer Sam Spiegel had dangled in front of him.

Spiegel had called Foote in Texas and told him he wanted to turn *The Chase* into a movie if Foote would write the screenplay. The producer promised him a top production team and an all-star cast. Foote told him he would think about it. From his early encounters with the big studios, Foote had been afraid of falling into the Hollywood trap that many writers from Faulkner to Williams had stumbled into—of becoming a "writer for hire," which was how most studios viewed their screenwriters. But his experience in working on *Mockingbird* and now *Rain* had led him to believe that maybe Hollywood wasn't such a bad place after all. Foote did not think long before he called Spiegel back and accepted.

Foote always had a soft spot for *The Chase*. He had nursed high hopes for it on Broadway, and he had turned it into a novel. But neither of those venues had found a large audience. Perhaps, Foote thought, the movie would remedy that.

The cast that Spiegel lined up was led by Marlon Brando and included Jane Fonda, Robert Redford, Angie Dickinson, Robert Duvall, E. G. Marshall, and Martha Hyer. Arthur Penn was signed to direct.

As soon as the filming of *Rain* was finished, Foote returned to Nyack and began to work in earnest on the screenplay for *The Chase*. Almost from the beginning, things began to go wrong.

At the urging of Spiegel, Foote introduced some new characters and added new scenes, opening up the action beyond the two settings of the play. The thrust of the story, however, remained the same as the play. But everyone, especially the studio executives, found things to complain about. Spiegel, Penn, and Foote all disagreed about elements of the screenplay, and the studio heads added their own suggestions.

Finally, Spiegel decided they needed to bring in another writer to work with Foote on the screenplay. The writer chosen was another Southern playwright who had had success on Broadway, but who also had a reputation for being opinionated and for not getting along with other writers. Lillian Hellman had been blacklisted in Hollywood during the 1950s for her politics, and she was most famously known for refusing to cooperate with the House Un-American Activities Committee and retorting to the Communist-baiting Senator Joe McCarthy, "I do not cut my politics to the fashion of the times."

As soon as Hellman was brought in to work with Foote on the screenplay, she quickly took over and began to make changes in the script without even telling Foote. She not only changed the names of the characters, she changed the characters themselves. In Hellman's version, the escaped convict Bubber ended up being a misunderstood misfit instead of the cold-blooded killer Foote had created. Rather than return to the town to kill Sheriff Hawes in an act of revenge, she had him trying to flee to Mexico and start a new life. Hellman even invented a torrid love affair between two of the minor characters.

It was as though Hellman believed she had been brought in not to collaborate with Foote, although that was the way it was first described to Foote, but to create her own adaptation of his play. In fact, Foote never even met Hellman the entire time *The Chase* was being made.

Hellman seemed to think it was now her movie, and the studio backed Hellman at every step. Spiegel sympathized with Foote, but told him that his hands were tied. The studio wanted to go with Hellman's version, not least because it felt Hollywood owed her a debt for the years she had been blacklisted.

Once, when Foote walked into Spiegel's office, the producer was on the telephone, obviously listening to a diatribe on the other end. Spiegel rolled his eyes and motioned Foote around to the side of his desk and handed him the phone. Foote could hear Hellman on the other end of the line ranting about a line in Foote's screenplay that referred to "chopping cotton." Foote put the phone to his ear, and Hellman was sputtering on the other end of the line. "Maybe in Texas they *chop* cotton, but in Louisiana we *pick* cotton," she shouted. The writer who wore her Southern credentials on her sleeve didn't know the difference. (Chopping cotton stalks and picking its bolls are separate processes in harvesting the plant.)

Nonetheless, Foote tried at the start to work with Hellman and Spiegel and Penn, if only to protect as much of his original voice as possible. And Spiegel tried to accommodate Foote. Early in the shooting, the producer asked Foote to visit the set to check it for authenticity. The scene being filmed that day was set in the drugstore, and Foote found it generally acceptable. As he was about to leave, however, he saw an extra sitting at one of the tables dressed as a Native American woman.

Foote rushed to Spiegel's office and said, "What is an Indian squaw doing in a drugstore in Harrison, Texas?" Spiegel called in the set designer, who explained he had seen a postcard of an early drugstore in Texas and there was an Indian woman in it. He added that Penn and Hellman both thought it added a nice touch. He even produced the postcard. One look at it and Foote pointed out that it was a postcard from West Texas, near the New Mexico border, where there is a large American Indian population, not the Gulf Coast, where there is none. While all this was going on, Penn had already shot the scene, and Spiegel said it would cost too much to reshoot it without the Indian woman in it. The film was released with a Comanche woman sitting at a table in a South Texas drugstore.

It wasn't long before Foote realized he would have no influence over the film. He left the movie and Hollywood and returned home dejected.

During his trials over *The Chase*, the finished film of *Baby, the Rain Must Fall* opened. If the Broadway critics didn't quite know what to think of the story of the ex-con who wants to return to his wife and child but can't change his wayward life, movie critics were equally at a loss. Some dismissed it outright, while others found similarities between Henry Thomas and Chance Wayne, the rebellious protagonist in Tennessee Williams's *Sweet Bird of Youth*. Although the film received mixed to lukewarm reviews, it had a core of admirers who felt it was insufficiently appreciated.

It also was a big success financially, grossing over $1.2 million, a lot for those days, and proving the drawing power of a big star like McQueen. It also proved the Hollywood adage that nothing succeeds like success, especially at the box office, and Foote had barely unpacked back in Nyack from his misadventure with *The Chase* when he got a call from one of Hollywood's biggest producers.

Otto Preminger had been working on getting a movie made of a K. G. Glidden novel about a ruthless Southerner who sets out to grab all his cousin's lands by any means available. The movie, which was being shot in England, was titled *Hurry, Sundown*, and had a cast that included Michael Caine, Jane Fonda, Faye Dunaway, Burgess Meredith, and George Kennedy.

Preminger was dissatisfied with the various scripts he had, and he knew the one writer who was still considered the master at Southern drama. His call was to ask Foote to come to London and write a new screenplay.

Foote at first rejected the offer. The bitterness over his experience with *The Chase* was very fresh, and he had been disappointed in the critical reception for *Baby, the Rain Must Fall*, although that was mitigated by the fact audiences seemed to like it. He used several excuses, not least that he had been away from his family for some months on the last two movies and he didn't want to leave them again for any extended period of time.

Preminger, however, was not a man easily dissuaded. He told Foote he would pay for his entire family to come to London with him. It would be like a summer vacation for the whole family. The only problem was that none of the children wanted to go. They were all looking forward to spending the summer swimming and being with their friends in Nyack. For Foote and Lillian, however, it was an exciting offer. In the end, it was one Foote couldn't resist. He packed Lillian and the children together and they spent three months in England while he worked on a new version of the screenplay.

After finishing it, Foote returned home and waited. It was some weeks before Preminger called. He was very apologetic and told Foote that he preferred his screenplay to all the others. It was, the director said, by far the best he had to work with. But he reluctantly had decided in the end to go with one of the earlier versions. He felt that Foote's version wasn't commercial enough—a complaint Foote often heard.

Despite the rejection, Preminger made an odd request. He asked Foote if he would still allow his name to appear in the credits as one of the writers. Foote's immediate reaction was to say no. However, since the director had been so nice about the whole thing, even taking the trouble to call in person, and had paid for his family to spend the summer in London, he reluctantly agreed.

In the final print, not a single word of Foote's was used, although he was listed in the credits.

After his experiences with *The Chase* and *Hurry, Sundown*, Foote renewed his vows that he would not work for the studios again. But Foote always had a great sense of loyalty, and it was mainly as a gesture of gratitude to Alan Pakula, Robert Mulligan, and Gregory Peck that he took an assignment the following winter to go to California to work on a screenplay for a movie titled *The Stalking Moon*, which was also an adaptation of a novel.

The story was about a white woman who had lived with the Apaches and is seeking to escape with her young half-breed son. The boy's Apache father comes after them, and the woman is aided by a U.S. Army scout. Pakula was producing the film, Mulligan was its director, and Peck starred as the army officer who becomes the hero. Eva Marie Saint, who had first worked with Foote in the stage version of *The Trip to Bountiful*, played the woman.

Foote spent several weeks in California, staying in the Beverly Hills Hotel in a room that cost twenty-six dollars a day. His letters were full of his usual homesickness, and he wrote Lillian that while he enjoyed working with Pakula, Mulligan, Peck, and Saint again, the plot of the movie was formulaic and did not interest him very much.

In May, Lillian was able to join Foote in California for what he thought would be the final days of shooting, and he moved to the Westwood Sovereign apartments on Wilshire Boulevard so they would have a kitchenette and some semblance of home life. She stayed for three weeks, then returned home when it became clear Foote would have to stay longer. The movie was not going particularly well, and Foote had to remain in California through most of June working on almost daily rewrites.

When the film was finally finished and he returned home, Foote felt defeated once again. He had been working on a new play during his free time from the movie, but no one was rushing forward to stage it. It was 1968 and tastes were changing. Theater producers wanted only offbeat plays. Hollywood studios decreed there had to be action and sex if a movie was going to make money at the box office, and screenplays had to be tailored to meet those demands. Original drama on TV was now a thing of the past, footnotes to be written in the history of television. There seemed to be no place left for the kind of story Foote wrote. The reviews of his life's work seemed to be in, and the result was that, in the words of Preminger, he was "not commercial enough" for stage, screen, or television. He privately wondered if his career as a writer was over.

CHAPTER 9

New Hampshire Exile

In the mid-1960s Foote and Lillian began thinking about buying a house in the countryside as a weekend retreat. They both loved to take excursions into New England, driving back roads and looking at antiques and Early American art and artifacts. They had looked at several houses on weekend trips, but never found one they thought was quite right. On one such visit they met a couple, Roger and Ruth Bacon, who ran an antique shop. The Bacons also loved the theater, and the two couples became friends. Foote and Lillian had just about given up their search when the Bacons phoned one day and said they had seen a house on the market they thought the Footes should look at. Foote and Lillian drove up to New Hampshire the following weekend and found their dream house.

It was located outside a small town called New Boston. It was a 1740 frame house with three floors, located at the end of a road on fifty acres of woods. The nearest neighbor was a mile away, and it was so secluded that in years to come visitors trying to find it invariably had to call, often twice, to ask directions. They bought it on the spot for nineteen thousand dollars and began furnishing it with a few small items they brought up from Nyack and some other pieces they bought in antique shops in the area.

They had spent only a few weekends there when Foote received Preminger's offer to go to England for the summer to work on *Hurry, Sundown*. When the family returned from England, they had a call from the Bacons informing them that in their absence there had been a small fire in the New Hampshire house. They drove up immediately and discovered that in addition to the fire, several of the items with which they had furnished the house had been stolen.

Fortunately, the thieves were inept as arsonists. The fire was contained to one room, the keeping room, as it is called in New England, and had not spread to the rest of the house. The perpetrators weren't much better as robbers, either. Only a few antiques were stolen, and not the most valuable ones.

The fire and robbery, however, prompted Foote and Lillian to contemplate a permanent move to New Hampshire. They had become disenchanted with Nyack. They found its upper-middle-class competitiveness, especially in the schools, and its country-club mind-set unappealing. In addition, the drug culture was making inroads in the town, and several of the children's classmates were falling to drugs. The setbacks in Foote's career were weighing heavily on him, and he felt increasingly estranged from a theater that was rejecting him. The isolation of the New Hampshire woods was a lure.

In the fall Foote and Lillian decided to put the Nyack house on the market and live full-time in New Hampshire. They were in the process of making the move when Foote left for California to work on *The Stalking Moon*. That the movie failed to fire his imagination was partly due to the fact that his heart was back in New Boston.

Foote's and Lillian's correspondence during his work on that movie were full of domestic concerns. Lillian wrote about the details of the remodeling of the new house and the repairs on the damage caused by the fire. They had not been able to sell the Nyack house immediately, and they were trying to rent it until they could find a buyer. Lillian worried over whether to ask $375 or $400 in rent, saying in one letter that they could use the extra $25 if they could get that much. Lillian also had been looking to buy a car, and there was an exchange over whether they should get a station wagon or a sedan. They ended up getting the station wagon.

Another concern was how the children, Barbara Hallie especially, would settle into their new schools. Their elder daughter had just started her junior year in high school, and she made no secret to her parents how much she opposed the move. At one point she went to her father and said, "I just want you to know that you've ruined my entire life."

Foote was nearly in tears and pleaded with her to understand that the move would end up being a good thing for all of them. Barbara Hallie retaliated by letting her schoolwork slide and immersing herself in the small-town New Hampshire culture into which she was thrust. She made new friends, and except for her academic pursuits, ended up adapting to the move quickly.

Horton Jr., who was in the ninth grade, had not initially opposed the move. Even he had found the prevalence of drugs at school in Nyack alarming. But the culture shock of adjusting from upper-middle-class life in Nyack to small-town New Hampshire proved more challenging for him than for his big sister. For one thing, his whole wardrobe changed. In Nyack, Horton Jr. had adopted a sort of antiestablishment demeanor and dressed accordingly. In New Hampshire, his mom bought him preppy clothes—a white denim jacket and striped trousers—so he would fit in with the kids there.

The crowning blow, however, was being told at his new school that he would have to get a haircut. He appealed to his mother to delay it until their next visit to Nyack, so he would still have long hair when he saw his friends there. In the end, he ended up shaving his head.

Walter and Daisy, both younger, took the move more in stride, Daisy even preferring her New Hampshire school to the one in Nyack. Daisy and Walter also found new activities they both pursued with a passion. For Daisy it was horses. One day shortly after the move, Daisy was outside on the dirt road that ran in front of the house when a woman rode by on a horse. She stopped, introduced herself, and told Daisy she was going to be teaching horseback riding. Daisy begged her parents to let her take lessons, and they let her start on a pony. Walter, who was growing tall in a hurry, joined the school's basketball team, a sport that he began to work at with such enthusiasm that Foote and Lillian hired a contractor to build a half-court for him to practice on.

Lillian, however, was worried over changes in the children's report cards, especially those of Horton Jr. and Barbara Hallie. Horton Jr.'s grades, especially, spiraled downward, and he was getting back at his parents for the move by playing the rebel in school. While Foote was in California working on *Stalking Moon*, Lillian wrote about her growing concern, but she reported in one letter that she had been gratified that Barbara Hallie had begun to confide in her, talking to her woman-to-woman about two boyfriends she had at school and how she was torn between them.

On the movie set, Foote agonized that he had agreed to a project that kept him away from home at such a difficult time for his family, and that he had left Lillian to cope with the upheaval alone. In an effort to exert parental authority from three thousand miles away, he wrote his elder son from California that he wanted him to send carbon copies of his English homework so his dad could look over them. It partly worked. A few weeks later, Foote wrote Horton Jr. about his latest report card: "I am grateful for the improvement and especially pleased by the conduct reports—but they have to be better (the grades, that is). D in math is not good enough. I can't help it if every other person in the class is making an F." Another letter from Foote to Horton Jr. said he was "delighted" with his English grades and told him about going to Gregory Peck's house one night for a chili dinner.

Walter and Daisy both joined basketball teams, and Horton Jr. began to play soccer. Foote tried to rebind his ties with his displaced children by taking an avid interest in the sports, the first time he had ever taken much interest in any kind of athletics, and asked in every letter home about the results of their games.

Lillian kept Foote up to date on all the daily activities that were taking place back in New Hampshire. She had consulted a local landscaper and was making plans for a large garden at their new house. Horton Jr. was grounded for some minor infraction, but he was also taking driver's education at school and working part-time as a handyman's helper for $1.50 an hour, saving the money so he could buy a car when he got his license. Walter was campaigning to go to a Bob Cousy basketball camp that summer, and the concrete for the court they were building him was being laid. Daisy often came into Lillian's room at night and slept with her mother.

The town of New Boston embraced its newest residents, and while Foote was in California that spring, a local community center arranged a screening of *To Kill a Mockingbird* and invited Lillian to appear at a Q-and-A session afterward. Lillian took Daisy with her. Daisy hid her head in her mother's lap during the scary scenes with Boo Radley, even when Scout sat on the front porch with him at the end.

Lillian sensed Foote's loneliness and feeling of isolation during that last California venture, and in one letter tried to comfort him by quoting her favorite Bible verse: "Trust in the Lord with all thine heart and lean not unto thy own understanding." She ended by reminding him of the life they had built together: "I think, my darling, we must continue to be grateful for all the good in our lives. I love you more than you'll ever know."

After returning from California that summer, Foote took stock of his life and career. He was fifty-two years old, and time was eroding all that had nurtured him through the ups and downs of his writing career. There were other problems preying on his mind. Letters from his mother in Wharton brought the news that his father was not well, was becoming forgetful and sometimes behaving strangely.

Barbara Hallie, and then his other children, one after the other, would soon leave home for college. Although he had a small nest egg from his earnings as a writer, college tuitions and the medical needs his parents would be facing would soon deplete that. Also, a new addition to the family brought some extra expenses.

Daisy had outgrown her pony and was now ready for her own horse. Foote and Lillian bought her a quarter horse but warned her that she would have to take care of him—feed him, water him, groom him, brush him down. But the addition of the horse to the family meant boarding costs. And the basketball camp Walter wanted to attend would not be cheap. Foote considered taking other jobs in order to bring in the money he and Lillian would need in the future.

Once again, it was Lillian who calmed the turbulent waters of his self-doubt. She told him in no uncertain terms that he would continue to write, and to write what he had always written. Sooner or later, she argued, art would prevail, and there would be a place again for Foote's plays on the stage or the screen, either big or small. Lillian began taking courses to become a real estate agent. In a rare departure from the normal domestic economic arrangements for that time, she would sell houses to bring in the family paycheck. Foote was to keep writing.

The problem was that he didn't know what to write. Foote went through a sort of crisis of the soul, casting about for an inspiration.

In the interim, however, one project came up that kept him from being idle. Herbert Berghof, who with his wife, the actress Uta Hagen, ran the HB acting school in New York, had long been an admirer of Foote's work. Not long after Foote returned to New Hampshire from California, Berghof approached him and asked about turning his teleplay of Faulkner's story "Tomorrow" into a stage play.

Berghof told him that his planned production would be based on the "idea of compressed time." Foote had no idea what Berghof meant by that, even after it was explained to him. Foote had met Berghof a few times but did not know him well. However, he had a great respect for his theatrical instincts and directorial ability, and he was an ardent admirer of Hagen as an actress. Foote agreed to let him do it.

Berghof had already cast the two main characters—a newcomer named Olga Bellin to play Sarah, and Robert Duvall for Jackson Fentry. The play was presented at the HB theater on Bank Street in Greenwich Village. Foote and the whole family came down to New York on the train one day from New Hampshire and saw a dress rehearsal.

Foote was very taken with what Duvall did with the character of Jackson Fentry. Duvall brought a depth to the backwoodsman that went beyond what Richard Boone had done in the television version. Foote was also impressed by Bellin in the role of Sarah. In an interesting footnote, a young actor who played one of the smaller parts in that production was Romulus Linney, who was soon to start writing plays of his own.

The trip to see the play provided the opportunity for the whole family to spend a weekend in the city. The outing would have a lasting impression on Daisy, who at the age of eleven had never had a clear idea of exactly what it was her dad did for a living. She knew he wrote, but the main connection she had with that fact was that he was gone a lot. She hated the shift that would take place in the house when he was not there, especially if her mother went away as well, as she had done for a few weeks on Foote's last California trip, and she missed him terribly. The performance made a strong impression on her, and when she was introduced to Duvall afterward she was relieved to discover he wasn't actually scary like Boo Radley.

The family went to a Mexican restaurant after the performance— a treat for Foote and Lillian, since New Boston had no Mexican restaurants—and Walter created a commotion when he drank some hot sauce straight from a bottle on the table. Since they couldn't afford a hotel, they stayed overnight at Valerie Bettis's house. The whole experience planted a seed of desire in Daisy to become a writer herself, and as soon as they returned to New Hampshire she began to write poetry.

Daisy was not the only budding artist to see and draw inspiration from the stage production of *Tomorrow*. David Mamet, then an acting student at the Neighborhood Playhouse, and Robert De Niro, a struggling actor in New York, both saw performances, and years later each told Foote it had been one of his most moving experiences.

A few weeks after the play opened, Foote got a call from two independent film producers, Paul Roebling and Gilbert Pearlman, who wanted to turn the HB stage version of *Tomorrow* into a feature film, using both Duvall and Bellin to reprise their roles as Fentry and Sarah. They asked Foote to write the screenplay.

Foote met with them. They explained that they wanted to open up the story even more, and that they planned to shoot it on location in Mississippi, in black-and-white, in an effort to maintain its authenticity. Roebling also was married to Bellin, and his main interest in getting the film done was to help his wife's career. One of the things they wanted Foote to undertake in the screenplay was to expand the character of Sarah even more. Although Foote had already turned Sarah into a major character from the minor role she plays in Faulkner's story, she disappears in the original teleplay after the birth of her son and her death. Roebling wanted her also to be a presence in the second half of the film.

Another stipulation was that they did not want Berghof to direct the movie. The producers felt that Berghof was too mercurial and they wanted a calmer hand in charge of the movie. They suggested Joe Anthony, Foote's old and close friend, as director. Foote was torn over this latest demand. He couldn't argue with the choice of Anthony as director, and he felt he could make Sarah a character in the second part of the film. He had always been fascinated by the woman, and he had been strongly impressed by Bellin's performance in the stage version. But he also felt a sense of loyalty to Berghof, whose idea it had been to move the teleplay to the stage in the first place and who Foote thought had done a good job directing.

Berghof had been born in Austria and came to the United States as a young man. He never felt quite at home in America, and never was entirely comfortable with the English language. He spoke it with a heavy accent, and he and Hagen still spoke German to each other privately. He had an uneven temperament and sometimes let his frustrations spill over into anger when he was directing. Horton Jr., who years later took acting classes at the HB Studio, recalled a rehearsal in which Berghof screamed at a young actress, calling her "stupid, stupid," sputtering in her face, and reducing her to tears.

Foote informed Roebling that he would not be the one to tell Berghof he wasn't going to direct the movie. Foote also insisted that Roebling convey to Berghof that he, Foote, opposed the decision. Duvall, however, who had become personally involved in the project, agreed with the producers.

In the end, it was Gilbert Pearlman, the coproducer, who told Berghof in a letter of their decision to use a different director. In it, to comply with Foote's demands, Pearlman said, "Although his request cannot be met, we must tell you that Horton immediately suggested that you be engaged to direct the film." The letter went on to say that financing for the movie could not be obtained "without a firm guarantee that we would secure the services of a director with previous screen directorial credits." Berghof was bitterly hurt, and his relationship with Foote cooled for some time.

After his recent unhappy experiences with the movies, Foote was surprised to discover that he enjoyed working on one again. For one thing, despite his uneasiness over Berghof's abrupt dismissal, he was happy to be collaborating with Joe Anthony. Over the years, Anthony had become one of Foote's closest friends, and when the two of them flew to Mississippi to begin scouting locations around Tupelo that they could use for exterior shots, they were like two college students on spring break. They would get into the car each morning and just drive around the countryside. One day their rental car got stuck in the mud and Foote had to walk to a nearby farm and persuade the farmer to come pull them out with a tractor.

Foote liked driving and looking at old houses and farms. It reminded him of being a boy and riding the back roads around Wharton with his grandfather and, later, with his grandmother in their old Studebaker, visiting the farms they owned. He felt like he was home in Texas, mainly because there were so many farms around Tupelo that were still producing cotton. He found a small café in the town that offered homemade chili and he went there for a bowl every chance he got. One night after returning to his motel from a chili dinner, he wrote Lillian that he thought of her every time he ate there, since she had grown to love the official dish of the state of Texas as much as he. "They make it very good here and I kept thinking how much you would enjoy it," he wrote.

By the end of the first month in Mississippi, however, he was again homesick. He had grown fond of the country life in New Hampshire, and he wrote Lillian how much he missed having breakfast with her, watching the evening news with her, and listening to her help Daisy with her homework. Barbara Hallie, who was by now away at college, visited while he was gone and he regretted he had not been there to see her. He wrote Lillian, "We are very blessed in that child, as we are in all of our children, mainly I think because for some reason we have made them feel they are the most important thing to us, as I guess they really are."

In opening up the screenplay, Foote began the film with the trial of the man who killed Buck Thorpe, the young man whom Sarah's son had become. He added a scene in which Douglas, the lawyer defending Buck's killer, gives his closing arguments to the jury, and another in the jury room, when Fentry refuses to vote an acquittal. Foote also wrote several small scenes for the second half of the film in which he tried to keep the memory of Sarah alive, but most of them were cut in rehearsal before shooting began.

There was, however, a lot of new material for Sarah in the film, and Foote took advantage of the location shooting to write several scenes between Sarah and Fentry outside the cabin—the two of them walking in the woods, with Fentry showing Sarah where he planned to build their house; another of them caught together in a rainstorm; and a flashback after Sarah dies when Fentry walks home with the baby and a goat. He also added several scenes between Fentry and Sarah's child as a little boy to establish the bond between them before Sarah's husband's family comes to take him away.

As Robert Mulligan had done with the children's roles in *Mockingbird*, Joe Anthony hired a young boy who was not a trained actor to play Sarah's son as a child. His name was Johnny Mask, and he was painfully shy. Duvall spent long hours with Johnny on and off the set to establish a rapport, like Peck had done with Mary Badham. When the cameras began to roll, however, Johnny became self-conscious at having to say his lines, and the scenes were rigid. Duvall got around the boy's awkwardness by letting Johnny talk spontaneously, then improvising the scene as it was being filmed.

The movie had been budgeted at three hundred thousand dollars, a ridiculously small amount for a film in 1970, and Roebling undertook most of the preproduction work himself to save money. The shooting schedule was very tight, and everyone on the set was conscious of the monetary restrictions. Shortly after filming had begun, Foote wrote home: "I have never seen a more cooperative bunch of people in my life. It is very much like the old television days, or one in summer stock. Everyone works together very well."

Apart from their close friendship, another reason Foote was happy to have Anthony direct was that he had an innate sense of detail that brought scenes to life. Although Anthony's meticulous approach created authenticity, it was a slow and time-consuming process. As a result, there was a break in the shooting for a few months when the money began to run low. And when the first cut of the film was finally finished, it ran much too long. Roebling, Pearlman, and Anthony worked for days with the editor to pare it to a manageable hour and a half.

For *Tomorrow*, however, there was no Gregory Peck to insist that the movie open at Radio City Music Hall, and there was not then the cachet for independent films that would come later. Finding a distributor took some time, but when the movie was released in 1972, nearly two years after it was begun, it was for the most part hailed by critics with rave reviews. Only Vincent Canby in the *New York Times* had reservations. Duvall's performance as Fentry vaulted him to Hollywood stardom, and it is a general consensus that the film version of *Tomorrow* is the best screen adaptation of Faulkner ever made.

It was a satisfying experience all around for Foote, but back home he faced a growing list of worries, chief of which was the failing health of his father. Letters from his brother John Speed told a grim story of his father's behavior and the effect it was having on his mother, who was trying to cope with the situation alone.

Although they had not previously been close, Foote now was in frequent touch with his brother about the status of his father's illness. John Speed was driving to Wharton from Houston almost every weekend, as much to comfort his mother as to care for his father. After one such visit, John Speed wrote Foote about taking their father out for a drive. "Truthfully, I can't see any improvement in Dad. Last Sunday he got mixed up several times—with both mother and me." He added, "Mother is starved for someone to talk to."

Foote had hired a young man named Elrese Kendricks, who had had some medical training and was the son of a woman who had once worked for Foote's grandmother, to live in his parents' house and help look after his father. But he had also been thinking that perhaps he should bring his parents to live with him in New Hampshire, and Lillian supported him in that decision.

Foote's reticence to discuss the problem with other relatives, however, led to a family rift. Nan Outlar, one of Foote's favorite cousins, had lived in Wharton her whole life, but she traveled frequently, even to New York, and was a big theater buff. It was she who had been young Foote's biggest supporter in his desire to become an actor, and no one in the family was more proud of his achievements. She also wrote for the local newspaper, knew all the town's gossip, and had a sharp tongue.

In the fall of that year, Nan wrote Foote to report that his father had suffered a dizzy spell and brief paralysis at a party he and Foote's mother had attended. She said the other guests had helped get him home, and that Foote's mother had said there had been two similar episodes prior to that. Nan suggested Foote come home and help get medical attention for his father.

Foote already had heard about these episodes from both his brother and mother and did not respond to his cousin's letter. His mother had informed him that she at first thought the seizures, which had been brief and infrequent, had been the result of his father becoming nauseated by the smell of tar that workers were using to put a new roof on a building next to his father's store. But now she was alarmed.

A couple of weeks later, Nan wrote back, chiding him for not answering her earlier letter. "Can't you write anything but plays?" she said. She reported further that his father had had several of these blackouts, and that his mind was deteriorating fast. Although the symptoms would make one think today of Alzheimer's, the doctors at the hospital where he was taken for tests thought the cause of his father's mental lapse were small blood clots forming pressure and damaging his brain. She said that although the periods of confusion were infrequent at first, Foote's father was now going downhill fast—he had started to wander off and get lost, and he wasn't making sense in conversations. Once, they found him walking along the old riverbed of Caney Creek. Although he had not run his store for some time, he still tried to walk into town every morning to open for business. "He is completely incompetent of leading a normal life," Nan wrote. She further castigated Foote for not being more thoughtful of his mother, who bore the brunt of looking after him alone, and described Elrese as a "lazy good-for-nothing."

Foote replied sharply that he was well aware of what was going on at home, that he knew the situation "in great detail," and that plans were under way to bring his parents to New Hampshire. Nan answered contritely, apologizing for her outburst and saying she had been wrong about the help Elrese was giving Foote's mother.

That winter Foote flew to Wharton to bring his parents to New Hampshire to live with them, along with Elrese. Foote's father made the flight from Houston to New Hampshire, which involved a change of planes, without any incident. But problems arose almost from the minute he arrived.

On the first evening there, Foote's father began running up and down the stairs of the three-story house like an angry child, screaming that he didn't want to stay there, that he wanted to go home. He didn't even recognize Foote.

The episode nearly broke Foote's heart. He said later that it was the worst night of his life, seeing his father, with whom he had enjoyed a close and affectionate relationship his entire life, behave as though he were a total stranger to him, shouting that he wouldn't stay in his house and that he was being held prisoner there.

The behavior of Foote's father began to infect the whole house, and in order for the rest of the family to pursue some semblance of a normal life, Foote moved his parents into an apartment he and Lillian had converted from an empty room over the garage. Horton Jr. had been living in the space, but with Barbara Hallie away at college, he now moved into her old room back in the main house.

Foote's father still kept trying to flee at every chance. In the mornings when Horton Jr. and Walter would come down for breakfast, they would find Pap-Pap, as they called their grandfather, standing in front of the door, dressed to go out, although there would be two feet of snow on the ground.

"Where are you going, Pap-Pap?" they would ask.

"I'm going to the post office and then to open the store," he would snap back. "Just like I've done every day of my life."

The boys would talk him back into the kitchen.

Foote and Lillian decided to hire a local man, a French Canadian whom they knew only as Leo, to drive Foote's father around town, so that he would not feel the need to run away. Leo, who had probably never seen a black man in his life, and Elrese became sort of odd-couple buddies and got along famously, sometimes going to the races together if they had some time off. Once, however, when Elrese and Leo took Foote's father into Manchester for the day, they went off on their own and left him alone in the car. He saw a Catholic priest on the street and got out and told the priest that he had been kidnapped and was being kept locked up in a strange house, and that the people who lived there had hired two guards to keep him from escaping.

Foote's father recognized no one except his wife, and as time went on, sometimes not even her. Daisy spent her afternoons after school visiting Nana, as the children called their grandmother, in the apartment above the garage, talking to her about anything that would take her mind off the situation that was only getting worse.

As his father's condition deteriorated, Foote's mother said she wanted to take him back to Texas. Foote finally and reluctantly decided to let them return to Wharton. His mother assured Foote that she and Elrese could tend to his needs there, and he would be less trouble to look after in Wharton than in New Hampshire. The following spring after his return to Texas, Foote's father died at home and was buried in the town cemetery.

Foote visited Wharton shortly before his father died, and although his father still didn't recognize him, he looked up from his bed, smiled at his son, and said, "You have a nice face."

CHAPTER 10

Old Letters
and Faded Photographs

Throughout the year his parents lived with the family in New Hampshire, the phone still wasn't ringing for Foote. Lucy Kroll was continuing to send out his scripts, and he had begun work on a new play, but there was nothing on the horizon in the way of a writing assignment. For the first time in many years money again became a major concern for Foote and Lillian.

It was not until the spring of 1972 that a theater producer called from London asking Foote if he would consider coming to England to undertake writing the book for a musical version of *Gone With the Wind*. It was to be a big production, with music and lyrics by Harold Rome, to be staged at the Drury Lane Theatre in the West End.

Ordinarily, it was not an offer that would tempt Foote to leave his family, but the dearth of other projects prompted him to accept it. Foote felt he had to earn some money, if for no other reason than that Barbara Hallie had become engaged during her last year at the University of New Hampshire and was planning a summer wedding.

Foote flew to London in March and stayed at the Washington Hotel on Curzon Street. He was to be paid a lump sum for the job and given a daily allowance for his expenses. Frugal as always, he immediately began living on a bare minimum and saving what he could from his per diem in the hopes of bringing Lillian over to join him.

Trying to bring the epic movie to the stage was a huge and complex task, and rehearsals were running twelve hours a day. Foote was constantly doing rewrites as the producers and director changed their minds, discarding whole scenes and demanding new ones. In each of his letters home, Foote brought up the idea of Lillian joining him for the last week or two before the opening. He found out he could get a double room at the hotel for eight pounds a night, or about nineteen dollars at the time, and that included breakfast. He figured they could both live on his per diem, so the only real expense would be Lillian's airfare.

The family's financial situation, however, did not immediately pick up. Foote did not receive the money for the musical in advance, and Lillian had not yet got her real estate license. In fact, she had been cramming for her final exam. Lillian told Foote that their bank balance was down to six hundred dollars and she was thinking of taking out a short-term loan of two thousand dollars to tide them over until Foote got paid.

Foote and Lillian had always shared a love of antiques, and one of their favorite pastimes was to browse through shops and barns and garage sales in New England, acquiring old furniture for their home. As money grew tighter, Lillian wrote that she was going through the house looking for things to sell, and decided on letting go of a pair of hooked rugs they had bought on one of their excursions that were now in Daisy's room.

The most immediate crisis that spring, however, concerned Horton Jr. His mediocre grades in high school had limited his choice of universities, and he ended up enrolling at Plymouth State College after graduating. He took his rebel streak with him to college, where he and academic life did not get along. He was reading voraciously, but he didn't attend many classes. After two months, he dropped out.

With his student deferment gone, however, he was suddenly eligible for the military draft. The Vietnam War was still raging, and it was the concern of every parent that their draft-age son would be sent to Southeast Asia to fight and possibly die in that unpopular conflict. Peace talks were about to begin in Paris, but Foote was convinced they were only window dressing for Richard Nixon's bid for reelection, and that North Vietnam would not make any concessions at the negotiating table until after the American presidential elections that fall. When Horton Jr.'s draft notice arrived, he received a very low number—seventeen—in the lottery, and he was considering enlisting in the army rather than wait to be drafted.

The local army enlisting officer had promised Horton Jr. that if he signed up for three years instead of the normal two, he would be sent to Germany, France, or Turkey after his basic training, and not to Vietnam. Foote was dubious. He reminded Lillian in one letter from London about some friends whose son was given the same assurances but ended up being sent to Vietnam anyway.

The country was so torn over the war that many young men, often with their parents' blessing, were fleeing to Canada or other countries rather than going to fight in Vietnam. Some made public displays of defiance by burning their draft cards. Those who fled were labeled draft dodgers and faced the prospect of prosecution if they ever returned to the United States.

For the next few weeks, Horton Jr. went back and forth over whether to enlist or take his chances with the draft. Early in April, he finally decided to enlist. The recruiting officer repeated his pledge that if he signed up for three years instead of the usual two, he would be posted to Europe after his basic training. Horton Jr. informed his mother that if the army went back on its word and tried to send him to Vietnam, he would refuse to go. Lillian wrote her husband that she would back up her son on that decision. She also said she felt she should stay in New Hampshire and be with him when he left for the army, rather than come to London for the opening of the musical.

Foote responded that he agreed with her that Horton Jr. should not go to Vietnam under any circumstances, and that she should be there to see him off when he reported to the army. On April 17, Foote wrote a letter to his son:

Mom and Barbara Hallie have kept me in touch with your plans and both report you seem in very good spirits now that you have made your decision. I feel very far away from you all at times like this, of course, and wish I could be there with you, but it is gratifying to me to see how maturely you worked this out for yourself. Dad thinks of you every day and I want you to know I am very proud of you.

As the day for his departure neared, Lillian wrote Foote that Horton Jr. had been "tense and apprehensive, but I am sure that's normal as it's quite a step he is taking." As soon as she returned from taking him to the train to report at Fort Dix in New Jersey, she wrote Foote an account of his last two days. Barbara Hallie had been home from college so the family could have a final dinner together. On his last day, Horton Jr. went to get a haircut, then spent the whole afternoon shooting baskets with Walter on the court outside the house. She described the trip to the train station:

We had to avoid discussing his going away as he had asked me not to talk about it. This morning's leave-taking was very simple—I didn't want to wake the children because I knew it would be too hard for him. We drove on into Manchester and when we got there he just said good-bye—didn't kiss me—and I slid over into the driver's seat and went on. It was difficult to watch him walk up those steps and through that door. I felt a part of my life had passed by, but I do feel it can be a positive experience for him. He's a friendly, warm fellow and he'll get along fine.

On the day Foote received Lillian's letter, Alan Pakula happened to arrive in London from New York. He went straight from the airport to Foote's hotel and the two went to have breakfast. Foote opened the letter in the taxi and began to cry as he read his wife's account of his son going off to the army. Pakula, who was always a sympathetic friend, burst into tears himself.

As spring moved toward summer and Foote was still in London, Lillian wrote him almost daily about family affairs. Walter had signed up for the Red Auerbach basketball camp. Barbara Hallie was having fittings for her wedding dress. Lillian passed her real estate exam and sold her first house. Money was still tight, however, and she sold a Martha Washington chair to help pay an unexpected tax bill.

In one letter Lillian reported that the children were fine—"They really are good kids"—but that she hoped Daisy would soon get out of "the 12-year-old syndrome or whatever it is—you can't make a statement that she won't challenge." In another, she recounted how she was driving Walter to a friend's house the day after Horton Jr. left for Fort Dix, and she casually said, "Well, I guess Hortie is in New Jersey now." Walter, who, if the Vietnam War went on much longer, might face the same draft dilemma as his brother, responded, "Yeah, New Jersey or Canada."

Walter was next to get his driver's license, and he had been working after school to save money. Lillian reported that he had spent forty dollars—nearly a week's salary—on a dress as a present for her. With Horton Jr. now gone, Walter had taken on the role of protector of his younger sister. In one letter Lillian told Foote that Walter had come to her and reported that Daisy was creating quite a stir among his male classmates. "She's becoming quite a beauty," Lillian said. "Walter said a lot of boys at school have their eyes on her. I think he's a little worried."

The musical of *Gone With the Wind* finally opened with a charity performance for which the producers had brought over the mayor of Atlanta. Princess Anne attended, representing the royal family. They and other honored guests came backstage after the performance, and Foote was presented to Her Royal Highness. But he left for home the following day.

Foote returned to a household in upheaval over Barbara Hallie's impending marriage to Jeff MacCleave, a young man she had met in college, scheduled for July 1. The money he finally received for his work on the musical of *Gone With the Wind* ended up paying for the wedding.

Foote felt his world was rapidly shrinking. After their marriage, Barbara Hallie and Jeff went to live in Boston; Horton Jr. had indeed been posted to Germany after his basic training and was now serving as an MP there. Only Walter and Daisy were still at home, and Walter would be leaving soon for college. In addition to the basketball court for Walter, Foote and Lillian had since built a barn for Daisy so that she could keep her horse, Dude, at home, rather than board him elsewhere. When Daisy wasn't out riding and Walter out shooting baskets, the two younger children spent a lot of time together.

In the summer they would fish together in a pond behind the house, and in the winter when the pond was frozen, they, against strict rules not to, would sneak out when their parents were away and skate on it. Walter was always full of mischief as well. Once, when their mother and father brought home an antique table they had bought from their friends the Bacons, Walter hid it in the woods to see if his parents would even miss it. They did; it was retrieved and Walter was grounded.

Lucy Kroll continued to keep in touch, but it was mostly out of friendship; there were no offers for movies and theaters were not asking for Foote's work. Joe Anthony and his wife, Perry Wilson, also stayed in close contact, and Anthony wrote frequent and funny letters to Foote in New Hampshire, lampooning the glitterati of the day, trying to cheer up his old friend; he always did. Once, for example, Anthony wrote about going with Perry to see a performance of the Living Theatre, the epitome of the avant-garde theater of the day, at BAM in Brooklyn. "That's where not the actors but the audience takes its clothes off," he explained. "I understand Walter Kerr did a token disrobing by loosening his tie."

In another letter, Anthony wrote about him and Perry going to a high-powered sit-down dinner for sixteen at Jean and Walter Kerr's house with Bennett Cerf, the television celebrity head of Random House, as guest of honor. Anthony's connection with the Kerrs began when he directed Jean Kerr's play *Mary, Mary* on Broadway. "Perry and I are the nonentities," Anthony wrote. "I introduce her and myself and they acknowledge the introduction but do not introduce themselves. We're supposed to *know* who they are. And what do these mighties talk about? Their insurance, taxes, diets."

Anthony always exhorted Foote not to be depressed by the theatrical fads of the times, what he described in one letter as "the anything-goes theater—where the silly, the irreverent, the non-think-four-letter-word-no-place-no-people-no-prepositions anti-writers hack away at what's left of our stages."

The spring of 1973 was the lowest ebb in Foote's exile in New

Hampshire. In May, his father died, shortly after Foote paid a final visit to see him. He had no projects on his desk and he felt his inspiration was drying up.

Horton Jr., who wrote frequent letters to the entire family, addressing them as "Dear Feet," had been informed of his grandfather's death only in a letter from Walter. Horton Jr. chastised his father and mother for not calling him with the news and wrote about the feeling of helplessness he had in being so far away from the family. "In the future when anything like this happens, you must always notify the Red Cross and I will be notified within a few hours," he wrote. "I could have possibly come home on an emergency leave to attend the funeral."

After Foote's father's death, his mother had become depressed. In an attempt to bring her out of it, Foote arranged for her to take a trip to California that summer to visit relatives there, and while in Los Angeles she saw a production of the musical version of *Gone With the Wind*.

But once she returned to Wharton, she again became despondent. Without her husband to care for, his mother seemed to lose the will to carry on and was growing more feeble with each passing week. She also was having troubling dreams about his father, in which he would say things like "I can't live without you." Foote was afraid that her dreams were bringing on a death wish, and he finally decided to bring her back to New Hampshire to live with him and Lillian. But less than a year after his father died, Foote's mother passed away. Foote took her body back to Texas for the funeral and she was buried next to his father.

On top of everything else, Foote's own family was going through a lot of transition as well. Barbara Hallie was not happy. She was living in Boston with Jeff and working in a public relations firm there. But she began to have panic attacks and kept wanting to go home to New Hampshire.

Although she had previously disdained the theater, possibly a residual act of resentment toward her father and mother, she suddenly decided she wanted to be an actress. She had heard of an acting teacher named Peggy Feury who ran the Loft Studio in Los

Angeles with her husband, Bill Traylor, and her plan was to move there and take classes. Foote and Lillian told Barbara Hallie they would help pay her tuition. Jeff was less enthusiastic about Barbara Hallie's acting ambitions. But he, too, was ready for a change of scenery, and in 1974 Barbara Hallie and Jeff packed an old van they had bought when they first married and moved to California.

Walter was now in college, so Daisy was the only child still living at home. Foote once again felt his world was slipping away. In a letter to Joe Anthony in the fall of 1974, Foote spoke about a sense of abandonment:

> It was a weekend of farewells—Barbara Hallie and Jeff leaving for California, Walter for college. We were all trying to be gay and brave but not doing too good a job of it. It's unbelievably quiet around here now. We haven't heard the sound of a basketball for weeks, and as much as I used to curse the constant thumping, I would welcome it now. Oh, it's too quiet, Joe.

Apart from the emotional strain from the death of both Foote's parents, money problems again began to surface. Besides the normal domestic expenses and another round of college tuition, Barbara Hallie and Jeff were having financial difficulties in California, and Foote and Lillian were sending them money on a regular basis.

Jeff was out of work a lot of the time. He had one job at a meat company, but he left it and was trying to get employment as a mechanic at a Harley-Davidson dealership in Long Beach. Barbara Hallie got a one-line part in a movie that paid little but earned her a Screen Actors Guild card. She also had one day's work as an extra, swimming in the ocean in the background, for a movie called *Lifeguard*. But acting jobs were few and far between, and she took a job as a salesclerk in a Beverly Hills clothing store for the Christmas holidays. In one letter she wrote that Brock Peters, who had known her father when he played the role of Tom Robinson in *To Kill a Mockingbird*, had come into the store, but she couldn't talk long with him because she had to wait on customers.

In January, she and Jeff sold their van for two thousand dollars, and Barbara Hallie got some work modeling for a clothing catalog. All of their jobs were temporary ones, and over the course of the next two years, Foote and Lillian kept sending checks to California. Barbara Hallie's letters were full of updates about her acting class and her efforts to break into acting jobs. She changed the name she planned to use as a professional actress several times—first, it was to be Hallie Brooks, then Barbara Hallie, then Hallie MacCleave. It was only later she settled on Hallie Foote. She had a shot at a small part in Sidney Lumet's film *Network*, but it didn't come through.

Through the whole period, Jeff was still trying to find steady work. Nothing he started seemed to last. He quit several jobs after a few weeks, or even a few days. A motorcycle buff, he talked at one point about trying to open his own motorcycle repair shop, but it never materialized. At another point, he decided to go back to school and finish his degree, and he started taking classes at UCLA. All of this was costing money, and Barbara Hallie continued to take odd jobs, working at a typing agency and as a temp at an insurance company, to supplement what her parents were sending. She applied for food stamps.

In the summer of 1975, Jeff returned to the East Coast for an operation on his leg, which he had broken in a motorcycle accident, and Barbara Hallie got a friend from acting class, Kathy Cronkite, the daughter of the CBS News anchor, to move in with her to share the rent. Barbara Hallie visited her parents in New Hampshire that August, but she returned to California alone to resume her acting studies. Jeff came back toward the end of the year and resumed classes at UCLA. In May, he went on a motorcycle trip with an old chum, and when he returned he announced he was going to start a construction company. Barbara Hallie asked her parents for a loan to help him get started. But it never got off the ground.

Barbara Hallie felt that Jeff had never really supported her acting ambitions, and he wanted her to give up her lessons and get a full-time job. Also, Jeff was beginning to run with a crowd of bikers Barbara Hallie regarded as dangerous. The end was inevitable. By the end of the year, there was no mention of Jeff in Barbara Hallie's letters home, and it was clear she was living alone. Shortly after the

New Year, Barbara Hallie wrote her parents that Jeff had come by, and that they "talked about the divorce."

Daisy went to visit Barbara Hallie after the separation and ended up staying several months, during which they became best friends.

Throughout Barbara Hallie's trials, Foote and Lillian responded with understanding and encouragement. Foote had great faith in his elder daughter's talent and knew she would find her way. He recalled how his own parents had been patient and indulgent with him as he tried to make his way, first as an actor, then as a writer. In fact, it was in his memories of them that he drew the inspiration that would jump-start the second act of his own career.

After the death of his mother, Foote stayed in Wharton and began the task of going through all his parents' belongings. The house in which Foote was raised was now empty. In their wills, Foote's parents had left the house jointly to him and John Speed. At the time of his mother's funeral, Foote and his brother discussed what to do about it. Neither particularly wanted to sell it, but though each might have considered moving back into it at some point, neither of them was able to do so at that time. Foote and Lillian had talked several times about moving to Wharton, a town that Lillian had grown to love and where she now had as many friends among the local population as her husband.

But with Daisy about to finish high school, Foote and Lillian did not want to uproot her again. John Speed had always liked Wharton, preferring small-town life to big-city life in Houston. But his wife, Betty, was adamantly opposed to it. In the end, the brothers chose to rent the house until they could decide what to do with it.

Foote spent a couple of weeks in Wharton, going through his mother's and father's things, the accumulations of a lifetime, discarding the minutiae that his loved ones had loved, holding on to the small things that had personal meaning to him. There was a plethora of material—boxes of letters, photographs, and other mementos his parents had collected over their lives. In the end he packed it all up and sent it to New Hampshire.

Foote spent several weeks that winter going through the boxes, reading over the letters and staring at the old photographs. There were pictures of his grandmother, Baboo, and of his uncles Brother and Speed, his aunts and great-aunts, and, of course, his mother and father when they were young.

Although Foote's parents had not spent more than a week apart throughout their nearly sixty years of marriage, they were separated most of the year of their courtship before they eloped. At the time, Foote's father was a traveling salesman, and he spent weeks calling on his company's clients in Texas, Louisiana, Arkansas, and Mississippi. While on the road he wrote Foote's mother regularly. They had to keep their correspondence as secret as possible because of her parents' objection to the relationship, but Foote's mother had saved every letter, including one she had torn up following a lovers' spat. When Foote found the letters, the pieces had been carefully taped back together.

Over the next two years, beginning in the summer of 1912, there was a steady exchange of letters, those from his mother addressed simply "Mr. A.H. Foote," followed only by the name of the town in which he was staying—Waco, Texas; Dallas; Fort Smith, Ark.; Crowley, La.; Vicksburg, Miss.—but they were all delivered. In the beginning they were polite, with a salutation of "Dear Horton" and signed "Sincerely." As the correspondence grew, the salutation became "My Own Dearest Horton" and the sign-off "Much love."

Whenever Foote's father visited a large town, he would buy sheet music of the latest popular songs and send them to Foote's mother, who played the piano with a passion. In thanking him for one batch of songs, she pined in a thinly disguised wish for him to return home, "I wish I had someone to sing them to." In the fall, she reported on the Wharton county fair and the daily horse races, which she said "are the most terribly exciting things in the world." In August 1914, Foote's mother went on a vacation to Galveston with her family, and by then had let all formality drop. "Do you miss me?" she asked, adding, "I am always missing you." They married the following Valentine's Day, when the letters abruptly stopped.

The nostalgia inherent in such an undertaking started Foote thinking about his parents' lives—the strength of a love that led them to defy his mother's parents and elope; the heartache his father felt his entire life at being abandoned by his mother and over the death of a father he barely knew; his father's determination to have a headstone erected over his own father's grave; the anxiety the whole family experienced over the troubles his uncles created; the hardship his parents endured during the Depression; the loss they suffered with the death of his brother in war.

They had lived through so much change, yet they had adapted to it without complaint, had come through the other side with dignity and with their love for each other and their family intact. And they were not alone. Thousands, even millions, of other families lived similar lives. This was the real drama of life, the only drama that could speak across time. It might be funny or it might be sad, but it was the drama that everyone in every generation can identify with and understand.

He began recalling all the family stories that he had heard around supper tables, in kitchens, and on the front porch after dinner. A photograph of his father as a child made Foote think of the dis-appointments that child had experienced as a boy. He recalled the story of how his father had tended his chickens with loving care as a boy, only to come home one day and discover his mother had killed them all, and how as an adult his father had kept chickens at home.

Foote remembered Stark Young telling him after seeing *The Night of the Storm* on television, the teleplay that was based on his father's childhood, that he should adapt it for the stage. An idea for a play came to him. Then another one. Then another one. Perhaps it would be a trilogy. Foote put aside the boxes of letters and snap-shots and began to write.

CHAPTER 11

The Orphans' Home Cycle
and *Tender Mercies*

THE ENTHUSIASM Stark Young had expressed after seeing *The Night of the Storm* on television in 1961 had been diminished in Foote's mind at the time by David Suskind's dislike of the teleplay. Although Foote told Young he would think about the critic's suggestion that he turn it into a stage play, Foote put the script in a drawer and forgot about it. Now, thirteen years later, he took it out and read it again.

After rereading it, he realized he would now have to rewrite large parts of it. For one thing, the character of the boy's mother—based on Foote's paternal grandmother—was portrayed more sympathetically in the teleplay than he now understood her to be, and he would have to more sharply define her character. However, he now agreed with Young. It could be adapted for the stage, and he decided it would be the first play, the starting point, for the project he had in mind.

When the teleplay had been published after being shown on television, Foote returned to the title of "Roots in a Parched Ground," and that was what he decided to call the stage version.

The thread that would tie all the plays together was the story of his mother and father's marriage, viewed mainly through the prism of his father's life. While *Roots in a Parched Ground* would be the first play in the cycle chronologically, it was not the first he began working on. Since it would involve considerable rewriting, he decided to leave *Roots* for later and began on a new play.

As he worked alone in his study in the New Hampshire woods, Foote began to pore over the episodes of his parents' marriage and found himself working on two or three plays at the same time. As he would recall a particular event, he would develop a scene in one play, then at another recollection he would turn to a scene in a different one.

Most of the plays were set in the fictional town of Harrison, Texas. All the plays dealt with the saga of the three families from which his parents had sprung. Foote used the name Horace for his father, the same as in the original *Roots in a Parched Ground*, but now called his family Robedaux. He christened his mother Elizabeth and gave her family the name Vaughn. The other family that figures in the plays is that of Horace's mother, who divorced Horace's alcoholic father and later remarried. They were named the Thorntons, and, like Foote's paternal grandmother's family, they boasted antecedents who went back to the early settlers in Texas and included the former lieutenant governor.

The first play he completed was *1918*, which takes place during the deadly influenza epidemic that swept the country that year, on the eve of America's entry into World War I. It is the seventh play in the cycle, although at the time Foote did not realize he had begun such an epic undertaking.

The second play he completed was called *Convicts*, and it is the second play in the cycle. It takes place in 1904 on an old cotton plantation outside a town called Floyd's Lane, which is near Harrison. Horace, who is thirteen, has gone to work for the plantation owner, a violent drunkard named Sol Gautier, in order to save money to buy a tombstone for his father's grave. With slavery abolished, Gautier uses black convicts to work his plantation, and he mistreats them mercilessly.

This play also became the first in the cycle to be read by anyone outside the Foote family. Foote rarely left New Hampshire during the period he was writing the plays, but Herbert Berghof lured him to New York to see a production of *A Young Lady of Property*, one of Foote's early teleplays that Berghof was staging at his HB Studio in Greenwich Village. Berghof and Foote had patched up their rift over the movie of *Tomorrow*, especially after Berghof realized Foote had not supported his dismissal as director. Berghof was still an ardent admirer of Foote's plays and he wanted the playwright to see an actress named Lindsay Crouse in the title role of *Young Lady*.

At the performance, Foote ran into Robert Duvall, who was also seeing the show. Foote told him he had just finished a play called *Convicts* and there was a part in it for him. Duvall asked to see the play, and Foote sent it to him. Duvall called him the next day and said he wanted to stage it immediately. But Foote wasn't ready.

Over the course of two years, Foote worked steadily on his cycle of plays. At the end, he had written eight, and he had visions of them all being done together. He figured that theater productions were out of the question and thought the only place he might find the will, not to mention the money, to do them all as a cycle was public television. About the only outlet left for drama on the home screen at that time was the *American Short Story* series on PBS, and Foote sent the plays to Robert Geller, the show's producer.

After reading them, Geller called Foote and told him he liked them but felt there should be a ninth play to round out the series. Foote then sat down to write what would become *The Widow Claire*, chronologically the fourth play in the cycle. When he was finished, Foote decided the entire opus should have a name. He had been reading the poetry of Marianne Moore at the time, and a line from her poem "In Distrust of Merits" gave it to him: "The world's an orphans' home."

In chronological sequence the plays and the year in which each is set: *Roots in a Parched Ground* (1902); *Convicts* (1904); *Lily Dale* (1910); *The Widow Claire* (1912); *Courtship* (1915); *Valentine's Day* (1917); *1918* (1918); *Cousins* (1925); and *The Death of Papa* (1928).

With the cycle now complete, Geller set about to persuade his masters at PBS to produce them all for *American Short Story*. In the interim Geller enlisted Foote to write an adaptation of Flannery O'Connor's story "The Displaced Person" for his show. That project, starring Irene Worth and John Houseman, eventually aired in 1977 on the *American Short Story* series.

During the two years he was writing the cycle, Foote had also

187

dealt with settling the last of his parents' estate and getting their house rented. First, the house had to be painted and repaired, and most of this fell to Foote to undertake by long distance from New Hampshire or on quick trips to Wharton, because his brother John Speed had a back operation that left him incapacitated for months.

As he was waiting for final word from Geller, Foote received distressing news from one of his oldest friends. Agnes de Mille sent a note describing how she had collapsed just before a performance in what turned out to be a stroke that paralyzed her on the right side. The dancer and choreographer recounted how her husband had been told that she was going to die and wouldn't last through the night. "It was just awful," de Mille said. "But finally I didn't die. So my days are not numbered yet."

In the end, despite hard lobbying by Geller, financing for the *Orphans' Home* project on PBS was not forthcoming. Foote had nine full-length plays sitting on his desk in New Hampshire staring back at him, and he had no idea how to bring them to life.

The commercial theater at the time, even the regional theaters that were beginning to come into prominence as producers of new plays, was simply not equipped, financially or artistically, to mount the entire cycle as Foote envisioned. In the end, Foote decided to trim his sails. He chose three of the plays that he thought might have the best chance at a stage production—*Courtship, Valentine's Day*, and *1918*—and began to think about actors he would like to see in them, especially the two principal characters of Horace Robedaux and Elizabeth Vaughn. He had several people in mind for Horace, but he was at a loss for an actress to play Elizabeth.

Although he had worked with some of the greatest actresses of the day—Kim Stanley, Geraldine Page, Eva Marie Saint, Julie Harris, and Joanne Woodward, to name only a few—they were now all past the age of playing the young Elizabeth.

Barbara Hallie was still studying acting with Peggy Feury in Los Angeles, but after her divorce from Jeff, she was looking for a new place to live. Foote went out to visit her. Daisy was also staying with her sister, and Foote spent a few weeks with his daughters. During his time there, Foote went to see Barbara Hallie perform in one of his plays—by coincidence, also a production of *A Young Lady of Property*—at Feury's studio. He was genuinely awed by his elder daughter's performance, and he called Lillian back in New Hampshire the next day and told her, "I've found my Elizabeth."

Foote still had not heard any of his plays read, and during his visit to California, he enlisted a group of Barbara Hallie's friends to read *1918*, the only play he had brought with him on the trip. They met in Barbara Hallie's apartment, and after hearing her fellow students read through it, he became more eager than ever to get at least one of the plays in the cycle onstage.

When he returned to New Hampshire, Foote sent the three plays he had chosen as the most likely to get produced to Herbert Berghof, asking if he would consider doing one of them at the HB Studio. Foote added that he wanted to direct himself.

Berghof replied that he would like to stage all three of them. They decided to do them out of sequence because Foote wanted to emphasize that each play was self-contained and could stand on its own. He chose to do *Courtship* first. It was a play that had first come to him after reading the exchange of letters between his parents before they were married. At the end of the play, on the eve of the character Horace's departure on a lengthy sales trip, Elizabeth asks him, "May I write you?"

In the spring of 1978, Foote and Lillian took over a sublet on a small apartment in New York near the HB Studio. Barbara Hallie returned from California, and Foote began pre-rehearsals in the apartment with his daughter, who would play Elizabeth, and Richard Cottrell, who was cast as Horace. Three weeks later the rest of the cast joined them in full rehearsals, and his old friend Valerie Bettis was brought in to do some choreography for the production.

The theater at the HB Studio was a long, narrow room with a cement floor. Ninety-nine seats are arranged on risers at one end, and the stage is at the other end. It was listed as an Off-Off-Broadway house, and under its arrangement with Actors Equity, productions were limited to only ten performances—two weekends and the week in between. Nobody got paid—neither actors nor directors nor playwrights—and critics were not invited.

Courtship opened on July 5, 1978, and if any date could be cited to represent the start of Foote's second career, it would probably be that one. As it happened, New York was in the middle of a torrid heat wave, and the little HB theater had no air-conditioning. Somehow, however, actors and audience both survived, and the production played to capacity houses throughout its brief run. Audiences were so enthusiastic that Berghof immediately asked Foote to direct both of the other plays he had sent him, one in each of the next two seasons.

This was very gratifying to Foote. He was excited to be back working in the theater. In fact, he was enjoying just being back in New York. The American theater and cinema had changed since he left it a decade earlier for his exile in the New Hampshire woods. The writers who had cut their teeth on the minimalist experimental plays that had been the mainstay of the late sixties and early seventies had matured and were writing more serious drama. New plays now almost never opened on Broadway. The new voices in theater got their tryouts in Off-Off-Broadway houses, or in theaters in Chicago, Seattle, La Jolla, or Houston. In film, independent film companies had sprung up across the country, shooting movies in the most unlikely places rather than on Hollywood back lots.

When Foote had decamped from New York years earlier, the general refrain had been a sort of dirge bemoaning the death of the theater. Suddenly there was a revival of interest in the theater. Now everyone was talking about this or that new writer—people like Sam Shepard, John Guare, David Mamet, and others, all of whom were writing, some even producing their own plays, which were performed in coffeehouses, bars, storefronts, basements, converted garages, even living rooms.

As satisfying as it was for Foote to have a successful play on the boards, the fact that he was not making any money out of it meant that finances once again became a major consideration. In order to be able to afford to continue working on the plays in *The Orphans' Home Cycle*, Foote would have to find a way to earn some money.

Lucy Kroll suggested he write a screenplay. At first he was dismissive of the idea, explaining to her he was so excited about his own plays that he didn't want to do another adaptation. Kroll said she meant an original screenplay. She told him that if he came up with an idea for a movie, she felt sure she could get him an advance from a Hollywood studio.

Foote had always liked to have words on paper to show a prospective producer, and the idea of just verbally describing a story had never appealed to him. The only time he had "pitched" a story was when he told Fred Coe about his idea for *The Trip to Bountiful*. However, he needed money, so he began to think about an idea for a screenplay that he could sell to a Hollywood studio executive.

Once again, it was family who provided an inspiration, though this time it was from an unusual branch of the family tree. Since he had been in closer contact with John Speed after the death of his parents, Foote and his brother had become more acquainted with each other's family.

Foote's nephew Tom—named by John Speed for his and Foote's brother who had died in World War II—had inherited his dad's love of country and western music. In fact, Tommie had started playing drums while a student at Texas A&M and was a member of a quartet that played gigs around Houston at any bar that would have them. Foote had just received a letter from his brother in which John Speed mentioned that Tom's quartet had just appeared at a honky-tonk in Houston for which Tom had been paid ten dollars for the night's work, and that they had another three-night engagement coming up for which he would earn twenty-five dollars. His nephew's struggles to break into country music reminded Foote of what he had gone through trying to begin an acting career. He decided to write a screenplay about a group of four young men trying to get a country band started.

Kroll was as good as her word and got Foote an appointment with Dave Putnam, a producer at Twentieth Century Fox. Alice (Boatie) Boatwright, who had known Foote since she worked on the movie of *Mockingbird* (she had conducted the talent search that found Mary Badham to play Scout), had put Kroll in touch with Putnam, who knew and admired Foote's work. Foote flew to California to "take the meeting," as they said in Hollywood.

When Foote went into Putnam's office, however, he was nervous. It was almost like his first audition for a Broadway play. He fumbled for words and spoke so softly that the producer had to ask him to repeat himself a couple of times. The pitch must have made sense, however, because Putnam, to Foote's genuine surprise, called Kroll afterward and asked her to come to Los Angeles the following week and draw up contracts. He wanted to produce the film.

In their meeting, Putnam had offered one suggestion for Foote to consider in writing the screenplay. The producer said he thought there should be an older man in the picture, someone the struggling young singers look up to, a character to anchor the story.

On the way home, Foote began to think about the advice. Another factor entered Foote's thinking. America was still trying to come to grips with the aftershocks of the Vietnam War. Families had been torn apart over America's involvement in the war, and young men who had fought in the conflict faced open hostility from many Americans. Veterans were often blackballed from jobs if they had served in the military in Vietnam, and the guilt of the survivor was a widespread feeling in both those who had opposed the war and those who had fought in it.

As soon as he returned, Foote began work on the screenplay. The story that emerged was about a washed-up, alcoholic country singer who is thrown together with a young Vietnam War widow who is trying to make ends meet and raise her young son by running a motel and gas station in Texas. The singer, Mac Sledge, is visited by a group of boys who are trying to start a country band. Foote called his story *Tender Mercies.*

When Kroll flew to Los Angeles to work out contract details, she happened to pick up a copy of *Hollywood Reporter* at the airport. To her surprise and consternation, the lead item in the trade newspaper was that Dave Putnam, the producer with whom she was to meet and draw up contracts for the movie, had been fired by Fox. The studio was no longer interested in green-lighting the movie.

By this time, however, Foote was full of the story and immersed in writing the screenplay, so he tightened his belt and continued to work on it. When he finished it, a chance conversation with Barbara Hallie convinced Foote of the actor he wanted to play the lead. When he told his daughter the rough outlines of the plot, she mentioned by way of passing, "You know Bob Duvall can sing."

Foote immediately showed the screenplay to Duvall, and the actor was eager to do it. Since the studio was no longer interested, Foote and Duvall agreed to try to produce it themselves. First, they had to find financial backers.

During this time, Foote and Lillian decided to move back to New York permanently. Daisy had graduated from high school the previous spring and spent the summer with Barbara Hallie in California. She was returning to begin classes at Dickinson College in Carlisle, Pennsylvania, that fall. Suddenly, the New Hampshire house had become too large for just Foote and Lillian. The basketball court was silent and the horse barn was empty. When Lillian accompanied Foote to New York as he prepared for the production of *1918*, the second of the three plays from the cycle that would be staged at the HB Studio theater, they became full-time New Yorkers once again.

At the time Foote began directing *1918* at HB, Duvall was busy working on a film called *Angelo, My Love*. Neither writer nor actor had much time to make the rounds asking for money for *Tender Mercies*.

The HB production of *1918* had much of the same cast as the production of *Courtship* the previous season. Richard Cottrell again played Horace, Barbara Hallie was again Elizabeth, and James Broderick reprised his role as Mr. Vaughn, Elizabeth's father. One new addition to the cast was a bright young actor named Devon Abner, who had been studying at HB Studio, in the part of Brother, Elizabeth's profligate sibling.

One night after a rehearsal Abner asked Barbara Hallie to dinner, and it was during the run of *1918* that they started dating secretly. Barbara Hallie insisted on keeping the relationship from her parents, much as her grandparents had done when they first started walking out together. There was no rational reason for her reticence. Abner was a few years younger than Barbara Hallie, and for some reason she thought her parents would object if they knew she was quietly seeing the young actor playing the part of Brother.

When the run of the play ended, Abner returned to California, and Barbara Hallie went her way.

Once again, the actors all worked without pay for an abbreviated run of ten performances. Once again, it played to sold-out houses. One of the people who came to see the play was a documentary filmmaker named Philip Hobel, who was looking to expand his horizons into feature films. Hobel was so taken with the play that he went backstage after the performance and told Foote he wanted to make a movie out of *1918*. Foote agreed to meet with him to discuss it.

At the meeting, however, Foote told Hobel that while he was flattered by his interest, he was too involved in trying to get *Tender Mercies* before the camera to even think about turning *1918* into a movie. Hobel asked if he could see the screenplay for Foote's other project.

Hobel read *Tender Mercies* and immediately said he would like to help Foote get it produced. Hobel had an office and a secretary and a lot of experience raising money for film projects. He also had a lot of enthusiasm for the screenplay and an inexhaustible supply of optimism.

The cameras, however, didn't roll for nearly three years. Hobel went from studio to studio, but each one rejected the project. Money wasn't the only obstacle facing Foote, Duvall, and Hobel. Finding a director for the movie proved nearly as daunting. The script was sent to several leading directors—among them Arthur Penn, Dan Petrie, Delbert Mann, even Robert Mulligan, who had directed *Mockingbird* and was a great Foote fan and a friend—and one after another turned it down. With each rejection, Foote grew more despondent. He was especially hurt by Mulligan's refusal. Foote had great faith in the screenplay, but he had all but given up that it would ever be made. His past experiences with Hollywood studios had not given him much confidence. Hobel, however, kept assuring Foote that the movie would ultimately get produced.

Through all the uncertainty and anxiety over the movie, Foote continued his climb back into the theater. *Valentine's Day*, the third of the cycle of plays he had sent to Berghof, was staged at HB Studio in 1980, a year after the *1918* production. This time there were some changes in the cast, although Barbara Hallie again reprised the part of Elizabeth and James Broderick continued as her father, Mr. Vaughn. Granger Hines took over the role of Horace Robedaux and Matthew Broderick, James's son, became the new Brother, giving a father-and-son acting team the chance to play father and son.

In addition to *Valentine's Day*, Berghof also opened his stage that season to a new full-length play by Foote called *In a Coffin in Egypt*, a two-hander starring Sandy Dennis and Bonita Griffin, and a one-act called *Arrival and Departure*.

Foote was writing in all his spare time, and the following year saw two of his plays staged at Peggy Feury's Loft Studio in Los Angeles. The first was *The Man Who Climbed Pecan Trees*, which was based on the true story of a man who used to go to the Wharton courthouse square on Saturday nights and climb the huge pecan tree on its lawn, to the general amusement of townsfolk who came downtown just to see him. The second was *Blind Date*, which was directed by Feury. Back in New York, two more plays went on the boards. *The Roads to Home*, starring Barbara Hallie, was produced by the Manhattan Punch Line Theater, and *The Old Friends* was staged at HB Studio.

While all the theater work was keeping Foote busy, the status of *Tender Mercies* remained in limbo. Every door Hobel knocked on seemed to be locked, and every turn he made seemed to lead to a dead end.

Even Hobel's unflagging optimism was beginning to wear thin. Then one day Foote received a call out of the blue from John Cohn, a producer at EMI. He said he had been flipping through a stack of screenplays from the slush pile and saw the name Horton Foote on one of them. Cohn had known Foote's work from years back, and he pulled *Tender Mercies* from the stack and started reading it. He told Foote EMI would finance the project.

Even with a committed checkbook, the movie still had a long way to go before it reached the cameras. For one thing, there was still the question of finding a suitable director. Within the space of a few days, Hobel, Duvall, and Cohn all called Foote and asked him to go see a movie called *Breaker Morant*, which had been directed by

Bruce Beresford, an Australian. They wanted Foote's permission to send Beresford the screenplay of *Tender Mercies*.

Foote saw the movie and liked it, but had doubts about whether an Australian would understand either Texas or the country music culture. After reading the script, Beresford cabled back that he loved it and wanted to meet the author. If they got along, he said, he wanted to do it.

Beresford flew to New York from Australia, and he and Foote hit it off. It is an interesting footnote that in the scores of productions Foote was involved in throughout his career, whether for stage or film, almost everyone he ever worked with liked Foote instinctively. He was always friendly and courteous and open to any suggestions, although he could be adamant on any point that he felt compromised the artistic integrity of a project.

After meeting in New York, Foote and Beresford flew down to Dallas together and spent three days just driving around the North Texas countryside, stopping in small towns, eating in local diners, and chatting with townspeople. Everywhere they went, Beresford would exclaim, "It's just like Australia."

They returned to New York and began preproduction chores. Although the screenplay was set in Texas, Hobel wanted to shoot the film somewhere in the Deep South—Georgia, Louisiana, possibly even Florida. Money was his main consideration, since production costs and hiring technical crews would be cheaper there than in Texas. But in one of those instances where Foote was adamant, he insisted that it had to be shot in Texas. Beresford and Duvall, who was an integral part of the planning for the film and would be listed, along with Foote, as a coproducer in the credits, backed Foote, and Hobel finally agreed.

Beresford and Foote, in consultation with Duvall, agreed on the actors for the other major roles and most were filled in New York. Betty Buckley was cast as Dixie, the country and western star from whom Mac is divorced, and Ellen Barkin as their grown daughter. Duvall especially wanted Wilford Brimley in the movie, and he was cast as Dixie's agent. They then flew back to Dallas to set up shop, hire cameramen and technicians, and complete the casting. Tess Harper, who played Rosa Lee, the young widow with whom Mac Sledge, Duvall's character, finds redemption, and Allen Hubbard, who played her son, were cast in Dallas.

If Dallas became the stand-in for a Hollywood studio for making *Tender Mercies*, then the town of Waxahachie was its back lot. Located about thirty miles south of Dallas, Waxahachie is one of those dusty little county seats that thrived during the 1920s and '30s, when cotton was king in Texas. During its heyday, there were fifty cotton gins working in the area, and not even the Great Depression made a dint in its affluence. By the 1980s there was only one cotton gin left, and the last time it was used was as a set in a movie—Robert Benton's *Places in the Heart*.

As a result of its prosperity during the cotton era, however, the town was filled with beautiful old houses with wide front porches, which, in the wisdom of the town fathers, were not torn down in the 1960s and '70s for parking lots or fast-food eateries. The town also boasted a huge granite county courthouse and an old cemetery full of live oak trees that has since become one of the most photographed graveyards in America.

Waxahachie was first used as a movie set for Benton's *Bonnie and Clyde*, and when Foote and Duvall showed up to scout locations for *Tender Mercies*, Foote fell in love with the town. He would return to shoot three more films there over the next few years. Beresford, however, did not use any of the town's museum homes for *Tender Mercies*, and other scenes were shot in nearby Palmer, Texas.

Foote rented a house in Waxahachie for him and Lillian to stay in for the duration of the filming. Since all the children had flown the nest, it was the first time in his career that he would have Lillian with him for the duration while he worked on a movie. The agonizing letters home over being separated from his family were a thing of the past.

Much of the film was shot outdoors, on the flat landscape of northeast Texas. Rather than try to find a suitable location, they decided to build from scratch the gas station and motel that Tess

Harper's character runs on an open stretch of land by the side of the highway. The set was so realistic that cars frequently pulled into it with their drivers wanting to fill up their tanks.

If Foote especially wanted Duvall to play Mac Sledge, the actor responded by embracing it as an alter-ego. Duvall was always a perfectionist, and in preparing for the role he wanted to get his character's accent just right. Even before shooting began, Duvall drove around northeast Texas, listening to farmers and ranchers talk in diners. When he heard the accent he wanted to use as Sledge, he sent a tape recorder and some of the scenes from the screenplay and asked the man to read some lines into the recorder. The farmer sent the tape back to Duvall, and while Duvall did not exactly copy the accent, he used the tapes to develop Sledge's voice.

There were frictions on the set almost from day one of shooting, with Duvall and Beresford often at odds on how scenes should be set up. Beresford worked out storyboards for the scenes, but Duvall felt that inhibited how he would play his character and tended to work by instinct. Beresford also kept trying to speed up the tempo of the film, while Duvall and Foote both knew that things didn't move that fast in Texas. And arguments arose over the pauses in some scenes.

More disputes arose over Duvall's objections to close-ups, which Beresford knew the studio heads wanted. In one scene, for example, after Mac has a tense reunion with his daughter, in which she recalls him singing her "a song about a dove" when she was a girl, Duvall quietly sings to himself a chorus of Bob Ferguson's classic "On the Wings of a Dove" while staring out a window, his back to the camera. The shot, which was Duvall's inspiration, brilliantly increases Mac's sense of isolation. When the studio executives saw it, they wanted it reshot as a close-up with Mac's face to the camera. This time, however, Duvall and Beresford agreed and the original was kept.

Brimley also kept tension high on the set. Once, when Beresford, who was always urging his cast to move the action and dialogue more rapidly, told the actors to "pick up the pace," Brimley shot back, "I didn't know we'd dropped it."

The differences between star and director became so strained that at one point, Beresford left the set and was about to quit the movie altogether. Their feuding reached the breaking point as Beresford was about to shoot a scene between Harper and Barkin. Beresford left the set to take a telephone call from Duvall. Shouting ensued and Beresford said, "If you want to direct this, then go ahead," and stalked off the set.

Hobel raced to Foote and pleaded with him to try to smooth things over. Foote and Duvall were old and close friends, and Foote managed to calm the actor down. He then tried to placate Beresford. In the end, an uneasy truce was somehow arranged, though there were more eruptions before the shooting was completed. There were times when Foote thought he might leave the set himself, but Lillian's presence helped him keep his own temper. Foote himself, for example, had been uncomfortable with the fast pace Beresford took with the opening of the movie. But by the time the final print was in the can, everybody was happy with the film.

The rest of the cast got along well, and, much as Gregory Peck had done with Mary Badham on *To Kill a Mockingbird,* Duvall assumed a sort of surrogate father role with Allen Hubbard, a nine-year-old local boy who played Sonny and whose own father had recently died. Duvall, a real country music enthusiast who sang all of his character's songs himself and even wrote two songs for the movie, taught Hubbard to play the guitar between scenes, and the boy often visited with Duvall in his trailer.

Duvall even kept up the relationship after the movie was finished, and when Hubbard celebrated his tenth birthday a month after shooting was completed, Duvall paid him a surprise visit and gave him a guitar as a birthday present. It changed Hubbard's life. He took his music seriously and later became a guitar teacher.

If cast and crew were pleased with the film, however, they were about the only ones associated with it who were. Universal had a deal with EMI to distribute the movie in theaters. Once again, however, studio executives were unhappy, and getting final distribution for *Tender Mercies* proved to be almost as difficult as finding a producer to back it and a director to direct it had been. Universal opened the movie in only three theaters in three cities—New York,

Los Angeles, and Chicago—and that was where it played throughout its run.

The complaints were familiar ones to Foote. "It's too long." "It's too slow." "Nothing happens." "Where's the action?" Universal was the same studio that had complained about *To Kill a Mockingbird* and balked over its release. This time, however, there was no Gregory Peck to throw his star-power weight around to make sure the movie got red-carpet treatment and opened in first-run houses. In fact, Universal first announced that they would not open the movie in the United States at all and planned to release it only in Europe, and even that was only to fulfill its contract obligations with EMI.

At one point, a marketing executive at Universal tried to explain the studio view to Foote. "We know how to sell *The Best Little Whorehouse in Texas*," he said. "But how do you market *Tender Mercies*?"

For reasons Foote never learned, Hobel ultimately persuaded the studio brass at Universal to change their minds, and when the movie finally opened it received an avalanche of rave reviews in the three cities it played. Even with all the good notices, the executives at Universal dismissed the movie and spent little on its promotion.

Tender Mercies is a story about redemption, and Mac Sledge became one of Foote's own favorite characters. He once explained, "I think the world of Mac Sledge. Mac is a very hurt, damaged man and silence is his weapon."

Sledge, a onetime country star who lost his wife and career because of drink, finds his way back to life through the love of Rosa Lee and Sonny, and through his connection to the young musicians who come to him for advice about starting a band. Redemption, however, always comes at a price. For Sledge, it comes with the death of his grown daughter in a car accident.

Sledge cannot fathom or understand why he has been delivered at the cost of so much pain and suffering to others. In a heart-wrenching scene toward the end, he tries to explain his doubts to Rosa Lee. Holding a hoe with which he has been weeding the garden, and with the great infinity of a Texas sky behind him, Mac delivers what is nothing less than a lamentation for his loss of faith in the American promise of happiness:

I was almost killed once in a car accident. I was drunk and I ran off the side of the road and I turned over four times. They took me out of that car for dead, but I lived. And I prayed last night to know why I lived and she died, but I got no answer to my prayers. I still don't know why she died and I lived. I don't know the answer to nothing. Not a blessed thing. I don't know why I wandered out to this part of Texas drunk and you took me in and pitied me and helped me to straighten out and married me. Why, why did this happen? Is there a reason that happened? And Sonny's father died in the war. My daughter killed in an automobile accident. Why? You see, I don't trust happiness. I never did, I never will.

That scene was also shot full in wide angle, with Mac and Rosa Lee standing apart in the little patch of garden she had planted next to her gas station and motel. When the studio heads back in Hollywood saw it, they demanded to see the close-ups. Beresford, who again agreed with Duvall on this camera angle, explained there weren't any. The scene was shot the way both he and Duvall wanted it.

By the time the Academy Award nominations were announced, *Tender Mercies* had already been pulled from distribution in theaters. To the surprise of many except critics, audiences, and those involved in making it, *Tender Mercies* received five nominations, a remarkable achievement for a film that was shown in only three cities several months earlier. They included nominations for Best Picture, Best Actor, Best Director, Best Original Screenplay, and Best Original Song. In the end, it won two Oscars—to Duvall for Best Actor and to Foote for Best Original Screenplay.

Unlike *Mockingbird,* the Oscars did nothing to change the minds of the Universal studio executives. They had already sold the cable TV rights to the movie even before the Academy Awards were announced, which meant the film would not gain any further theater distribution, even if it won any Oscars. None of the studio heads ever expressed any regret to Foote, the stars, or anyone else involved in getting it made over their lack of faith in the film, not when it won critical acclaim and not when it won its Academy Awards.

Despite all the anxieties that accompanied the making of *Tender Mercies*, the movie proved to be a great crash course in filmmaking for Foote. It was the first movie he had ever worked on in which he was both writer and producer, and it was a great learning time for him.

Foote loved being on the set every day, then watching the dailies every night. He learned about budgets and shooting schedules. He enjoyed working with editors and the technical side of filming. In short, he discovered he enjoyed just about every aspect of making a movie except for raising money and haggling over contracts.

Independent films were slowly coming into their own in the 1980s. The days of studio dominance, when they decided which movies were made and how, was gradually disappearing. Foote and Lillian sat down and had a long talk about the prospect of making movies on their own outside the studio system. They decided it was worth a try.

CHAPTER 12

Waxahachie:
Family Reunion

THE 1980s SAW the beginnings of what might be called the Foote Revival. After years of sitting on the sidelines, Foote was back in the game. He was writing daily, working on plays and screenplays, and often had two or three projects going at the same time. Producers were again putting his work before the public.

In 1982 alone, four of Foote's plays were staged in New York and Los Angeles. A trio of one-acts under the collective title *The Roads to Home* were presented by the Manhattan Punch Line Theater in New York, comprising *A Nightingale*, *The Dearest of Friends*, and *Spring Dance*. That was followed by *The Old Friends*, again at the HB Studio, and two plays at the Loft Studio in Los Angeles, *The Man Who Climbed Pecan Trees* and *Blind Date*.

The following year, two plays from *The Orphans' Home Cycle* were staged—*Cousins* was produced in Los Angeles, and the Actors Theatre of Louisville did a revival of *Courtship*.

One small project gave him a big break. In 1985, the Ensemble Studio Theatre in New York, a nonprofit, Off-Off-Broadway venue that each year presented a festival of new one-acts, included a play by Foote called *The Road to the Graveyard* in its season's lineup. Roberta Maxwell agreed to star in it, and Frank Rich, the chief drama critic for the *New York Times*, strayed from his usual Broadway beat to see it. In his review, Rich said: "Horton Foote has been writing about a changing Texas for decades. This work may be among the finest distillations of his concerns, accomplished with a subtlety that suggests a collaboration between Faulkner and Chekhov."

Though all these stage productions and the response they were getting were gratifying, they were not bringing in much money, and Foote and Lillian began to focus their efforts on making their own movies. They had been so impressed with the technical crew in Dallas that had worked on *Tender Mercies*, they decided to make their headquarters there, and for the next few years Foote and Lillian became virtual commuters shuttling between New York and Waxahachie, Texas.

The idea at the back of Foote's mind was that they would be able to make the entire *Orphans' Home Cycle* as independent films, using local crews and Waxahachie as a setting for Harrison.

When Foote and Lillian first moved back to New York, they lived in a small apartment on Waverly Place. They had been looking for something more permanent, however, and Lillian finally found an apartment in a building on Horatio Street in the Village that she liked and that fit their needs. It had a doorman who could hold or forward their mail during the periods they were away in Texas shooting a movie. At first they decided to keep the New Hampshire house for the reasons they originally bought it, as a weekend place. But now there were fewer and fewer free weekends to spend there, and they began to consider selling it.

Their first task in getting the movies before a camera was to find a director. The lead cameraman for *Tender Mercies* was Jerry Calaway, and he suggested they take a look at the work of a local filmmaker named Ken Harrison. They flew back to Dallas and drove the thirty miles south to Waxahachie. They spent the entire day in the Brookshire Hotel watching three short films that Harrison had directed. They liked what they saw and hired him on the spot.

Foote and Lillian chose *1918* for their first movie venture, and they set about trying to get the money with which to shoot it. For the next several months, they went from one production company to another, flying between New York and Texas. At each stop, starting with Ross Milloy of Guadalupe Enterprises in Austin, Texas, they were referred to someone else, until they finally ended up back in New York talking to Lewis Allen and Peter Newman. Allen and Newman read the screenplay for *1918* and liked it very much. However, they said they would like to produce it first as a play at the Kennedy Center in Washington.

Foote was torn. He thought he would never find himself saying no to producers wanting to put one of his plays on the stage, especially one as prominent as the Kennedy Center. But he did. He told Allen and Newman that it had already been done as a play. What he now wanted was to make a movie of it.

In the end, Milloy, Allen, and Newman agreed to arrange the financing for the movie and joined Foote and Lillian as coproducers. Throughout all the discussions for obtaining financing, Foote had spent time in Waxahachie with Harrison scouting locations, deciding which of the old houses they wanted to use for exterior shots, and working out shooting schedules.

If the town of Waxahachie was a perfect walk-on set for period pictures, one of its leading citizens was a perfect stage manager. On an early trip there, Foote made the acquaintance of L. T. Felty, the vice president of the Waxahachie Bank & Trust, and the man who almost single-handedly made the town a backdrop for nearly a dozen movies.

Felty, who always introduced himself simply as T. Felty, was a former high school principal, science teacher, and football coach who could have stepped out of one of Foote's plays. A jovial, friendly man, he was also someone who got things done. Once, during the filming of a movie called *Square Dance*, the director wanted to shoot a crowd scene the following morning. He called Felty that night about suppertime and said he needed eight hundred extras on the set at first light the following morning. Felty got on the phone to everyone he knew, and some he didn't, and had eight hundred people on the set the next day. If a director wanted a train in a shot, Felty had a friend at the Texas Railroad Commission who could tell him the exact time the next one would pass through town. He knew every vacant house and Model T car in town, and which ones could be used for filming exteriors or interiors.

Felty even acted as an extra in several of the movies made in the town, and he liked to tell how he had lain in a ditch for three hours playing a duck hunter while David Byrne shot take after take after take for his movie *True Stories*. Foote ended up using Felty as a flag waver in the parade scene in *1918*. (Another bond that united Foote, Lillian, and Felty was that they shared a love for chili. Felty actually boasted the official title of Chili Adviser to the Governor of Texas.)

Foote and Lillian had hoped to start filming *1918* that fall and had rented rehearsal space in New York to work on the script before the cast moved to Texas for the filming. The main parts for the movie had been cast: Barbara Hallie would be Elizabeth; William Converse-Roberts was signed to play Horace; and Matthew Broderick would reprise the role of Brother, which he had played in the HB stage production of *Valentine's Day*.

On the first day of rehearsals in New York, Foote got a call from Newman asking him to come to his office immediately. Foote had a sinking feeling as he took a taxi uptown, and when he was ushered into Newman's office he knew from the look on his face that the news was not good. Newman asked Foote if he would be willing to postpone the filming of *1918* until the spring and gave him a list of reasons, most of which involved money.

Foote went back downtown and had to tell the actors that the filming was being delayed by six months. For anyone associated with making movies, the announcement sounded more like a death knell for the entire project. None of the actors thought the movie would ever be made.

Foote and Lillian had a hard decision to make. They had taken out a lease on a house in Waxahachie, and they now had to decide whether to break it and return to New York or to keep the house in Texas in the hopes the movie would indeed get under way the following spring. In an act of supreme faith, they decided to stay on in Waxahachie and continue work on the film during the intervening time.

As it turned out, the delay was a blessing. The winter of 1983–84 in North Texas was one of the worst on record. Snow and ice covered the ground and stayed for weeks. Since much of the story takes place and was to be shot outdoors, the filming would have been halted several times and they would have gone way over budget.

Through the winter, Foote and Lillian worked alone in New York and Texas. Their children had all scattered and were facing problems of their own.

Barbara Hallie was in a new relationship that was proving unsatisfactory, and she was looking forward to working on the movie in Texas as a possible escape route. Once, when she was at her parents' apartment in New York, she saw a letter on her dad's desk with a California return address and the name Devon Abner above it. She was surprised to see his name and nearly picked up the phone and called him, but resisted. Still, she wondered why Abner was writing her father from California.

For his part, Horton Jr. had been somewhat at loose ends since leaving the army, trying one thing and then another. He had first settled in Boston, but after breaking up with a girl about whom he had been serious, he drove to Los Angeles and got a job in an exclusive men's clothing store on Rodeo Drive, where many movie stars shopped. He first thought he would make a career of it. After all, his grandfather had owned a haberdashery in Wharton. But after a year and a half, he tired of it and decided he wanted to act.

He went to see Bill Traylor, who with his wife, Peggy Feury, ran the acting studio at which Barbara Hallie had studied, and told him he wanted to be an actor. Traylor asked him what kind of roles he thought he could play. Horton Jr. thought a moment and said, "Al Pacino." Traylor laughed out loud, and Horton Jr. left in a huff. Traylor eventually took him on, however, and for several months he took acting lessons in Los Angeles. He later studied with Herbert Berghof at the HB Studio and appeared in several plays, including two by his father—*The Man Who Climbed Pecan Trees* at the Loft Studio in Los Angeles, and *The Old Friends* in New York.

It was during rehearsals in California for *The Man Who Climbed Pecan Trees* that Horton Jr. nearly killed himself. There was a large crane on a construction site near the theater, and one night after a few drinks, he decided to climb it, like the title character of the play did with pecan trees. He reached the farthest end of the giant crane, but then couldn't get down and nearly fell before he could be rescued.

At the time Foote and Lillian were preparing for *1918*, Horton Jr. was again between engagements, as hopeful actors put it, and was trying to find a direction in his life. His parents asked him if he would like to join them in Texas once the filming started.

But it was Daisy who was giving her parents the most concern. Daisy's years at Dickinson College had been a roller-coaster ride. She entered her freshman year as a serious young woman who was contemptuous of the swirl of social life that occupied so much of her classmates' time. She was writing seriously and reading voraciously and couldn't understand why the other girls only wanted to make the rounds of fraternity parties when they could stay at home and read Joyce or Chinese poetry. She even tried going to a frat party, but when she saw the president of the student body wearing a grass skirt and serving drinks, she was put off.

She tried dating—there was a Chris, a John, and a Jay whom she wrote home about—but she would soon drop each one when she realized all they wanted to do was drink beer and party, among other things. By the spring of her sophomore year, however, she adopted an if-you-can't-beat-them-join-them attitude. She pledged the Delta Nu sorority and went with some of her girlfriends to Florida for spring break. There she met a new boyfriend who was on the lacrosse team and who, she wrote her parents, "is really nice." He, too, however, was soon on the growing list of ex-boyfriends.

By her junior year, Daisy had become such a party girl that, along with some classmates, she decided to stay at school and hang out when the nuclear accident at nearby Three Mile Island was forcing thousands to evacuate their homes. Foote was so concerned that he telephoned Walter Cronkite, the anchor of CBS News and the father of Barbara Hallie's former roommate, to ask just how serious the threat of a nuclear meltdown was. Advised there was a real possibility of a disaster that could devastate much of Pennsylvania, Foote finally laid down the law with his daughter. He called Daisy and in no uncertain terms told her, "Young lady, you get in a car and get home this very day." She retreated as far as New Jersey.

But it was when she informed her parents in her senior year that she was seriously dating one of her professors at the college, a medievalist named Tom Reed, that Foote and Lillian genuinely became alarmed. When she told her mother—she was afraid to tell her father first—that she and Tom were engaged and would get married as soon as she graduated, her mother burst into tears on the phone. They were not tears of joy.

There were problems in the marriage from the outset, not least among them Daisy's determination to be a writer. She had been getting rejection letter after rejection letter for stories she had sent out, but very much her father's daughter, she had not let them deter her. Foote always encouraged her in her writing, believing she had real talent. When she wrote her first play, Daisy sent it to her father and he had been genuinely impressed. He suggested she take a course from Herbert Berghof, who later became a sort of mentor, and her first play, *The Villa Capri*, based on her experiences working in an Italian restaurant in New Hampshire, was produced at HB Studio. She felt her husband, unlike her father, offered little support or encouragement.

In the spring of 1984, Daisy decided to end her three-year marriage, and Foote and Lillian invited her to come to Texas to work on the movie. However, her husband had a sabbatical to Oxford University for six months, and he persuaded Daisy to accompany him to give the marriage one last chance. In postcards and letters from Wales and Oxford, Daisy wrote her parents that both she and her husband had come to terms with the marriage breakup. "Tom and I were so angry about everything, and now we have calmed down and both are much happier" about the divorce, she wrote. She also reported that she had finished a new story, "my best yet," that she was working on a play, and that she was eager to come to Texas to work on the movie. "Count me in!"

By the time the cameras finally rolled on Foote and Lillian's first venture as independent producers, the set of *1918* was almost like a family reunion. Only Walter, whose dreams of becoming a professional basketball player had been scuttled by a knee injury and who was now in law school, was absent.

1918 concerns the conflicting loyalties of nation versus family during the year of the title. America is entering World War I and much of the nation is also suffering from a deadly influenza epidemic. Patriotic fervor is sweeping Harrison, Texas, along with most of the country, and Horace is being pressured by his father-in-law, Mr. Vaughn, to enlist in the American Expeditionary Force and go fight the Germans. But Elizabeth has just given birth to their first child, and Horace does not want to leave his wife and daughter and join the army.

When the film was released later that year, it had mostly good reviews, though some critics felt it would be seen to better advantage on the small screen rather than in a movie theater. The box office receipts were respectable, if not staggering, for a movie shot on a modest budget. But if Foote was in any way dejected by its reception, he could take comfort in a parallel project that had arrived out of the blue during the months he had been waiting to get *1918* in front of the cameras.

It was during that winter-long delay on *1918* that Foote had a call from Peter Masterson, a theater director who was also a distant cousin of Foote's. Masterson had been wanting to try his hand at directing a feature film, and he told Foote he wanted to make a movie of *The Trip to Bountiful.*

Over the years, Foote had been approached several times about doing *Bountiful* as a feature film, and while he thought it would transfer well to the big screen, he had always insisted that Lillian Gish play the role of Carrie Watts, since she had created it in both the television and stage versions in the 1950s. That insistence had always proved to be a stumbling block. Gish had a reputation of unreliability among Hollywood studio producers, and none wanted to take the risk of backing a movie that depended on her showing up and working to schedule.

The prospect of a movie version of *Bountiful* had not come up for many years, however, and when Masterson called with his proposal, he prefaced his appeal to Foote by pointing out that Gish was now more than ninety years old.

"Who would be your second choice for Carrie?" Masterson asked.

"Geraldine Page," Foote said without hesitation.

Masterson liked that choice and a deal was quickly reached for him to direct the film with Sterling Van Wagenen and Foote as coproducers.

With little to do on *1918* until the spring, Foote returned briefly to New York and began writing a screenplay for *Bountiful*. It did not take long, and he called Page only after he finished it, saying simply that he had something he wanted her to read. He told her he would put the script in the mail. Page, who had been a great admirer of Foote's since working on *Old Man* for television nearly twenty-five years earlier, replied that she would get on the subway and come down to get it immediately.

It was early December, and when Foote handed her the screenplay, she clutched it to her breast and said, "Thank you for my Christmas present."

"I don't know about that," Foote said. "You'd better read it first."

She called Foote back an hour later to accept.

After *1918* was completed, Foote and Lillian began work on their second independent film, which was to be *On Valentine's Day*. This time they did not have to wait for the financing, and over the course of a year, Foote was juggling work on three separate films—all in Waxahachie and nearby North Texas towns, actually shooting two of them at the same time. Foote would often drive back and forth between the sets for *On Valentine's Day* and *Bountiful* several times on the same day.

If *1918* and *On Valentine's Day* were strictly low-budget, independent films, *Bountiful* had the full backing of a major Hollywood studio. Unlike Universal had been with *Mockingbird* and *Tender Mercies*, MGM got behind the movie and promoted it strongly. In addition to Page, the cast included John Heard as Carrie's son, Ludie, and Carlin Glynn, who was married to Masterson, as Ludie's wife, Jessie Mae, and Rebecca de Mornay as Thelma, the young woman who befriends Carrie at the bus station.

When the movie was released it drew rave reviews, one calling it "perfect on just about every level." *Variety* said Page gave "the performance of a lifetime," and the film earned two Academy Award nominations—including another one for Foote, his third for Best Screenplay, and one for Page, who won the Oscar for Best Actress.

With the modest success of *1918* and the enormous triumph of *Bountiful*, Foote and Lillian had high hopes for *On Valentine's Day*, which chronologically immediately precedes *1918* in the nine-play cycle and tells the story of Horace and Elizabeth's first Christmas together after their elopement the preceding February 14. At the time the movie takes place, Elizabeth is pregnant and the main thread of the film concerns her reconciliation with her parents, who had not spoken to her since she married Horace in the face of her father's opposition.

There is a subplot involving Horace's uncle, George Tyler. George is suffering from some form of dementia, and his behavior is the cause of growing concern to family and friends. At one point, he runs off to the river with a pistol, clearly crazed, shooting wildly. On another occasion he walks around the town square, handing out envelopes full of hundred-dollar bills to the town's black residents as a way of personal atonement for slavery. The character, brilliantly and poignantly acted by Steven Hill, mirrors the declining mental faculties of Foote's father.

Like the other plays in the cycle, Foote's three profligate uncles are collapsed into the one role of Brother, whose drinking and gambling are the bane of his father's and mother's existence. Matthew Broderick repeated that role, and his wonderful deadpan performance provided the comic element in both *1918* and *On Valentine's Day*.

The year working on those three films in Waxahachie was one of the happiest of Foote's life. He loved making movies, but his greatest joy came in having Lillian and three of his children with him daily. Barbara Hallie was the star of both movies, and with Mom and Dad as producers, Horton Jr. and Daisy both found work on and off the set, in front of and behind the camera.

When Horton Jr. arrived in Waxahachie at the start of *1918*, Foote introduced him to an assistant director, who offered him the job of second assistant director. Horton Jr. took it with visions of at least being able to direct some of the crowd scenes. The job, however, turned out to consist mostly of guarding the refreshment table for cast and crew and keeping Dixie cups filled with Kool-Aid. He promptly quit and was about to return to Los Angeles when Foote intervened and got him a job on the technical crew, operating a boom.

Later, Horton Jr. did get some directing work on a crowd scene, working with Felty to organize the extras for a big parade that takes place in the movie, and in the credits he was listed as "casting assistant." Eventually, he appeared as an actor in one scene playing Brother's ne'er-do-well friend and gambling partner, Jesse.

By the time *On Valentine's Day* was shot, Horton Jr. was a long way from either the Kool-Aid table or a boom mike. He was cast as Steve Tyler, Horace's cousin and the son of George Tyler. It was a full supporting role, and Horton Jr. was impressive in it.

Foote put Daisy to work with the costume department on the two movies, and she is listed in the credits of *1918* as "production assistant" and in *On Valentine's Day* as "wardrobe assistant." Being a wardrobe assistant consisted mostly of washing the actors' dirty laundry every day. But Daisy was happy just to be away from the trauma of her divorce and in the company of her parents and big sister and brother.

There were other compensations for Daisy, as well. When she first showed up in Waxahachie, Daisy renewed an old acquaintance-ship with Matthew Broderick. She had known the actor from the time his father, James Broderick, appeared in a couple of her father's plays. When they were thrown together on a movie set in a small town in Texas, the friendship blossomed into romance, an affair that lasted for two years, and then took another three years to end.

No sooner had they wrapped *On Valentine's Day* than Foote and Lillian began planning for a third movie, *Courtship*, which again goes back in time and precedes the other two plays in the cycle, recounting Horace's pursuit of Elizabeth and her decision to marry despite the opposition of her parents.

These were the same three plays from the cycle that Foote had chosen to direct for the stage at HB Studio, and they were the three he first wanted to get in front of a camera. Although they had brought in *1918* and *On Valentine's Day* at budget, under $1 million each, financing for the third movie proved elusive, and it appeared that *Courtship* would not get made until Lindsay Law, the producer for the *American Playhouse* series on PBS, came to the rescue with the necessary money. Law wanted to show all three movies on the PBS series.

For *Courtship*, however, Foote and Lillian insisted on some changes in the production team. A problem had come up at the end of filming *On Valentine's Day*. Although Ken Harrison is listed as director on both *1918* and *On Valentine's Day*, it was Foote who had rehearsed the actors in the scenes back in New York and who essentially directed the performances. Harrison's main contributions had been to set up the scenes to be shot once they were on location. Frictions arose during the second film when Harrison, backed by one of the producers, sought to exert control over the final cut.

The situation came to a head when Harrison, with the support of Calvin Scaggs, who was listed along with Lillian as a producer on the film, asked Barbara Hallie to record some new material for the movie as a voice-over. When she saw it, Barbara Hallie realized it was not from her father's screenplay, and she became alarmed. She called Peter Newman of Guadalupe Productions in New York, and he told her not to record the voice-over. It emerged that Harrison and Scaggs wanted to cut some of the scenes from the movie and use the voice-over from Hallie as a bridge to cover what they wanted to delete. The situation was resolved and the movie remained intact as Foote wanted it, but it was the last time he would work with Harrison or Scaggs.

For *Courtship*, Howard Cummings was signed to direct, and the filming was moved from Waxahachie, Texas, to Brookhaven, Mississippi. One member of the creative team was retained, however. Van Broughton Ramsey was a native of Wharton and had known the Foote family all his life. He also had a keen eye for wardrobe detail and knew what the townsfolk of Wharton wore. Foote kept Ramsey as costume designer for all three films.

In addition, another key character was added to *Courtship*— Elizabeth's sister, Laura—and Amanda Plummer was signed to play the role. The rest of the cast, however, remained the same, although the character of Brother is absent from *Courtship*.

Daisy and Horton Jr. also came along for the filming of *Courtship*, extending the family reunion. Horton Jr. reprised the character of Steve Tyler, although he appeared in only one small scene toward the end. And Daisy got in front of the camera for the first time, playing the cameo role of Allie, one of Elizabeth's friends.

Of the three films, *1918* got the best reviews and *On Valentine's Day* received the most attention. It was the official American entry in 1986 at the Venice Film Festival, at the Toronto Film Festival, and at the U.S. Film Festival. When Law aired them on *American Playhouse* on PBS in 1987, he divided them into a five-part miniseries and gave it the overall title of *The Story of a Marriage*.

Although they still hoped to make films of all nine plays in *The Orphans' Home Cycle*, Foote and Lillian took a break from movie production after the completion of *Courtship*. But in the fall of 1986, two plays from the cycle were staged in Off-Broadway theaters. *Lily Dale* was mounted at the Samuel Beckett Theatre on Theatre Row with Molly Ringwald, then a hot young movie star and member of what was known as the "brat pack," in the title role; and *The Widow Claire*, the afterthought that Foote had written to round off the cycle with nine plays instead of eight, was produced at Circle in the Square.

Just as a Brooks Atkinson review had given Foote a boost nearly half a century earlier, it was the continued attention of another *New York Times* critic that eventually helped bring Foote back to Broadway. Frank Rich was an exacting, demanding, and very knowledgeable critic. As demonstrated by his review of *The Road to the Graveyard* the previous year, Rich had long been familiar with Foote's work and considered him a vastly underappreciated playwright.

The first of the two plays to be staged that fall was *Lily Dale*, and Rich had serious misgivings about most of the production, which he called "generally inadequate." He found most of the acting "modest," at best, with the exception of Don Bloomfield in the role of Horace, comparing his performance to those of Robert Duvall and Geraldine Page in more well-known Foote works. Rich added, however, that the play was a "modern, psychologically subterranean drama" that in the character of Horace conveys "the spirit that ennobles Mr. Foote's characters—a blind, unshakable faith that nothing, not even death, can derail the pilgrim who must go home again."

A month later, *The Widow Claire* opened, and Rich reviewed it for the *Times*. He admired this production, directed by Michael Lindsay-Hogg, especially the "perfect" performance of Hallie in the title role and that of Matthew Broderick as Horace, a very different part than that of Brother, which he had played in the movies of *1918* and *On Valentine's Day*.

Rich began his review by repeating an old complaint about Foote's plays. "Of course, almost nothing happens in 'The Widow Claire,'" he said, then went on to refute it. "Those attuned to Mr. Foote's style, however, may find another, more moving drama percolating beneath the placid surface." Rich said the play was "the work of an artist who knows just what he wants to do and how he wants to do it."

Productions of Foote's plays began to proliferate around the country, and several collections of his plays and screenplays were published. The most important result of all this renewed attention, however, was that it spawned in Foote a period of productive creativity. He was constantly writing, on sets and off, at night or whenever he found a bit of spare time in the day. For the next few years, every season had a new Foote play. And now they all found producers wanting to stage them.

Foote himself directed *The Habitation of Dragons*, which had its premiere at the Pittsburgh Public Theater, with Hallie and Horton Jr. both acting in it. *The Land of the Astronauts* was staged at the Ensemble Studio Theatre in New York. *Dividing the Estate*, a comedy in which the avaricious relatives of an aging family matriarch hover around her, trying to convince her to part with her wealth, was presented at the McCarter Theatre in Princeton, New Jersey. *Talking Pictures* was staged in Sarasota, Florida. *Night Seasons* premiered at the American Stage Company in Teaneck, New Jersey.

Even with all the activity on the stage, Foote was still pursuing his independent film efforts. *The Widow Claire* was the next play from the cycle that Foote and Lillian targeted to go before the cameras. For once, the financing seemed to come together rather quickly. An investor with what he described as "Israeli money" told Foote he would back the project provided he could again bring it in under $1 million.

Foote returned to Waxahachie, planning to shoot the movie there. He signed contracts with the technical crews and again rented a house for him and Lillian to stay in during the filming.

As preproduction work was proceeding, however, the "Israeli money" fell through and the prospective producers pulled out. Foote and Lillian had to cancel the lease on the house in Waxahachie, and it was only out of respect for Foote that he was allowed to break his contracts with the technical unions in Texas with no penalties. But there were hard feelings involved.

Foote's previous mistrust of the big Hollywood studios had been assuaged by his experience with MGM in the making of *The Trip to Bountiful*, and the studio was eager to repeat that success by making another movie of a Foote play, with Masterson again directing.

Robert Duvall's interest in *Convicts*, the second play in *The Orphans' Home Cycle*, had never waned. The main character of Sol Gautier was a plum role, and Duvall had wanted to get it made as a film for years. It was suggested to MGM as a possible project, and the studio agreed to do it.

In many ways, *Convicts* made a better movie than a play. In opening up the play for the camera, Foote was able to take the audience to an old-time sugarcane plantation at the turn of the twentieth century and show the life of black convicts who were assigned to work the fields. Sweeping shots of the plantation, its houses, the barnlike shacks where the convicts lived, the plantation store, and the wide expanse of the cane fields gave the film a stark reality that could never be achieved on a stage.

They decided to shoot the movie in Louisiana, and Lillian joined Foote for the filming. Masterson and Foote found an old, abandoned farm not far from New Orleans, right next to the Mississippi River, that they used for location, and much of the movie was shot outdoors. The only factor they did not consider was that the Mississippi was still a vital waterway with a lot of steamship and barge traffic on it, and they frequently had to halt the filming, sometimes in the middle of a scene, for the boats to pass down the river and clear the camera shot.

The play is set less than forty years after the abolition of slavery, when many of the old plantations used black convicts to work them. As a boy, Foote had seen chain gangs at work in the fields around Wharton, mostly picking cotton. He also had heard many tales about such arrangements and the treatment the convicts had to endure.

Once again, Foote made use of details from his father's life—working on his uncle's plantation in his teens, and living with a black family of sharecroppers—as the circumstances for his young hero, Horace Robedaux, in the film. Horace's mission to earn enough money to buy a tombstone for his father's unmarked grave, also taken from Foote's father's life, becomes a character objective that is echoed in later plays in the cycle as Horace grows into manhood and courts and marries Elizabeth Vaughn.

In its unvarnished depiction of Southern country life, *Convicts* is a dark comedy that brings to mind the best of Faulkner, especially in the character of Sol Gautier, the illiterate, mean, and irascible owner of ten thousand acres of cane fields. Sol exists in a perpetual state of inebriation, his brain so softened by liquor that he can't remember the names of people he is talking to, let alone what they were talking about, from one minute to the next. He walks around with a shotgun under his arm and a pistol near at hand every waking moment and treats his own relations, especially his alcoholic niece, Asa, with the same rough contempt he does the black convicts who work his land. His minders are a black trusty named Jackson, a murderer who has been on the plantation for years; a black family retainer named Ben, who was born during slavery and whose parents are buried on its land; Ben's wife, Martha; and the thirteen-year-old Horace.

Duvall gave a brilliant performance, as always, as Sol Gautier, and the rest of the cast—including James Earl Jones as Ben, Mel Winkler as Jackson, Starletta DuPois as Martha, and especially a young

Lukas Haas as Horace—were no less inspired. Toyomichi Kurita, the director of photography, beautifully re-created a bygone world.

The action takes place on Christmas Eve 1902, on Sol's plantation on the Gulf Coast, not far from Foote's fictitious Harrison, Texas. In a riveting opening montage, a black convict is running through the swamps at night, trying to escape a posse, led by Sol on horseback, who are chasing him with bloodhounds. Young Horace, who is living with Ben and Martha, wakes and hears gunshots.

The scene dissolves to the following morning and an old buggy bouncing through a rutted road that runs through the cane fields, carrying Asa to Sol's house, past Jackson digging a grave for the dead convict. Horace spends the day following Sol around, trying to collect the $12.50 Sol owes him for the past six months of work, so he can go into Harrison for Christmas.

Sol is obsessed with his own death, which he believes to be imminent, and orders Jackson to have the convicts stop chopping cane and build him a coffin. In a darkly humorous sequence that is reminiscent of Faulkner's *As I Lay Dying*, Sol climbs into his coffin, even having the lid secured in place, to see if he will fit into it. Sol also gives instructions for his funeral, or at least a list of things he does *not* want. He doesn't want any members of his family to attend, especially his niece, Asa. He doesn't want to be buried in the family graveyard but in an unmarked grave with no tombstone. He doesn't want a preacher to preside over services, or any hymns sung or prayers said.

Just prior to starting work on adapting *Convicts* for the screen, Foote had written a teleplay of *Madame Bovary* for the BBC. In reading and rereading Flaubert's novel for the teleplay, he was reminded of the importance of small details in creating a different time and making it authentic for the audience. The details in *Convicts*—from little touches like Martha tossing feed to scrawny chickens as Asa's buggy passes her shack, to the use of songs the convicts sing while they work—are central to the dramatic effect the film achieves.

Foote had always used music to augment or enhance a mood he was striving to achieve in a particular work—country music, obviously, in *Tender Mercies*, and old hymns in *The Trip to Bountiful*. He

had also employed songs or ballads in the plays from *The Orphans'
Home Cycle* to create a certain ambiance, like "Tiger Rag" and "Lily
Dale" in the play of that name or "Waltz Me Around Again, Willie,"
which Martha Graham had once told him was her favorite song, in
The Widow Claire.

In choosing a song for *Convicts*, Foote recalled a conversation he
once had with Leadbelly. Foote had first met the great blues singer
one night in New York back in his struggling-actor days when he
had gone to hear Billie Holliday sing at a club. They began to talk
about Houston, and Leadbelly, who had served time on a prison
chain gang in Sugar Land, Texas, which is just outside Houston, told
Foote they used to sing "Rock Island Line" to pass the time. In *Convicts*, the black prisoners who work Gautier's plantation sing that
song while they are chopping sugarcane. At the end of the movie, as
Ben, Martha, Jackson, and Horace lower Sol's coffin into a simple
grave, Jackson notes that while Sol said he didn't want any hymns,
he didn't rule out other kinds of songs. In a touching final scene,
Mel Winkler sings an awkward rendition of "Golden Slippers."

But it is in a speech that Ben makes over Sol's unmarked grave
that Foote gives a poignant and memorable tribute to a man
unmourned. The words echo those of Carrie Watts, spoken when
she leaves her old home in Bountiful for the last time. Ben, played
by James Earl Jones, tells the others that Miss Asa plans to close
the plantation store and to move all the convicts who have been
working the land over to her father's farm, leaving Sol's place
untended:

> The weeds, the trees, the cane can take this land. Six months
> from now you won't be able to tell who's buried out here. Not my
> people, not the convicts, not Mr. Sol. Weeds, the trees, the cane'll
> take everything. Cane land it was called once. Cane land it'll be
> again. The house will go. The store will go. The graves will go.
> Those with tombstones and those without.

When the movie was released the following year, it received
mixed reviews from critics, many of whom seemed offended by the

realistic depiction of life on a plantation in 1902, and by the character of Sol, who treated the convicts who worked his farm the same way he had treated slaves just a few decades earlier.

If Foote was distressed by the reception *Convicts* received, he soon had another project to take his mind off it. Foote and Lillian were spending more and more time in Wharton, and at one point even contemplated moving to Texas full-time. John Speed, Foote's brother, had developed Alzheimer's, and Foote had bought out his brother's share in their parents' house. Foote had stopped renting it, and he and Lillian used it almost as a second home. Lillian had grown to love the town as much as Foote, and they were happy in the quiet life they found there.

They were in Wharton when Gary Sinise, a cofounder of Chicago's Steppenwolf Theatre, visited Foote and asked him to write a screenplay for Steinbeck's *Of Mice and Men* that he was planning to direct. Sinise said they already had a working script, but he was not happy with it, and he thought Foote was the one person who could adapt the story for the screen.

Foote had been working on another play, but he liked Steinbeck's story of the two brothers, George and Lennie, and he put aside the new play and began work on the screenplay. The movie was shot in California with Sinise directing and starring along with another Steppenwolf cofounder, John Malkovich.

It was while they were in Texas that winter that Lillian became ill.

CHAPTER 13

Grief and Carrying On

Foote and Lillian spent most of the fall and winter of 1991 to 1992 in Wharton, and it was while they were there that Lillian began to lose weight and experience some odd pains. She had little appetite, and as the weeks went by she seemed to make no improvement. It was alarming enough for them to return to the apartment on Horatio Street in New York and consult a Christian Science practitioner. The report was not good. Neither she nor Foote told the children exactly what was wrong, and each learned of their mother's illness almost by accident.

Barbara Hallie had been appearing out of town in one of her father's plays and she was about to return to New York when her father called her on the telephone. Even then, he was circumspect.

"When you get home," he said, "don't be surprised to notice that your mother has lost some weight."

Barbara Hallie was concerned by that cryptic comment. But when she entered her parents' apartment on Horatio Street that summer, Barbara Hallie was shocked to see her mother almost a ghost of herself. Likewise, Daisy, Walter, and Horton Jr. were informed of their mother's condition almost incidentally. Even as the illness progressed and their mother entered a Christian Science hospice in Princeton, New Jersey, there was little discussion, as the children deferred to their parents' adherence to Christian Science. As a result, none of the children ever had a definite diagnosis of their mother's illness, though cancer seemed almost certain.

Foote tried to keep up a brave front on Lillian's illness, going about his normal routine. He even made a couple of trips in connection with upcoming productions of plays, including a staging of *The Roads to Home* that he was to direct for a theater in Virginia and an eventual transfer to New York, as well as a television version of *Habitation of Dragons* for Steven Spielberg's company that was to be aired on the TNT cable network.

Foote's outward demeanor was so placid that Horton Jr. thought at the time that his father was being callous in the face of his wife's life-and-death struggle. Barbara Hallie and Daisy saw it more as an act of denial, or a silent acceptance of the inevitable. Foote visited Lillian daily when he was in New York, but he steadfastly, almost resolutely, declined to discuss the situation with the children.

Lillian Foote died on August 5, 1992, at around three o'clock in the morning in the hospice in New Jersey. She was sixty-nine. Foote was at her bedside at the time. Daisy and Walter were both asleep in a family waiting room down the corridor.

Horton Jr., who was in California, had only learned how serious his mother's condition was a few weeks earlier. In all of the telephone conversations, the reports on her illness had been so vague that he did not fully understand how grave it was. Whenever he had asked his father about his mom, Foote had been evasive and changed the subject.

In early August, after talking with Daisy, Horton Jr. had decided he should come home. But even on the day he was flying in from California, he was led to believe that her condition was not critical. He arrived at Kennedy Airport late in the evening and called Barbara Hallie, who was in Virginia acting in the production of *The Roads to Home* that her father had directed. She had heard from Daisy that their mother seemed improved that day. Daisy had even remarked on it to their mother, and Lillian had responded that she felt better.

After hearing Barbara Hallie's positive report, Horton Jr. decided he would go to bed for the night and visit his mother the following morning. When the phone rang in the middle of the night and woke him, he knew what the call was. Daisy was calling with the news that Lillian had died.

Barbara Hallie was torn. The run of *The Roads to Home* was about to end in Virginia, but she wanted to come back to New York immediately. She agonized throughout the day, then decided to play one last performance that night, after which the production closed and she returned home.

Lillian was cremated, and a small service was held in Foote's apartment on Horatio Street for only family and a few very close friends. Foote and the children then planned to travel to Texas, where Lillian's ashes would be interred in the Foote family plot in Wharton.

In the days immediately following Lillian's death, throughout the small service in New York and the preparation to take her ashes to Texas for burial, Foote had remained stoic, dry-eyed, almost detached from the events going on around him. Horton Jr. remembered thinking that his father's spiritual strength kept him from showing the grief he must be feeling.

When the plane carrying the family and Lillian's ashes arrived at the airport in Houston, Foote was walking through the terminal when he suddenly collapsed and began to sob. As the children rushed to him, he said through tears, "I can't go on. I can't take another step." They got him to a chair in the airport lobby, and he sat there, crying like a baby.

For days after the service in Texas, both in Wharton and back in New York, at least one of the children was always with him. Often during the night, they would hear him pacing his room, moaning and calling for Lillian. At one point, Foote told Michael Wilson, a young director who had become a close friend to both him and Lillian and had attended the services in Wharton, "I don't know if I'll ever be able to write again."

In the end, Foote took the Beckettian counsel of one of his own characters. In the final scene in *1918*, as Elizabeth is trying to come to terms with the death of her baby daughter in the influenza epidemic, she turns to her mother, who had lost two daughters in infancy. "Mama, help us," Elizabeth pleads. "How did you stand it when you lost your children?" Mrs. Vaughn, a character based on Foote's grandmother, Baboo, simply replies, "You just stand it. You keep going."

In the end, it was the theater that helped Foote keep going. Within weeks of the family's return to New York from Texas, the production of *The Roads to Home* that had been in Virginia was scheduled to open at the Lambs Theatre in New York.

The play, which consists of three connected one-acts, had been one of the first to be performed at the start of Foote's comeback in New York a decade earlier. The new production, which Foote was directing, starred Barbara Hallie and Jean Stapleton in the two main women's roles. Unknown to Barbara Hallie, Foote had also called a California-based actor, who had worked for him in the HB production of *1918*, and offered him a part in the revival. That actor was Devon Abner.

When Barbara Hallie arrived in New York to begin rehearsals for *The Roads to Home* before it moved to Virginia, Foote had asked his daughter if she wanted to know who else besides Stapleton was in the cast for the play. Barbara Hallie was so concerned with her mother's illness that she didn't even care to know who the other actors were.

"No," she replied. "Surprise me."

He did. When she first walked into rehearsals in New York and saw Devon Abner sitting there, Barbara Hallie nearly fell over.

The letter that Barbara Hallie had seen years earlier on her father's desk with Devon's return address on it was not the only missive Foote had received from the actor. Devon had written several times over the years since he had appeared in *1918* and he and Barbara Hallie had their brief backstage romance. Most of the notes were friendly congratulations to Foote on some success or another, as Devon followed the revival of Foote's career over the years. And usually there was a plug for a part in any future Foote play. "I'm still dying to work with you again," one note said. "If something should come along with my name on it, it's going to get my best shot," said another.

Some letters also extolled Hallie's talents. After seeing the film version of *Courtship*, Devon wrote Foote that he had been "especially impressed with Barbara Hallie's work." And in another letter he recalled to her father how, during his rehearsals with Barbara Hallie for *1918*, he had "learned more as far as great choices and how to approach a script in a few weeks with her than in months of Stella Adler's script class."

Whether the correspondence had any bearing on Foote calling him for a part in the revival of *The Roads to Home*, the result was that not long after rehearsals began in New York and performances were under way in Virginia, Devon and Barbara Hallie were dating again. This time, she did not hide the relationship from her father, and Devon was a source of strength and comfort to Barbara Hallie during the time of her mother's final illness and death.

The three connected one-acts that comprise *The Roads to Home* tell the story of three women living in Houston but dreaming of the small towns of their youth. In the case of two of them, that town is Harrison.

Frank Rich again came as the critic for the *New York Times*, and he began his review by saying, "Any list of America's living literary wonders must include Horton Foote." It went on:

> And here Mr. Foote is now, in a small playhouse in the shadows of the Broadway behemoths, directing his own script, meticulously tending to a vision that has deepened but not wavered throughout his long career. "The Roads to Home," a trilogy of related one-act plays first seen briefly Off-Off Broadway a decade ago, is modest Foote but *echt* Foote. The setting is Texas. The time is long ago (the 1920's). The lives on display are unexceptional, undramatic. And just when the audience is set to relax into an elegiac reverie that might resemble nostalgia, the playwright finds a way to make his characters' inner turmoil so ferociously vivid it leaps beyond their specific time and place to become our own.

Rich had special praise for Hallie's performance as Annie Gayle Long, the pretty young woman who drops in daily on her friend Mabel Votaugh, Jean Stapleton's character. Annie and Mabel are both natives of Harrison and they spend their days going over their memories of their hometown. Rich said Hallie gave "the central and transporting performance" in the plays, especially in the last one,

Spring Dance, in which Annie recalls dances of her youth, though by this time she is in an insane asylum near Austin.

The Roads to Home was an enormous success for the Lambs Theatre, and for Foote and Hallie. After Rich's review, producers lined up to come see the show, and one of them was a young man named James Houghton, who had just started his own theater in New York, an enterprise he called the Signature Theatre Company, which was dedicated to producing a season of plays that concentrated on one playwright.

Houghton had come to know Foote's plays when he was in graduate school at SMU in Dallas in 1983. Like many young students in the theater in the 1980s, Houghton knew Foote mainly through the movies that had brought him honor and fame, such as *To Kill a Mockingbird* and *Tender Mercies*. After all, Foote had been mostly absent from the stage, living in isolation in New Hampshire, through the years in which the young producers and directors of the 1990s received their calling to the theater.

During the time that Foote and Lillian had spent in Waxahachie making their first independent movies, a small theater in Dallas staged two of the plays that were being filmed just a few miles out of town—the two from *The Orphans' Home Cycle*, *1918* and *Valentine's Day*. Houghton had gone to see the stage productions and had been moved by what he later called the "gentle storm" that existed in the plays.

At the time Houghton came to see *The Roads to Home* the Signature had completed its first season of plays, devoted to Romulus Linney, a young playwright who also had begun his career as an actor and had once appeared in a Foote play at the HB Studio. The theater was preparing for its second season, featuring the work of Lee Blessing.

Houghton had first met Foote during the Signature's first season. Foote had come to see the theater's production of Linney's *The Sorrows of Frederick*, and Houghton, recognizing Foote, introduced himself at intermission. It had already occurred to Houghton that he would like to devote a season to Foote's plays, and he suggested it to him.

At the time, Foote had said he thought that would be fun, but was noncommittal. Houghton filed the conversation away, and nothing more was done toward making the suggestion a reality.

After seeing *The Roads to Home*, Houghton again approached Foote about a season at the Signature. The only stipulation the Signature required from its chosen playwright was that he or she take an active part in all the productions, which meant the writer would have to be available to the company for the entire theatrical season, attending all casting sessions and rehearsals and most of the performances. Foote had other irons in the fire for the upcoming year, but said he would be able to devote the 1994 to 1995 theatrical season to Houghton and the Signature.

Barbara Hallie had already begun to assume the role of protector for her father, a role her mother had always carried out before. When Foote told her that he had promised to do a season of plays with Jim Houghton, Barbara Hallie immediately set out to learn more about this young producer and his company. When she reported back that Houghton was legitimate and his theater had won critical praise, Foote chided her. "I could have told you that," he said. "I have seen his productions." She had not known her father had been to see Linney's plays there earlier.

In its third season the Signature showcased Edward Albee. One of his plays that season was a new drama called *Three Tall Women*, which won the Pulitzer Prize for Drama later in the year. At the start of Foote's season with the Signature, Albee had sent him a note:

Dear Horton: You will probably have a frightening experience with the Signature Company this coming season. You will discover you are working with eager, dedicated, talented, resourceful, gentle, and thoughtful people whose main concern will be making you happy. This will be frightening. Even more, they will succeed in making you happy. This will be even more frightening. Don't fret about it; just go with it. Have a wonderful season.

When Foote and Houghton began to discuss the four plays that would be produced during the season dedicated to his work, Foote said he also wanted to do only new plays, or at least plays that had not been seen previously in New York, and that one of them, possibly two, would be premieres of new works.

The first play in Foote's season with the Signature was *Talking Pictures*, a wistful portrait of a woman who played the piano at a small-town cinema during the era of silent movies, and whose life was changed by the advent of the talkies. The play had been staged twice—once in Florida and once in Houston—but it had never been done in New York. Carol Goodheart directed the Signature production, which starred Barbara Hallie as the movie pianist.

The second play was *Night Seasons*, which had been staged in Teaneck the previous year. Foote directed the Signature staging himself. Barbara Hallie also starred in that production, along with Jean Stapleton, and with Devon Abner playing the part of Lawrence.

It was during the run of *Night Seasons* that Barbara Hallie and Devon were married in a ceremony at city hall.

The third play Foote chose for the Signature season was one he had written a few years earlier and had held a reading of in Houston. It had never been staged. The play was called *The Young Man From Atlanta*. It is set in Houston in 1950, when Lily Dale and Will Kidder, who were young lovers in the play *Lily Dale* and are now in their sixties, face the biggest crisis of their lives: their only child, a son who had served with honor in World War II, drowns at the age of thirty-seven in Florida in odd circumstances.

Lily Dale Kidder, née Robedaux, is a character who appears in three of the nine plays in Foote's *Orphans' Home Cycle*. When audiences first get to know her in *Lily Dale*, she is a teenage girl being spoiled by her stepfather and wooed by the man she eventually marries, Will Kidder. She also appears as a young girl in *Roots in a Parched Ground* and as a woman in her thirties in *Cousins*. She is one of the few characters in any of Foote's plays whose name is the same as the real person on whom she is based, and Foote indulged in that mainly because he wanted to use the song "Lily Dale" in the play named for her.

Since many of his plays and characters were based loosely on real events and people, Foote had been mindful of those people's feelings and tried to avoid writing anything that would embarrass or hurt friends or relations back in Texas. He had written *The Young Man From Atlanta* only after his real aunt Lily had died, and Foote now felt unrestrained in telling the story of the great sadness in her life.

The young Lily Dale of the earlier play considers herself an accomplished pianist and even writes songs—ragtime music, mostly—one of which she names after her stepfather. The real Aunt Lily, Foote's father's sister, continued to play the piano and write music throughout her life. On several occasions over the years, she sent her piano compositions to Foote, asking him to help her get them published and performed. He once showed several of the songs to a friend in the music business and was told they were "interesting" but not very original. Foote never told her that, and his aunt always felt Foote had not done enough to get her music the attention it deserved.

Aunt Lily remained the stereotypical fussy, meddling, self-centered aunt throughout her life. Since she had, in fact, been spoiled by her stepfather and indulged by her husband, she felt superior to the whole family. She was a George Wallace supporter, and as a right-wing fundamentalist, she was always trying to "save" Christian Scientists from going to hell. She was always at the center of her own universe. When she saw *Night of the Storm*, the teleplay that later became *Roots in a Parched Ground*, she wrote Foote that she liked it, then went on at length about how *Reader's Digest* had rejected a first-person story she had submitted to a contest they were running. She sent Foote a copy of the story in case he could help her get it published. When Foote received his first Academy Award, for *Mockingbird*, she wrote a letter saying, "Congratulations on winning an Oscar. I have just won something, too," and proceeded to tell him how she had won a drawing after buying some new cookware.

In *The Young Man From Atlanta*, Foote took a family tragedy—the drowning of his aunt Lily's only son in circumstances similar to those described in the play—and constructed a poignant social and family drama. In the play, Will and Lily Dale are trying to come to grips with changing society in the 1950s and the grief they share over the death of their only son. After the war, their son, Bill, had moved away from Houston to live in Atlanta, a disappointment to his parents, who had hoped he would join his father in the wholesale grocery business. While on a business trip to Florida for the company he worked for, Bill had stopped at a lake in the middle of the day to go for a swim. Only he didn't know how to swim. He walked out into the lake until the water swallowed him. Will is convinced his son committed suicide, but he has not told his wife that.

After their son's death, Lily Dale and Will were contacted by his former roommate in Atlanta, the young man of the title. Will wants to have nothing to do with him, but the young man preys on Lily Dale's grief, telling her that her son had found religion, a comfort to his mother, and persuading her to give him thousands of dollars that Will had given his wife over the years and which she had saved. The play opens on the day Will, at the age of sixty-four, is fired from his job. He is offered a settlement by his company, but out of pride or stubbornness he refuses to accept it.

At the time, Will and Lily Dale have also just moved into a new house and are supporting Lily Dale's widower stepfather. In confronting the financial hardships that lie ahead after his firing from the company he helped found, Will asks Lily Dale if he can use some of the money he had given her over the years to start a new business of his own. It inevitably comes out that Lily Dale has given most of those savings to Bill's former roommate. The stress of being fired and the disclosure that Lily Dale had been in secret contact with his son's roommate, even giving him large amounts of money, induces a mild heart attack in Will and creates a rift in his and Lily Dale's marriage.

The unspoken understanding through the course of the play is that Bill was a closet homosexual, and his young roommate was a predator who had taken his, and now his grieving mother's, money and possibly had been the reason Bill committed suicide. The tender poignancy of Foote's drama is in Will coming to terms with the fall his pride has precipitated and the sadness and emptiness that his son's death has left him with.

Toward the end of the play, Will gives a cri de coeur that any father can understand:

> I failed him, Lily Dale. Some way I failed him. I tried to be a good father, but I just think now I only wanted him to be like me. I never tried to understand what he was like. I never tried to find out what he would want to do, what he would want to talk about. Life goes so fast, Lily Dale. My God. It goes so fast. It seems like yesterday he was a baby, and I was holding him in my arms, and before I turned around good he was off to school, and I thought, when he comes back he'll come into the business and I'll be close to him. I was never close to him, Lily Dale. How was your day? Fine, son, how was yours? And then he was gone. I want my son back, Lily Dale. I want him back.

Peter Masterson, Foote's cousin who had directed the film versions of *The Trip to Bountiful* and *Convicts*, was chosen to direct the Signature staging. Masterson's wife, Carlin Glynn, was signed to play Lily Dale in *Young Man*, and Ralph Waite took on the role of Will Kidder. Devon Abner, Foote's new son-in-law, played Will's business partner, Tom Jackson.

The play opened at the Kampo Cuitural Center in the East Village on January 27, 1995. It was an instant hit. Vincent Canby, who had gone from being film critic to drama critic at the *New York Times*, said the play was "one of Mr. Foote's most serious and seething works . . . a work that will haunt you long after the performance." John Leonard, referring to Foote in his review in *New York* magazine, said:

> He's so quiet we have to slow down to hear him, and then what he says is not so much surprising as confirming. I still believe every syllable of Horton Foote, and envy him. He doesn't know how to lie.

There was much talk about possibly moving the play to Broadway, and there was also an offer from CBS to make a television movie. Performances at the Signature were sold out, and the run was extended. But discussions on a transfer to Broadway became bogged down.

When Foote met with CBS executives to discuss a TV movie, the network's producers told him they wanted him to make some changes in the script. For one thing, they wanted him to introduce the title character into the play at some point, to write a part for the young man from Atlanta so that he would appear onstage at the end. Foote would have loved to make a movie of the play, but he had to turn down the proposal. He tried to point out that it was essential to the drama that the young man from Atlanta, and both the resentment he raises in Will and the hope he represents to Lily Dale, remain in the audience's imagination. A movie was never made.

The play won the Pulitzer Prize for Drama that year.

The final play of the Signature season was another new play called *Laura Dennis* with Missy Yager in the title role, and Barbara Hallie playing her alcoholic cousin, Velma. Jim Houghton directed the production, and Horton Jr. also had a part in it. A long one-act, the play returns to the theme of loss. The Dennis clan is the one that according to family legend stole the Hortons' property, and they have now fallen on hard times. Laura is living with another family, and Velma seeks comfort in a whiskey bottle.

The play received polite notices, with Ben Brantley, now the chief drama critic at the *New York Times*, saying that while interesting, it was one of Foote's "lesser works." Clive Barnes, writing in the *New York Post*, said the play had "no real moral, except to say life is difficult at best, hell at worst, and survival is only a temporary blessing." Coming immediately after *The Young Man From Atlanta*, the major attraction among the four plays mounted by the Signature, *Laura Dennis* paled by comparison.

As the Signature season drew to a close, Frank Rich used the occasion of Foote's Pulitzer to issue an indictment of the economics of Broadway that would deny one of America's greatest playwrights a forum that would bring one of his most incisive plays to a larger audience. Rich by this time had moved from the chief drama critic's desk to the Op-Ed page and had turned his critical eye from the theatrical stage to the broader cultural and political one. His column, which appeared shortly after the Oklahoma City bombing that year, began by giving a brief history of Foote's achievements:

> Fifty-four years ago this week a young man from Texas named Horton Foote made his playwriting debut in New York with a drama called "Texas Town." Brooks Atkinson, the critic of The Times, declared it a "feat of magic."
>
> Last week and some 50 plays later, Mr. Foote, now 79, won the Pulitzer Prize for Drama for "The Young Man From Atlanta." In the intervening half century he has passed through Broadway during its Golden Age . . . and won two Oscars in Hollywood. But incredibly, Mr. Foote is now in some ways back where he started in the theater. Not only is he still writing about the same Texans but his Pulitzer-winning play, just like "Texas Town," was staged on a shoestring in a tiny Off-Off-Broadway playhouse.
>
> Though the play received good reviews, no producer moved it to a larger home off Broadway, let alone on, for an extended run—so financially risky has it become to mount a serious drama requiring nine actors in the commercial theater. Even now, post-Pulitzer, "The Young Man From Atlanta" is not assured a future New York production. If Mr. Foote's plays have much to tell audiences about the psychic fissures lying just beneath the surface of middle-class American life in this century, what does it also say about America that playwrights of his stature must now fight to be heard?
>
> If "The Young Man From Atlanta" could be seen now, what a catharsis it would offer audiences whose lives or hearts have been touched by the horrors of Oklahoma City. Set in the cocky Houston of 1950, it tells of a couple whose bedrock belief in America and in God takes them just so far when their only son, a World War II hero, inexplicably kills himself.
>
> Months after seeing this play, I can still hear Mr. Waite's gruff voice swell unexpectedly on the line "I just want my son back,"

keeping company with the rest of us who have known inconsolable grief. Great artists like Horton Foote give us this, and more. Why do we give them so little in return?

Whether because of Rich's column or in spite of it, a little over a year later, a Broadway production of *Young Man* was in the works. It would be Foote's first play on Broadway in more than forty years, but it did not turn out to be the happy return to the Great White Way the playwright had been anticipating.

David Richenthal made plans to put it on Broadway after tryouts in Houston, Boston, and Chicago. Inevitably, the producer wanted changes in the play. These proposed changes did not, however, include writing a part for the absent young man of the title and bringing him onstage, and Foote could live with the suggestions. The cast, however, was to remain the same, with Ralph Waite and Carlin Glynn repeating their performances as Will and Lily Dale Kidder. Masterson was again to direct the Broadway-bound production. But trouble began in the tryouts.

The producer was not happy with the way the play had been going in Boston. Masterson was sometimes absent from rehearsals, and Foote tried to talk to his cousin and caution him that Richenthal might fire him. Masterson, however, took little notice of the advice.

Foote's warning to his cousin had not been an idle one. Richenthal ended up dismissing Masterson, Glynn, Waite, and all but one member of the rest of the cast from the Signature production. Robert Falls was hired as director, Rip Torn was signed to play Will, and Shirley Knight was brought in to replace Glynn as Lily Dale.

Masterson was upset and Foote felt badly. Apart from the family connection, Foote felt that Masterson understood his work. They had experienced happy collaborations together, not least of which were the films of *Bountiful* and *Convicts*, and a new TV movie version of the play *Lily Dale* that was about to begin shooting and in which Masterson was directing his daughter, Mary Stuart Masterson, in the title role.

That TV project, which was in preproduction around the same

time the problems began with the Broadway-bound staging of *The Young Man From Atlanta*, had sent Foote back to Waxahachie. There had been an earlier effort to get *Lily Dale* made into a movie, but the financial backing collapsed. This one was being financed by Showtime.

Hallie Foote was an executive producer on *Lily Dale*, and she had assembled a first-rate cast that included Stockard Channing, Sam Shepard, Jean Stapleton, and a bright young actor named Tim Guinee, who played the young Horace. Daisy Foote accompanied her father and sister on location in Texas, and she and Guinee began seeing each other off the set. It was a romance that blossomed, and two years later they were married.

Showtime allocated a shoestring budget for the made-for-TV film. They had offered Shepard a part in a different movie for four times what he was paid for *Lily Dale*, but he insisted on playing the role of Horace's stepfather at lesser money. The pecuniary attitude toward the Foote project infuriated Shepard. "Who are these people?" he fumed at one point. "Don't they know this is Horton Foote."

After Richenthal fired most of the cast from the Broadway-bound production of *The Young Man From Atlanta*, there were feelings among some that Foote should have stood up to the producer and insisted on keeping the original actors and director. There was little Foote could have done, however, except to pull the play from production. Foote had not had a play on Broadway in forty-five years, and he wanted *The Young Man From Atlanta* to reach as many people as possible. The episode created hard feelings between Masterson and Foote, and although relations were later restored to at least familial cordiality, they never worked together again after *Lily Dale*.

The newly cast and directed *Young Man* opened at the Goodman Theatre in Chicago in January 1997 to mostly favorable, though some mixed, notices. It played there two months then opened at the Longacre Theatre on Broadway in March.

Critics were not unkind, and some were even enthusiastic, though some who had seen the original Signature production found Torn's performance as Will Kidder lacking the depth and compassion that

Waite had brought to the role. The play was nominated for three Tony Awards, but the Best Play award went to Alfred Uhry for *The Last Night of Ballyhoo*. The producers abruptly closed the play when it did not win the Tony.

Two years earlier, on the night Foote was to receive the Pulitzer for the Signature Theater production of *The Young Man From Atlanta*, Jim Houghton hired a limousine to drive him and the playwright uptown to Columbia University for the awards ceremony. The prize was another feather in the cap of Houghton and his young company—the second play that won the Pulitzer in two years. It was also a crowning achievement for Foote.

Heading back downtown from Columbia in the limousine, Houghton noticed that Foote was staring out the side window sadly, tears welling in his eyes. It had been a glittering ceremony, and the award should have been a cause for celebration. Houghton asked him if anything was wrong.

Foote, still gazing out the window, said quietly, almost in a whisper, "I wish Lillian was here."

CHAPTER 14

New Plays
and New Audiences

Over the next few years, Foote collected a trophy case full of awards and honors from universities, institutes, and theaters around the country to go alongside his two Oscars and Pulitzer. A remake of *Old Man* for the CBS *Hallmark Hall of Fame* won an Emmy (the television awards had not yet been established when *The Trip to Bountiful*, *Tomorrow*, and the original *Old Man* had been shown on TV in the 1950s). He was elected to the American Academy of Arts and Letters and received its Gold Medal in 1998. The following year he was given a Lifetime Achievement Award by the Writers Guild of America.

Several film festivals dedicated seasons to his work, and universities lined up to give him honorary degrees or otherwise honor him for his canon of plays, films, and television dramas, among them Southern Methodist University, Baylor University, Brigham Young University, Dickinson College, Drew University, the University of Hartford, the University of the South, and the American Film Institute. He received the PEN/Laura Pels Foundation award, the Lucille Lortel award, the Humanitas Award, the Texas Institute of Letters award, the RCA Crystal Heart Award, the Texas Book Festival's Bookend Award, the Last Frontier Playwrights Award in Alaska, the Texas Film Hall of Fame Award, a Fellowship of Southern Writers award, and the New York State Governor's Award.

One of his proudest moments, however, came in December 2000, when he received the National Medal of Arts from President Clinton at the White House.

It was not the first time he had met Clinton. A lifelong Democrat like his father—his father once told Foote he would forgive him anything except voting Republican—Foote had been an ardent supporter of the forty-second president. Jim Houghton knew that Foote was a big Clinton fan, and earlier that year when he and Foote were planning a trip to Washington together, Houghton thought it would be a nice surprise if he could arrange for Foote to meet the president.

Unfamiliar with the corridors of power in Washington, Houghton called Frank Rich, by now as important a political writer as he had once been a theater critic, and asked him for advice. Rich told Houghton to get in touch with Sidney Bloomfield, one of Clinton's top aides. Bloomfield said he would see what he could do.

Houghton had not mentioned any of this to Foote in case the meeting fell through, and when he and Foote, accompanied by Daisy, arrived in Washington, Houghton still had not heard back from Bloomfield. He had just about given up hope of springing his surprise on Foote when he got a call the next morning from Bloomfield with a brief message: "The president will see you at two o'clock."

Foote was still in the dark when they took a taxi to the White House and presented themselves to the duty officer. Within minutes they were shown into Clinton's office. Foote, who had worked with the top celebrities in show business throughout his life, was almost speechless. Clinton was nothing if not a charismatic presence, and when he turned his full attention to someone, he had the ability to make that person feel as if he were the most important person on earth. Clinton spent about ten minutes chatting with Foote, Houghton, and Daisy, then invited them to join him on the White House lawn, where he was to sign the Patients' Bill of Rights Act before the media.

After the signing, the president insisted they accompany him back to the White House, where a limousine was waiting to take him to a meeting he had at the Pentagon. As he got into the presidential limo, Clinton looked back at Foote, waved, and said, "Great to see you, Horton."

When Foote returned to the White House later that year to receive his National Medal of Arts award, Clinton greeted him like an old friend.

Since the death of Lillian, Foote's world had begun to shrink even further. The decade of the 1990s at times seemed like one never-ending funeral. Agnes de Mille became ill shortly after Lillian died and was confined to a wheelchair. Foote visited her often and would take her on walks along the river, pushing her wheelchair and talking over old times. She died in 1993, the same year his old friend Joe Anthony died. Perry Wilson, Anthony's widow, visited Foote in Wharton for several weeks afterward. Foote's brother John Speed succumbed to Alzheimer's, and other friends and former colleagues died within a few years, including Herbert Berghof and Lucy Kroll.

Foote himself suffered a flare-up of the hernia that had kept him out of the army in World War II, and it became so serious that Daisy ordered him into a hospital in Boston to have an operation. Foote finally sold the New Hampshire house, and many of the antiques he and Lillian had acquired over the years along with it.

At the death of so many of his friends, Foote experienced a sense of abandonment that only survivors can understand. He went through a brief last-man-standing period, but the young directors and actors whom he had befriended in recent years rejuvenated him. And he still had stories to tell.

If anyone thought *The Young Man From Atlanta* had been a valedictory, or that the National Medal of Arts and all the other awards he traveled around the country collecting were an octogenarian's victory lap, he or she did not truly fathom Foote's passion for the theater. Foote had written nearly every day of his life from the time he gave up acting and became a full-time writer some fifty-five years earlier, and he did not stop just because the century he had chronicled with such incisive insight was drawing to a close.

One project that served partly as a cathartic for the losses Foote had suffered was a play he wrote for television about a widower trying to come to terms with the death of his wife. It was called *Alone* and was aired on the Showtime cable channel in 1997, starring Hallie, Hume Cronyn, Frederick Forrest, James Earl Jones, and Piper Laurie.

Two years later in 1999, Houghton was planning to mark the tenth anniversary of the founding of the Signature Theatre with a two-year celebration of new plays by several of the playwrights whose work had been showcased by the theater over the preceding decade. Plays by Foote, Lee Blessing, Romulus Linney, Sam Shepard, Edward Albee, and John Guare would make up the 2000–2001 and 2001–2002 seasons.

Foote's offering was *The Last of the Thorntons*, and it was staged in November 2000 with a cast that included Hallie, Estelle Parsons, Mason Adams, and Anne Pitoniak, with Houghton directing.

The Last of the Thorntons is set in 1970 in a nursing home in Harrison and is a final look back over the decades at the Thorntons, the third family that figures in *The Orphans' Home Cycle*, that of Horace Robedaux's mother. The Thorntons were stand-ins for the Hortons, the clan of early Texas settlers who boasted a lieutenant governor and who, according to Foote family lore, cheated the Footes out of their share of the family fortune. Alberta Thornton is the last surviving daughter, and she is now living in the nursing home, the once vast holdings of the family plantation fortune dwindled to a duplex in Houston that a cousin is trying to sell against her wishes.

Foote brings some characters from earlier plays together in the nursing home. Annie Gayle Long, for example, whom audiences had last seen in a mental asylum in the last act of *The Roads to Home*, is now also a resident of the nursing home in *The Last of the Thorntons*. Several old family tales are woven into the memories of the home's residents, and even the set—a frame house that had once served as a doctor's office and the town's hospital—was modeled after the one in Wharton where Foote had undergone his appendectomy as a young man.

Each of the residents lives on memories, even delusional ones, trying to come to terms with the changes that life has dealt them.

As the twentieth century drew to a close, Foote began to muse further on the changes that had been wrought in America, especially in its small towns, over the past hundred years, and how the most traumatic event in the nation's history, the Civil War, had influenced all that had happened. He had been rereading a lot of Chekhov, and *Three Sisters* kept coming back to him. He wondered what had happened to the sisters as they grew older, whether they had been disappointed or satisfied with the way their lives turned out.

For much of his career, starting with his first full-length play, Foote had worked on a large canvas from a palette rich with colorful characters, creating crowded scenes full of dialogue and interaction. In contemplating a subject as vast as the twentieth century, however, he began to think in simpler terms, a more modest and personal form, one that he had never before employed.

A couple of years earlier, the Alley Theatre in Houston had asked Foote to write an original play for a season they planned to dedicate to him and his work. Never comfortable with the concept of writing for commission, Foote had delayed until he had the inspiration for a new play. It now came to him, and with Chekhov's play clearly in mind, Foote wrote *The Carpetbagger's Children*, an elegiac drama told by three sisters—the daughters of the carpetbagger of the title—delivering alternating monologues.

Foote also knew who he wanted to direct the play. Michael Wilson was a bright-eyed young man who by his own admission was devoted to radical postmodern theater. Foote had first met him under improbable circumstances a dozen years earlier.

Throughout his travels across the country to pick up awards, Foote also had been asked to give lectures at various colleges or institutes honoring him. In May 1987, he was to deliver a lecture at the Southern Educational Communication Authority in Winston-Salem, North Carolina.

Michael Wilson was about to graduate from the University of North Carolina in 1987. He was at a crossroads in his life, about to leave a home and family he loved, and uncertain what direction he should take in his chosen career—whether he should pursue the stage, which was his great love, or the movies, or television, or even try to become a writer himself.

One night shortly before his graduation, Wilson and his sister saw *The Trip to Bountiful,* and by the end of the movie Wilson was sobbing. He knew that the writer of the play and film was lecturing in town, and he decided to go hear him. After the lecture, which was titled "What It Means to Be a Southern Writer," Wilson went up to Foote and asked him for advice on what he should do with his life.

"I don't give advice," Foote said, not unkindly. "But I can tell you that I have had my greatest personal satisfaction in the theater."

It was enough to point Wilson in the right direction. He spent a couple of years working as a house manager at the American Repertory Theatre in Cambridge, then got a job as an assistant director at the Alley Theatre in Houston. During Wilson's second year at the Alley, the theater presented Foote with an award and a retrospective of his work. Foote, Lillian, and their children all came to Houston for the occasion, along with Robert Duvall, Harper Lee, and a parade of other stars who had appeared in Foote's plays and movies over the years.

Wilson introduced himself to Foote and reminded him of their brief conversation in North Carolina four years earlier. Foote told Wilson he remembered him, although the young director doubted it. Foote and Lillian were both in residence in Wharton at the time, and they invited Wilson to drive over for dinner.

Thus began a relationship that deepened over time, to the point that Wilson became almost an adopted member of the Foote family. Foote and Lillian would often drive in to see productions at the Alley or other Houston theaters, including those staged by avant-garde directors. Wilson visited Wharton often and after a meal of Southern fried chicken prepared by Rosa, the Footes' cook and housekeeper, Foote, Lillian, and Wilson would talk theater long into the night.

If Wilson thought that Foote would be dismissive of the new experimental theater, he was pleasantly surprised to find that Foote understood it and even admired it. And Wilson learned from Foote. After they all saw a radical postmodern staging of Ibsen's *When We Dead Awaken*, for example, Foote told him of seeing Eva Le Gallienne in three Ibsen plays in Los Angeles sixty years earlier, and how it had changed his life.

Foote and Wilson's working relationship began in 1992 when

Foote asked Wilson to direct a reading at the Alley of a new play he had written. It was the first draft of *The Young Man From Atlanta*. That reading came not long after Lillian had died, however, when Foote was contemplating giving up writing altogether. The play was put away in a drawer and not brought out again until Foote decided to stage it for the Signature season.

Although Pete Masterson ended up directing the Signature production, the early reading at the Alley that Wilson had directed had gone well and confirmed Foote's opinion that Wilson understood his work like few directors ever had. A couple of years later, when the PlayMakers Repertory Company, a theater in Chapel Hill, North Carolina, that Wilson had been associated with during college, asked him to return and direct a show for them, Wilson asked Foote for permission to direct one of his plays.

Foote gave him *The Death of Papa*, the last play in *The Orphans' Home Cycle* and one that had never been produced before. Foote had turned down several offers to stage the play, mainly because he wanted Matthew Broderick to repeat his role of Brother, but until that time he had thought Broderick too young to play the character at an older age. He now believed the time was right and he chose Wilson to direct the first production.

The PlayMakers theater was ecstatic. Not only would they have a world premiere of a Horton Foote drama for their new season, but a top Hollywood star would be performing on their stage. Broderick's movie *Ferris Bueller's Day Off* had just been released and the actor was a very hot item on the celebrity scale. Hallie also acted in the production, along with Ellen Burstyn, Ray Virta, Nicholas Shaw, Polly Holiday, and Ray Dooley.

Although the play was a huge success, certainly the biggest in PlayMakers' history, the production was beset by problems. Broderick was an avid squash player, and one day during the rehearsal period, he took a tumble while playing a game and badly hurt his knee. He was out during most of the rehearsal period, and Burstyn, who played his mother, had to work with an understudy. When the play finally opened, Broderick played the part, first in a brace, then on crutches or using a cane. None of it dampened the enthusiasm of the audiences, however, and Wilson's handling of the crisis only strengthened Foote's conviction that he had found the right director.

After he finished writing *The Carpetbagger's Children,* Foote sent it to Wilson, who had since taken the job of artistic director of the Hartford Stage Company. The play, however, was intended for the Alley, and a deal was worked out whereby Wilson would direct it for the Houston theater, then move the production to his own theater in Hartford.

The play opened in the spring of 2001 at the Alley with Wilson directing Barbara Hallie, Roberta Maxwell, and Jean Stapleton as the three daughters of the carpetbagger of the title, looking back on their lives in alternating monologues, and occasionally addressing one another.

The story they tell is that of a family who lived, even after his death, in the shadow of their patriarch, Joseph Thompson. Thompson was a Union army soldier who returned to Texas after the Civil War and used his position as county treasurer and tax collector to acquire plantations that had gone bankrupt after the abolition of slavery. Thompson had forbidden his three daughters from marrying, and he ostracized the one daughter, Grace Anne, who defied him. He also stipulated in his will that the vast estate of land and farms he had built should never be sold. There is a fourth daughter in the play—Beth, the father's favorite—although she never appears, having died as a young woman. But her ghost haunts the family throughout their lives.

As each of the three surviving daughters tells her side of the family saga, including the slow mental breakdown of their mother and the loves and losses each sister endured, a recurring song that was their father's favorite creeps into their recitations. It is an old hymn that Sissie—the shy daughter, played by Hallie, who couldn't leave home even when she married and whose husband visits her on weekends—sings as a sort of dirge for the twentieth century:

> *O, the clanging bells of time,*
> > *Night and day they never cease;*
> *We are wearied by their chime,*

For they do not bring us peace;
And we hush our breath to hear,
And we strain our eyes to see;
If the shores are drawing near,
Eternity! Eternity!

Another thread running through the play is the inevitability of change in the face of time. One by one, other farmers have sold their land, which then turned into malls, and the houses on the street where the sisters lived were replaced by fast-food eateries and filling stations. As Cornelia, the daughter whom Thompson left in charge, tries to keep the family's lands intact, she has to make hard decisions that affect other people's lives. Tractors and cotton-picking machines have replaced the mules and farmhands. In one speech, Cornelia says:

> It almost killed me the day I had to go out and tell the tenants I had to change how I was farming or I'd lose everything. I don't know whether they believed me or not. Old Jake Tillman and his wife had been on their place nearly forty years and his daddy ten years before him, anyway they cried and I cried when I told them. Some of the others just didn't look at me while I was talking to them. Just stared down at their feet and I couldn't even see their faces. They all said they understood, but I'm not sure they did.

The play was rehearsed in Hartford, then moved to Houston just before the scheduled opening at the Alley. It was during the preview performances that disaster struck. If one believed in omens, the Alley staging of *The Carpetbagger's Children* would have doomed the play from the start.

Tropical Storm Allison hit the Texas Gulf Coast with a fury of torrential rains and high winds. Flooding was everywhere, and the streets of downtown Houston were waist-high in water. The stage of the Alley Theatre, which was situated in a cultural center in the heart of the city, was underwater. One picture of the news coverage of the flooding that appeared on the front page of the *New York*

Times showed furniture from the set of *The Carpetbagger's Children* floating around the theater.

Performances of Foote's play were canceled, and Wilson tried to salvage what he could of the production. At one point, as he was trying to drive slowly through the swirling eddies that engulfed the city, he had to abandon his car and wade through water waist-high to his hotel. The car was a write-off.

Within five days, the floodwaters had receded, but the Alley Theatre was in ruins. Wilson arranged to move the play to the Stages Repertory Company, a smaller Houston theater that was not as badly damaged, and it opened there to an enthusiastic reception. After the Houston run, with the help of Jim Houghton at the Signature, the play took a brief detour to the Guthrie Theater in Minneapolis before transferring to the Hartford Stage Company that fall.

Foote and Wilson were both hoping that the play would move on to New York, but finding a Broadway producer or a theater willing to take a chance on a play about three old women remembering a forgotten South was not an easy task. In addition, the terrorist attack on New York City on September 11, 2001, had a pronounced effect on the theater in general. Many New Yorkers simply were not going out—to the movies, to restaurants, to sporting events, to the theater. Attendance was off at all public events for weeks and months that fall, as many people decided just to stay home.

In fact, only one of the major New York drama critics came up to Hartford to review *The Carpetbagger's Children*, although a new Horton Foote play was by now a major theatrical event, even if it was being staged in Connecticut. The one critic who did make the trip was John Lahr of the *New Yorker* magazine, who said the play was "theatrically daring" and called Foote's writing "bittersweet music—a rhapsody of ambivalence." His review helped set events in motion that saw the play eventually move to Lincoln Center Theater.

Theatrical artistic directors don't tend to hang out together as a group, socialize at the same clubs, or drink in the same bars the way journalists, cops, firemen, or even actors often do. But Andre Bishop, artistic director of Lincoln Center Theater, had known Michael Wilson for years.

Apart from any other common interests, Bishop and Wilson shared a deep passion for the theater. When he was artistic director of Playwrights Horizons on New York's Theatre Row in the 1980s, for example, Bishop had instituted a series of new plays by emerging playwrights that he produced and offered for five dollars a ticket. It was a project designed to lure young people into the theater by giving them live drama for less than it cost to go to the movies.

Like Wilson, Bishop had first known the name Horton Foote from his movies. Bishop came into the theater in the late 1960s and early '70s, a time in which New York was a thriving mecca for the theater, with a class of new playwrights such as Sam Shepard, Edward Albee, David Mamet, John Guare, and Romulus Linney. Their plays were being produced anywhere that had free space—basements, lofts, bars, and churches. Money was not an issue. The play really was the thing.

At some point, however, the profit factor reared its head, and as a result fewer new plays were being produced in New York. Struggling young playwrights had to move elsewhere, to places like Seattle or La Jolla. One night in Los Angeles, Bishop had an epiphany. He had gone to see a new play in a small theater in a suburban strip mall and spent the evening afterward discussing its merits with locals. It was an experience that was once common in New York but had now vanished there, and he wanted to bring it back to the theater's natural home. His five-dollar plays were part of that effort.

Since moving to Lincoln Center, where he succeeded Gregory Mosher, the man who, together with Bernie Gersten, had revived the theater there, Bishop had always been on the lookout for new plays to stage in one of the center's two theaters. He had to answer to a board of directors, of course, and he had to keep an eye on the bottom line of the theater's ledger. But the theater thrived on new plays; and if they could not always be premieres, then he was always looking for new dramas that could be transferred from other theaters.

Wilson was constantly urging Bishop to come up to Hartford to see his productions there with an eye to moving them to New York. After *The Carpetbagger's Children* opened in Hartford, Wilson began badgering Bishop to come up. Bishop was ambivalent. He was not sure he wanted to make the trek to Connecticut to see three mono-logues, and the trip itself gave him pause. Because of September 11, Bishop was reluctant to leave his family, even for an evening. But Wilson kept calling, and after Lahr's review ran in the *New Yorker*, Bishop went up to see a matinee.

Bishop loved the play and the performances and returned to New York determined to move the show to Lincoln Center. The problem was that both theaters at Lincoln Center were fully booked for the entire season. Bishop's original plan was to include the play as part of a Monday night series of new dramas that were being staged on the theaters' dark night. Then, the show that had been planned for the smaller Mitzi Newhouse stage fell through, and Bishop quickly started work to fill the vacant slot with a full production of *The Carpetbagger's Children*.

By this time, there was some competition. Lynn Meadow, artistic director of the Manhattan Theatre Club, had also seen the play and expressed interest in it. In the end, Foote decided on Lincoln Center. Bishop had struck a sympathetic chord in Foote, and the playwright felt that it could be the start of a lasting relationship.

The Carpetbagger's Children opened at Lincoln Center in the spring of 2002 and became an instant hit. It was a happy experience, for Bishop and for Foote, as well as for his cast of three women. Critics and audiences alike responded to the play enthusiastically, and its run was extended. Bishop had become a new member of the Foote fan club.

The New York reviews were glowing. Donald Lyons, writing in the *New York Post*, called it a "small masterpiece," and Ben Brantley, the *New York Times* chief critic, said, "Few dramatists today can replicate this kind of storytelling with the gentle mastery that Mr. Foote provides." Brantley described the play as "both sentimental and ruthless, toting up the losses in one generation's life with warm compassion and a cold awareness that to live is ultimately to lose."

Foote continued to write. A full-length drama titled *Getting Frankie Married—and Afterwards* was produced at the South Coast Repertory. He also wrote his first purely autobiographical play. It was called *The Actor* and dealt with his early years of wanting to

become one. The play had its premiere at the Royal National Theatre in London in the summer of 2002 and was staged the following year by the American Conservatory Theater in San Francisco.

Apart from focusing on himself, the play also represented a departure for Foote in structure. The central character, a fifteen-year-
old Horace Robedaux Jr., addresses the audience in monologues—a
device Foote had not employed until *The Carpetbagger's Children*—
in which he explains the background and circumstances of scenes
with his schoolmates and family that are played out in between the
soliloquies.

The plot, even the dialogue, chronicles an episode straight from
Foote's life, from the time he was struck with the desire to become
an actor, and tells how his father, despite his opposition to his son's
ambition as a foolhardy whim, sold a house he had been renting for
income during the Depression in order to pay for Foote to go to the
Pasadena Playhouse to pursue his dream.

It is a wistful play that is an homage to his mother's and father's
love for him, and it brings his theatrical life full circle. The seed
that was planted in Foote's first performance—as Puck in his third-
grade teacher's backyard—came to bud in his "call" and struggle to
be an actor, blossomed in his conversion as a playwright, and flow-
ered into nearly a hundred plays, films, and television dramas that
defined twentieth-century America.

CHAPTER 15

American Storyteller

IF THE TWENTY-FIRST CENTURY began with another landmark Foote play in *The Carpetbagger's Children*, it proceeded with a steady stream of productions of old and recent works that confirmed Foote's place in the pantheon of American playwrights.

If there had been any doubts about the durability and timelessness of Foote's plays, they were easily put to rest in a revival of one of his earliest plays half a century after it was first produced on television and then on Broadway.

In 2003, James Houghton and his Signature Theatre Company faced an unexpected crisis. Houghton had been planning to stage a season of plays by August Wilson. When Wilson died suddenly, he was left without a resident playwright for the season or plays to perform.

Houghton came up with the idea of celebrating the theater's fifteenth season by doing "signature" plays by playwrights whose work had been showcased at Signature. There would be no time to write original plays, so the season would focus on previous works. Houghton chose *The Trip to Bountiful* for the Foote play.

Houghton considered directing it himself, but decided against it. Michael Wilson had other commitments at the time. Foote had in mind an actor-turned-director who previously had staged two of his one-acts at the Off-Off-Broadway Ensemble Studio Theatre—*The Prisoner's Song* and *The One-Armed Man*, both part of a trilogy called *Harrison, Texas* that Herbert Berghof had directed twenty years earlier. Foote had been impressed with those productions at EST, and Harris Yulin was signed to direct the revival of *Bountiful*.

There had been no hesitation about who would play Carrie Watts. Lois Smith was one of the leading lights in New York theater, and she was a perfect fit for the part. Devon and Hallie took the roles of Ludie and Jessie Mae, husband and wife playing husband and wife. Foote insisted that the play be performed without the intermissions that had been forced on it half a century earlier on Broadway, and Yulin's direction produced a poignant and unforgettable ninety minutes of theater.

The production played in Houston and Hartford before landing at the Signature in New York. As part of the theater's fifteenth anniversary observance, Houghton offered fifteen-dollar tickets, and the entire run of the show was sold out within days. Tickets were sold for patrons to sit on the steps in the aisles, and those, too, were snapped up. The run was extended once, and those performances also sold out.

As is often the case with a successful Off-Broadway production, there was talk of transferring it to Broadway, but Foote and Houghton were told there were no Broadway theaters available to move it to. The real reason the production didn't transfer probably had more to do with New York showbiz politics. The prominent Broadway theatrical producers had plays running for which they had Tony Award aspirations that season. If Yulin's staging of *The Trip to Bountiful* moved to Broadway, it stood a good chance of sweeping the Tonys—Lois Smith for Best Actress, almost certainly, but also Hallie, Devon, and Yulin for Supporting Actress, Supporting Actor, and Director, respectively, not to mention Foote himself and the play for Best Revival.

For anyone fortunate enough to have seen the Signature production, the play was a revelation. More than fifty years after it was written, the play left audiences standing and cheering, most with tears in their eyes. The audiences, far from being a gathering of card-carrying AARP retirees taking a nostalgic trip to a bygone era, were more than half filled with young and middle-aged theatergoers. That the play also spoke across geographic divides was evidenced by those who approached Foote night after night at the theater to tell him how the play had touched them. One middle-aged man in a yarmulke, for example, came up one night to the playwright, red-eyed from weeping, and told him the play had taken him back to the kibbutz in Israel where he had grown up.

If Broadway turned a deaf ear to transferring the play, Chicago did not, and the production was staged at the Goodman Theatre with the same cast two years later.

Nothing succeeds in theater like success, and the year after the Signature staging of *The Trip to Bountiful*, another Off-Broadway company called Primary Stages presented another Foote work, this time directed by Michael Wilson, who by now had secured his place as a foremost interpreter of Foote's work. The play was *The Day Emily Married.*

Foote had written the play some twenty years earlier, a full three-act drama, but had kept it in a drawer because some of the people on whom the characters were based were still alive. The play had been one of Lillian's favorites. At the time Foote wrote it, he had been in California and sent his wife a copy. She wrote him back that it was "fantastic" and that he had "written a major and most significant play, and I'm proud of you."

For *The Day Emily Married* Foote once again reached into his store of family lore to tell a sad tale of the heartache that comes to those who seek the false happiness and security they think only money can bring.

Emily Davis is the divorced only child of doting parents. Her first husband was an alcoholic layabout, and the play opens on the day before her second marriage, to Richard Murray, an oil field worker with whom her father seemingly has forged a special bond. When audiences first meet him, Richard is a polite, attentive, and caring husband and son-in-law. But the sunny hopes for Emily's future that shine brightly in the first act quickly cloud over in the second, and turn into a devastating storm in the third.

Emily's father, Lee, had made certain promises to Richard about investing in a business that the young man would run. Richard wants to put Lee's money in an oil venture, but Emily's father procrastinates. When the money is not forthcoming, Richard's real reasons for marrying Emily become apparent, and Lee's dreams of securing his daughter's happiness with a cash investment are dashed.

Running through the play, in the character of Emily's mother, Lyd, is the separate sorrow of those who try to cling to the past at any cost. Change—the inevitability of it and the loss that it brings—is again a major theme. In *The Day Emily Married*, it is manifest in old photographs of Lyd's large and once prosperous family that cover the sitting room walls. Lyd lives in constant fear that her impulsive daughter will carry out a threat she once made to burn all the pictures. In addition, Lyd adamantly refuses to sell the house that her great-grandfather built, even though it might save her daughter's marriage to Richard.

Early in the play, Lyd pines for a place and time that have disappeared and will never return. She recalls her own father and says "he wouldn't even recognize the town he was born in if he came back." She remembers some trees her father had planted around the Courthouse square "and when those men came to cut them down, he took his gun and stood there for two days and nights guarding those trees. They cut them down, though, when he died. They say we have to have progress."

It is near the end of the play that Emily delivers a speech, foreshadowing one that Foote would write decades later in *The Carpetbagger's Children*, about dealing with the mixed blessings of progress. She is assuring her father that things will be all right, and that they will all survive the disaster that has hit them.

It'll all come out all right, Daddy. Do you remember when I was a little girl and you used to lie awake at nights and worry what would happen to people here when the mechanical cotton picker came along? We'll all be ruined, you used to say. I'd lie awake myself after hearing you and cry and cry and cry for all the tenant farmers and the sharecroppers and their jobs, that would be taken away from them. What will people do, you used to say. What will they do? Well, they got along. The cotton pickers came, and people went on and the world didn't stop. And I'm going to get along, Daddy. And you will. And Mama.

The production of *The Day Emily Married* was a big hit for Primary Stages. It received excellent reviews from the critics, and the run was extended. The company immediately wanted to present another Foote play. Once again, Wilson was chosen to direct, and the play would be staged first in Hartford, then in New York.

The play was *Dividing the Estate*, another that dealt with money and the folly of believing it is a panacea for life's woes. Unlike *The Day Emily Married*, however, the later play looks at the subject with a twinkle rather than heartache. *Dividing the Estate* was one of the few straight comedies Foote had written, and it had first been staged at the McCarter Theatre in Princeton, New Jersey, some fifteen years earlier.

The story, set in the 1980s, centers on a matriarch who holds the purse strings to the family fortune, and her squabbling relatives who want her to divvy up the money before she dies. Elizabeth Ashley was cast as Stella Gordon, the octogenarian head of the family, with Hallie playing her youngest daughter, Mary Jo, and Devon taking the role of her grandson, known only as Son, who is the only member of Stella's extended family she can trust.

After the one-acts of *The Carpetbagger's Children* and *The Actor*, in *Dividing the Estate*, Foote was again back at work on a large canvas with a full-length play and a cast of a dozen, painting a humorous family portrait of greedy, avaricious, even larcenous relatives all clamoring for a variety of reasons to get their hands on Stella's estate. The matriarch loosely resembles Foote's grandmother, Baboo, and there is more than a little of his various aunts and uncles among the squawking family members in the play.

The play opened at Primary Stages' home at the 59E59 theater in 2007. This time Wilson did not have to cajole Andre Bishop to come see the production. The Lincoln Center director had become an avid Foote admirer. As with *The Carpetbagger's Children*, Bishop saw a matinee performance, mainly for his own enjoyment, since he did not have any immediate thought of moving it to one of Lincoln Center's two theaters. As things often happen in the theater, however, a series of unforeseen events made him think about the possibility of a transfer.

A revival of *South Pacific* was being designed specifically for the space in the Vivian Beaumont Theatre at Lincoln Center that season. Bishop had taken an option from the Shuberts on one of their Broadway houses for a second musical that was being planned for the fall of 2008. When that project collapsed, Bishop was faced with the task of finding a show to put in the Broadway theater he had leased.

His first thought was to move the *South Pacific* revival. That show had been a huge success and was now extended to an open-ended run. But the cost of transferring it would have been monumental and very complicated. The sets, the choreography, the entire production had been designed specifically for the Beaumont, and it would not be the same show in a different theater.

Bishop came back to see *Dividing the Estate* a second time. He had loved the play and the cast, especially Hallie as Mary Jo, and he noticed that it was drawing a very diverse audience during its run at Primary Stages. By this time, however, he was one of several suitors wanting to move the play, either to an open-ended run Off-Broadway or to Broadway itself.

Foote had fond memories of the Lincoln Center production of *The Carpetbagger's Children*, and he sensed in Bishop another kindred spirit who shared his love for the theater, and he believed that Lincoln Center could become a home for his plays. Bishop began work on putting *Dividing the Estate* into the Booth Theatre the following season, and the show opened there on November 20, 2008.

Ben Brantley called it "one of [Foote's] masterworks" and cited Hallie's performance as one of "true comic genius." He praised the whole production and its direction as "an ideally balanced ensemble piece, with acting that matches and magnifies Mr. Foote's slyly and acutely observant writing."

The Broadway staging coincided with the collapse of the American economy in the fall of 2008. Almost overnight, theater attendance dropped dramatically and shows began closing one after another—a total of eight plays folded on one day early in 2009. Still, *Dividing the Estate* was drawing good audiences, and Lincoln Center was eager to extend the play's run. However, Andre Bishop was told by the Shubert Organization that the Booth Theatre would be unavailable, so the Broadway production closed.

When the Tony Award nominations were announced in the spring, *Dividing the Estate* received one for Best Play and Hallie was named for Best Featured Actress.

Wilson, however, arranged to move the show to his own theater up in Hartford in the late spring. The only major change in the Hartford staging of *Dividing the Estate* was the casting for the role of Stella, the family matriarch. When it became clear the Broadway run would not be extended, Elizabeth Ashley agreed to appear in another play and was unavailable to do the role in Hartford.

In the interim, Wilson mounted a production of *To Kill a Mockingbird* at the Hartford Stage Company. The director had wanted to try to unravel the decades-old snarl over the stage version of "Mockingbird." At the time Harper Lee's novel was first published, the rights to adapt a play from the book were sold to Christopher Sergel. After Foote's screenplay was published, many theater directors used it in preference to Sergel's stage version, although royalties for the play were paid to Sergel and, after he died, to his estate. Although Foote's screenplay was often the text used on the stage, he never received any money for it. Wilson wanted to rectify this.

Foote, however, resisted. It was an old scar, and one he did not want to reopen at this late date. Foote and Lee had been lifelong friends, and he knew that she had felt badly over how the sale of the stage rights had been handled. It was not worth the strain it might put on his friendship with Lee to revisit the issue.

Wilson had another project in mind, however, that would fulfill one of Foote's lifelong dreams—a stage production of the entire *Orphans' Home Cycle*.

The possibility of such an undertaking first came to Wilson after he directed both parts of Tony Kushner's *Angels in America* for the Alley Theatre in Houston. The feasibility was reinforced when Wilson saw Tom Stoppard's *The Coast of Utopia* at Lincoln Center, which was performed as three three-hour plays.

Wilson's vision called for dividing Foote's nine plays into three segments, each of which would have a separate title. The first three would come under the heading *The Story of a Childhood*; the second would be called *The Story of a Marriage*, the same title given to the PBS broadcast of the three middle plays; and the final part of the trilogy would be called *The Story of a Family*. Foote was receptive to the idea and began work on distilling the nine plays into three long ones.

Wilson had reckoned on a budget of around $1.5 million to mount the three plays, but realized his own theater in Hartford could not bear the cost alone, and he began talks in the fall of 2008 with some other theaters to join in the project and share the financial expenses. The Alley Theatre in Houston and Lincoln Center in New York became possible candidates, along with Houghton's Signature Theatre. It was Bishop, after all, who had brought Stoppard's *Coast of Utopia* trilogy to Lincoln Center from London, and it had been a huge success.

Wilson's initial enthusiasm was dampened somewhat by the economic recession that riddled the United States and ricocheted around the world throughout that fall and into 2009. Theater companies across the country were trimming budgets rather than expanding them, canceling plans for productions, not budgeting for new ones. Wilson never gave up on producing and directing the entire cycle, however, and Foote, who knew a thing or two about the vagaries of financing artistic projects, continued to work on the script that would fulfill an ambition he once never thought possible.

Early in 2009, Foote had completed work on six of the nine plays, and Wilson held a sit-down reading of them in a rehearsal room at Lincoln Center, using many of the cast members from the Broadway production of *Dividing the Estate*. Among those who sat in on the reading was Jim Houghton.

By this time, Houghton had already told Wilson he was committed to the project and toward the end of January 2009, they jointly announced that *The Orphans' Home Cycle* would be coproduced at the Hartford Stage Company from August 27 to October 17, 2009, and at the Signature Theatre Company from October 29, 2009, to April 11, 2010.

The three three-hour parts of the cycle would be presented on alternating nights in repertory, as well as in some one-day marathons during which all three parts would be performed in the morning, afternoon, and evening.

Foote was excited by the prospect. It would be the culmination of a lifelong dream. He had already made progress on completing his adaptation of the final three plays of the cycle when he, Barbara Hallie, and Devon left New York for Hartford in January. Wilson had cast both Hallie and her husband in the revival of *To Kill a Mockingbird* so that they could stay in Hartford and Foote could continue working on the cycle without having to travel back and forth to California before *Dividing the Estate* opened in Connecticut.

The first few weeks in Hartford developed into a familiar routine. Hallie and Devon spent their days at rehearsal while Foote stayed at home and completed work on the plays. Early in February, however, Foote began to experience the return of some episodes of sleepwalking and memory lapse that had first surfaced briefly in California before Foote, his daughter, and son-in-law left for New York for the Broadway production of *Dividing the Estate*.

When it happened back in California, Barbara Hallie had not been overly concerned. It was hardly surprising that at the age of ninety-two a man might forget someone's name, and the sleepwalking incident had been isolated. In typical fashion, Foote had apologized afterward, telling his daughter, "I'm so sorry I frightened you."

As the incidents recurred in Hartford, however, Foote agreed to see a doctor. In the end, he saw three. He was examined first by a GP and then a cardiologist, the latter finding his heart very sound, although his blood pressure tended to fluctuate up and down. He was referred to a neurologist and had an appointment for Friday, February 20.

On February 19, Foote attended the opening preview of Wilson's staging of *To Kill a Mockingbird* and was ebullient. Foote was very happy with the production and told the director he thought it was "a triumph." He sat in an aisle seat and stayed there for about half an hour after the performance, signing autographs and receiving well-wishers and admirers who recognized him and stopped to speak to him. As he was leaving, the entire cast lined up in the lobby to greet him, and Foote stopped and talked with each actor, congratulating them on their performances. It was his last night in a theater.

The visit to the neurologist the next day did not go well. In unsparing clinical terms, the doctor told Foote that he might be suffering from the onset of some form of dementia. He told Foote that it was incurable, although there were treatments for it. Barbara Hallie tried to put a positive interpretation for her father on the doctor's report—that there was treatment to forestall the progress of the disease—but Foote was despondent. One of his greatest fears was that he might end up like his father, and over the course of the next week and a half, his condition went into a tailspin. He appeared depressed and had trouble concentrating and staying awake. The words "dementia" and "incurable" preyed on his mind. To Barbara Hallie it seemed as though he had lost the will to carry on.

On Wednesday, March 4, Hallie and Devon both went to the theater early in the morning. Hartford Stage Company presented 10:30 a.m. performances on Wednesdays, mostly for classes of students as part of a program to make theater available to city schoolchildren.

Foote had passed a difficult night. He had woken once, agitated, and seemed to be having a conversation with his grandmother. Barbara Hallie got into bed with him and she and Devon managed to calm him and he went back to sleep. The family had hired a home helper named Lucy McCollum to stay with him when Hallie and Devon had to be away, and Lucy called the theater during intermission to say that Foote had not yet woken that morning. Hallie told her that he had had a rough night and to just let him sleep. As Hallie was returning to the apartment, Lucy called her on her cell phone and got her just as she reached the lobby. Lucy said, "I think you had better come up." Foote had died in his sleep, ten days short of his ninety-third birthday.

Barbara Hallie had gone on in one of her father's plays the night her mother died, and she went on in *To Kill a Mockingbird* the night her father died. More than any showbiz credo about the show must go on, it was for Hallie a way of paying tribute to the work to which her father and mother had dedicated their lives.

The cast of *Mockingbird* held a sort of wake after that night's performance in Foote's memory. His body was cremated a few days later, but funeral plans were delayed until April, when the family could return to Wharton to bury his ashes next to Lillian's in the family plot of the local cemetery. A public memorial service was planned for May, and Andre Bishop offered the Vivian Beaumont Theater at Lincoln Center for the occasion. On the night after Foote's death, all the lights on Broadway were dimmed for a minute before the evening's performances in tribute to him.

Even in death, Foote got an extended run. The day before his scheduled funeral in Wharton, a Gulf storm accompanied by torrential rains dumped nearly a foot of water on the town in less than twenty-four hours. The local cemetery, where his ashes were to be interred next to Lillian's in the Foote family plot, became a marshy wetland, and the children decided to hold the service indoors.

Dozens of mourners—friends from New York and California as well as locals who had known him and Lillian—crowded into the front parlor and dining room of the house on Houston Street. His sons and daughters read from *Beginnings*, Foote's memoir of his childhood, and sang a hymn. Robert Duvall read a letter he had written to the man who gave him his first job in film and of whose work he was a consummate interpreter. After the service, as was the custom in Texas, everyone joined in a meal of fried chicken, potato salad, and deviled eggs. In the end, everyone agreed the deluge had been fortuitous. Foote loved the rain, and he loved having people visit him at home. It seemed only fitting to hold the service in the house Foote's grandfather had built for his mother and father and that Foote had regarded as his real home for over ninety years.

The following day dawned sunny and bright, and a small group of friends and relations who were staying an extra day in Wharton reassembled at Foote's house. Before the caravan of cars left for the cemetery, each took a handful of ashes and scattered them around the trees that Foote loved so dearly in the backyard of his house, a yard in which his father had once kept chickens and one he had traversed countless times as a child to his grandmother's home across the way.

At the cemetery, each of the children spoke again; then one after another of those attending were invited to share their own memories. What had been planned as a brief burial service the day before had become a two-day commemoration.

For the memorial in New York on May 11, 2009, about seven hundred friends and admirers filled the Vivian Beaumont Theater to hear actors and directors with whom Foote had worked read passages from his plays and other playwrights pay him tribute.

With a huge portrait of the man Harper Lee once said "looks like God, but clean-shaven" smiling from the back of the stage, Roberta Maxwell, Estelle Parsons, Elizabeth Ashley, Matthew Broderick, Devon Abner, and Lois Smith took turns reading from plays they had appeared in. Edward Albee and Romulus Linney spoke, as did Andre Bishop, Harris Yulin, James Houghton, and Michael Wilson. Robert Duvall talked about his long association with Foote, beginning with him being cast as Boo Radley in *To Kill a Mockingbird*. Betty Buckley sang "Blessed Assurance," one of Foote's favorite hymns. Each of the children spoke, recounting stories funny and touching in a loving remembrance of both their father and mother. Hallie read a passage from her father's play *A Coffin in Egypt*.

At the conclusion, Foote himself spoke—through a filmed interview Houghton had made nearly three years earlier for the playwright's ninetieth birthday. In it, as always, Foote told a story, and this one was about himself: Once as a boy he had told his mother he was going into town to see a movie of a Shakespearean play, but instead he sneaked off to see a risqué film set in a Chinese brothel. As he began to relate how his mother had found him out by questioning him about the Shakespeare he was supposed to have seen, Foote started to laugh and couldn't stop. It was a fond parting memory—Foote laughing and telling a story.

In his review of *The Road to the Graveyard* more than twenty years earlier, Frank Rich had compared Foote's writing to a "collaboration between Faulkner and Chekhov." It was not idle critical hyperbole for a writer Rich admired, but a fine appreciation of the similarities between Foote's work and that of the American novelist and the Russian playwright.

Foote had been likened to Chekhov in the past, but usually with an adjectival proviso that Foote's work is "rural" or "regional." In fact, Chekhov himself was a "rural" and "regional" writer. What Foote and Chekhov held in common was an understanding that the most personal drama is the family drama, and whether it involves selling a cherry orchard or cotton plantation acreage, the anguish of giving up a part of one's heritage is the same in Russia as it is in Texas. Likewise, the youthful yearning to go out into the world, whether it is to Moscow or to Houston, in search of fame, fortune, and true love is a constant in every generation. It is these human conflicts that make the plays of Chekhov and Foote universal and speak to audiences across time. It is the drama of the commonplace, and both playwrights are masters of it.

In his Nobel Prize acceptance speech, William Faulkner spoke of "the old verities and truths of the heart, the old universal truths lacking which any story is ephemeral and doomed—love and honor and pity and pride and compassion and sacrifice." He said that only "the problems of the human heart in conflict with itself . . . can make good writing because only that is worth writing about, worth the agony and the sweat."

Faulkner and Foote both knew what makes a story. On another occasion Faulkner spoke of understanding through the "means of childhood's simple inevitable listening," and as a boy, Foote learned to listen. Whether it was on the front porches of his various family members, or in the kitchens of the black families he visited, or to the men who dropped into his father's store, he listened. He heard tales, as he once put it, "of who killed whom and why, of who stole and got caught, of who stole and never got caught." He heard arguments over why one person prospered and another didn't, why some people behaved the way they did. He heard stories of murderers, drunkards, philanderers, some involving his own family, and all of which ended in heartache. Like Faulkner, Foote could look at the detritus it all left in its wake and find compassion for both sides.

Like Chekhov and Faulkner, Foote also observed the inevitable sadness that change brings in the lives of ordinary people. Foote once wrote that he first noticed the effects of change in his life as a young boy when his grandfather sold his horses, dismantled his barn, and built a garage for his car in its place. Soon after, the hitching posts were taken down on the town's main square.

Change haunts everyone, and whether it is for good or ill depends on one's point of view. Foote often told the following story about himself as a young man: He ran into a black friend in Wharton and commented about how terrible it was that the new cotton-picking machines were taking work away from field hands. His friend asked him, "Have you ever picked cotton?" Foote admitted he had not. His friend dryly observed, "Then don't ever think those machines are a bad thing."

Change in Foote's own life encroached even further early in the new century, when he had to give up the apartment on Horatio Street into which he and Lillian had settled after their full-time return to New York. When Foote and Lillian first moved there, Horatio Street was in a rough part of the Village, filled with prostitutes and drug dealers. But over the years, the far West Village had changed, too, had become more gentrified. The Meatpacking District had given way to boutiques, and new condos and co-ops began to command top-end prices. After watching his rent shoot up every two years, he finally left Horatio Street and went to live with Hallie and Devon in California. Before giving up the New York apartment, Foote held an auction to sell the last of the antiques and Early American art that he and Lillian had collected over the years.

Admirers have often pondered why Foote never became as widely known as some of America's more famous playwrights, such as Eugene O'Neill, Tennessee Williams, or Arthur Miller. One possible reason is that his private life never produced newspaper headlines or gossip-column material. His favorite libations were iced tea and Coca-Cola. He didn't use drugs and remained happily married to one woman. He adored his children and was always supportive and encouraging of whatever path they chose in life.

Daisy followed in his footsteps as a writer. She learned her lessons well, and her plays deal with the same inner conflicts that her father examined, except Daisy's point of geographic reference is small-town New Hampshire, where she grew up, rather than Texas. Walter became a successful lawyer and lives in Scarsdale, New York. Horton Jr. and a friend from California opened a restaurant in Greenwich Village that is known as a theater gathering place as well as a neighborhood tavern, although Horton Jr. also maintains some ties to the theater. Barbara Hallie is one of the theater's most respected actresses and has become a sort of unofficial keeper of the Foote flame.

Another reason for Foote's relative obscurity to the general public could have been his innate affability and humility. In an artistic field known for catering to egomania, Foote always put himself at the service of the story, rather than using the story to serve his own ends.

Andre Bishop recalled how during the run of *The Carpetbagger's Children* Foote would come to the theater every night. "I was astounded," Bishop said. "With some playwrights I wouldn't name, there is a sense that the theater owes them something, the theater should be grateful to them. With Horton, it is he who is grateful to the theater."

In his nineties, Foote still returned to Wharton as often as he could, now always accompanied by Hallie or one of his other children. He had earlier bought the house next door, and any visitors who might come to see him stayed there.

The town had changed almost beyond recognition from the one where Foote was born nearly a century ago. During one of his last trips home to the house his grandfather had built for his parents, Foote suggested to a guest that they drive to see some of the town's landmarks. It was like a guided tour of the plays, screenplays, and teleplays he had written over his life.

"That's the house from *Baby, the Rain Must Fall*," he said, pointing. "That's where Wilma lived in *A Young Lady of Property*," he added about a frame structure. "That's the *Dividing the Estate* house," he said, indicating another. "It's also the *Carpetbagger's Children* house." A bit farther on, he pointed again. "That's where the man who was tarred and feathered lived." The tour continued to the town cemetery and beyond, to neighboring communities like El Campo, Glen Flora, or Egypt. There was a story in each house, in each little town.

Back home after the drive around town, while Barbara Hallie prepared supper, Foote settled into an easy chair in what was once a

wide-open porch with a view across the backyard to his grandmother's house. The porch had by now been glassed in, heated in the
winter and air-conditioned in the summer. Two Oscars sat on a shelf
by the window, and a tall pile of papers teetered close to collapse on
a cluttered desk. To the end, Foote still preferred to write in longhand, and the day's labors rested on a TV tray next to his recliner.

As his guest asked Foote about his long life in the theater—from
playing Puck in the third grade to his years as an actor during the
Depression; to the Golden Age of Television; to his work in the movies, both with studios and as an independent producer; to the plays,
nearly sixty in all, staged in basements and on Broadway—Foote
merely smiled and shook his head at how it all came to pass.

"It was all miraculous," he said. "I look back and it all seems
miraculous."

Foote and his visitor were not long in conversation before a twinkle came to his eyes and a bashful, boyish grin crept across his face,
and he said, "that reminds me of a story . . ."

Acknowledgments

First and foremost, this book would never have been possible without the gracious generosity of Horton Foote, who not only shared his wealth of memories in numerous interviews but also extended his friendship and hospitality to me over many years. I am further grateful to his family—Barbara Hallie and Devon Abner, Horton Jr., Daisy, and Walter—for their cooperation and patience with a deluge of questions over the past year.

Russell L. Martin and his staff at the DeGolyer Library at Southern Methodist University gave invaluable assistance in providing access and helping to navigate the extensive Horton Foote archive of papers and letters.

Many of Foote's friends and colleagues were kind enough to recount their experiences, but especially Michael Wilson, Jim Houghton, Andre Bishop, Frank Rich, and Robert Duvall. I would like to thank Suzanne O'Connor for her help with some research.

I am especially indebted to Wylie O'Sullivan for her faith in the book, her meticulous editing, and her unflagging support, and to Al Zuckerman of Writers House for finding it such a welcoming home.

Bibliography

Foote, Horton. *Beginnings: A Memoir*. New York: Scribner, 2001.

Foote, Horton. *Farewell: A Memoir of a Texas Childhood*. New York: Scribner, 1999.

Foote, Horton. *Genesis of an American Playwright*. Edited by Marion Castleberry. Waco: Baylor University Press, 2004.

Porter, Laurin. *Orphans' Home: The Voice and Vision of Horton Foote*. Baton Rouge: Louisiana State University Press, 2003.

Watson, Charles S. *Horton Foote: A Literary Biography*. Austin: University of Texas Press, 2003.

Wood, Gerald C. *Horton Foote and the Theater of Intimacy*. Baton Rouge: Louisiana State University Press, 1999.

271

Index

About the Author

Like Horton Foote, Wilborn Hampton had a childhood dream of becoming an actor. At the University of Texas, Austin, he wrote theater and movie reviews for the student newspaper, *The Daily Texan*, and was working at a theater in his hometown of Dallas when he was hired by United Press International as a cub reporter.

He had been at UPI in Dallas only two months when he was thrust into the agency's coverage of the assassination of President John Kennedy. That experience led him to pursue another ambition, becoming a foreign correspondent. After two years in New York, he was posted to London, where he reported on the beginning of the Troubles in Northern Ireland, including the entry of British troops. Hampton was later assigned to the Rome bureau of UPI, from which he traveled frequently to the Middle East, eventually covering two wars—the so-called Black September civil war in Jordan and the 1973 Arab-Israeli war. After returning to New York, he joined the *New York Times* as an editor on the foreign desk. Later Hampton began to work on the culture news desk and the weekly Book Review. He also began to write theater reviews for the newspaper. He remains a contributing critic for coverage of Off-Broadway and Off-Off-Broadway theater.

The author has published four books with Candlewick Press, and he has written two biographies (one on Elvis Presley and the other on Babe Ruth) for Penguin's UpClose series. He lives in New York with his wife.